Girl Alone

CATHY GLASS

THE MILLION COPY BESTSELLING AUTHOR

Girl Alone

Joss came home from school to discover
her father's suicide. Angry and hurting,
she's out of control.

HARPER
element

Certain details in this story, including names, places and dates,
have been changed to protect the family's privacy.

HarperElement
An imprint of HarperCollins*Publishers*
1 London Bridge Street
London SE1 9GF

www.harpercollins.co.uk

First published by HarperElement 2015

1 3 5 7 9 10 8 6 4 2

A catalogue record of this book is
available from the British Library

ISBN 978-0-00-813825-7

Printed and bound in Great Britain by
Clays Ltd, St Ives plc

MIX
Paper from
responsible sources
FSC **FSC˚ C007454**
www.fsc.org

ACKNOWLEDGEMENTS

A big thank-you to my family; my editors, Holly and Carolyn; my literary agent, Andrew; my UK publishers HarperCollins, and my overseas publishers, who are now too numerous to list by name. Last but not least, a big thank-you to my readers for your unfailing support and kind words.

CHAPTER ONE

UNSAFE BEHAVIOUR

'I hate you!' Joss screamed at the top of her voice. 'I hate you. I hate your house and your effing family! I even hate your effing cat!'

Our beloved cat, Toscha, jumped out of Joss's way as she stormed from the living room, stomped upstairs and into her bedroom, slamming the door behind her.

I took a deep breath and sat on the sofa as I waited for my pulse to settle. Joss, thirteen, had arrived as an emergency foster placement twelve days earlier; angry, volatile and upset, she wasn't getting any easier to deal with. I knew why she was so angry. So too did her family, teacher, social worker, previous foster carers and everyone else who had tried to help her and failed. Joss's father had committed suicide four years previously, when Joss had been nine years old, and she and her mother had found his lifeless body. He'd hanged himself.

This was trauma enough for any child to cope with, but then, when Joss was twelve, her mother had tried to move on with her life and had remarried. Joss felt rejected and that her mother had betrayed her father, whom she'd been very close to. Her refusal to accept her new stepfather as her younger brother had been able to had seen family arguments escalate

1

and Joss's behaviour sink to the point where she had to leave home and go to live with an aunt. The aunt had managed to cope with Joss's unsafe and unpredictable behaviour for a month, but then Joss had gone into foster care. Two carers later, with Joss's behaviour deteriorating further, she'd come to live with me – the day after Danny, whose story I told in *Saving Danny*, had left.

It was felt that, as a very experienced foster carer, I'd be able to manage and hopefully improve Joss's behaviour, but there'd been little progress so far. And, while I felt sorry for her and appreciated why she was so upset and angry, allowing her to self-destruct wasn't going to help. Her present outburst was the result of my telling her that if she was going out she'd have to be in by nine o'clock, which I felt was late enough for a girl of thirteen to be travelling home on the bus alone. I'd offered to collect her in my car from the friend's house she was supposedly going to, so she could have stayed a bit later, but she'd refused. 'I'm not a kid,' she'd raged. 'So stop treating me like one!'

It was Friday evening, and what should have been the start of a relaxing weekend had resulted in me being stressed (again), and my children Adrian (sixteen), Lucy (thirteen) and Paula (twelve) being forced to listen to another angry scene.

I gave Joss the usual ten minutes alone to calm down before I went upstairs. I wasn't surprised to find Paula and Lucy standing on the landing looking very worried. Joss's anger impacted on the whole family.

'Shall I go in and talk to her?' Lucy asked. The same age as Joss and having come to me as a foster child (I was adopting her), Lucy could empathize closely with Joss, but I wasn't passing the responsibility to her.

'Thanks, love, but I'll speak to her first,' I said. 'Then you can have a chat with her later if you wish.'

'I don't like it when she shouts at you,' Paula said sadly.

'I don't either,' I said, 'but I can handle it. Really. Don't worry.' I threw them a reassuring smile, then gave a brief knock on Joss's door and, slowly opening it, poked my head round. 'Can I come in?' I asked.

'Suit yourself,' Joss said moodily.

I went in and drew the door to behind me. Joss was sitting on the edge of her bed with a tissue pressed to her face. She was a slight, petite child who looked younger than her thirteen years, and her usually sallow complexion was now red from anger and tears.

'Can I come and sit next to you?' I asked, approaching the bed.

'Not bothered,' she said.

I sat beside her, close but not quite touching. I didn't take her hand in mine or put my arm around her to comfort her. She shied away from physical contact.

'Why do you always stop me from having fun?' she grumbled. 'It's not fair.'

'Joss, I don't want to stop you from having fun, but I do need to keep you safe. I care about you, and while you are living with me I'll be looking after you like your mother.'

'She doesn't care!' Joss blurted. 'Not for me, anyway.' This was one of Joss's grievances — that her mother didn't care about her.

'I'm sure your mother does care,' I said. 'Although she may not always say so.' It was a conversation we'd had before.

'No, she doesn't,' Joss blurted. 'She couldn't care a toss about me and Kevin, not now she's got *him*.'

3

Kevin was Joss's younger brother. *'Him'* was their step-father, Eric.

'I know it can be very difficult for children when a parent remarries,' I said. 'The parent has to divide their time between their new partner and their children. I do understand how you feel.'

'No, you don't,' Joss snapped. 'No one does.'

'I try my best to understand,' I said. 'And if you could talk to me more, I'm sure I'd be able to understand better.'

'At least you have time to listen to me. I'll give you that. She never does.'

'I expect your mother is very busy. Working, as well as looking after her family.'

Joss humphed. 'Busy with him, more like it!'

I knew that with so much animosity towards her step-father it would be a long time before Joss was able to return to live at home, if ever. However, we were getting off the subject.

'Listen, love,' I said, lightly touching her arm. 'The reason you were angry just now wasn't because of your mother or stepfather; it was because I was insisting on some rules. As you know, when you go out I expect you to come in at a reasonable time. The same rules apply to everyone here, including Adrian, Lucy and Paula.'

'Adrian stayed out later than nine last Saturday,' she snapped. 'It was nearly eleven when he got back. I heard him come in.'

'He's two years older than you,' I said. 'And even then I made sure he had transport home. Lucy and Paula have to be in by nine unless it's a special occasion, and they only go out at weekends sometimes.'

'But they don't want to go out as much as I do,' Joss said, always ready with an answer.

It was true. Joss would be out every night until after midnight if I let her, as she had been doing with her aunt and previous foster carers.

'I don't want you going out every night, either,' I said. 'You have school work to do and you need your sleep. It's not a good idea for a young girl to be hanging around on the streets.'

'I like it,' she said. 'It's fun.'

'It's unsafe,' I said.

'No, it isn't.'

'Trust me, love, a teenage girl wandering around by herself at night is unsafe. I've been fostering for fifteen years and I know what can happen.' I didn't want to scare her, but she had no sense of danger and I was very concerned about her unsafe behaviour.

'I'm not by myself. I'm with my mates,' Joss said. 'You're paranoid, just like my aunt and those other carers.'

'So we are all wrong, are we, love? Or could it be that, being a bit older and having more experience, we have some knowledge of what is safe and unsafe?'

Joss shrugged moodily and stared at her hands clenched in her lap.

'I'm still going out tonight,' she said defiantly.

'I've said you can. It's Friday, but you will be in by nine o'clock if you are using the bus.'

'What if I get a lift home?' she asked.

'I offered that before and you refused.'

'Not from you – one of my mates' parents could bring me back.'

I looked at her carefully. 'Who?'

'One of my mates from school, I guess.'

'Joss, if you are relying on a lift then I would like to know who will be responsible for bringing you home.'

'Chloe's parents,' she said quickly. 'She's in my class. She's a nice girl. You'd like her.'

I continued to look at her. 'And Chloe's parents have offered to bring you home?'

'Yes. They did before, when I was at my last carer's. You can ask them if you like.'

On balance, I decided she could be telling the truth, and if she wasn't, questioning her further would only back her into a corner and make her lie even more.

'All right, then,' I said. 'I trust you. On this occasion you can come in at ten o'clock as long as one of Chloe's parents brings you home.'

'Ten's too early if I have a lift,' she said, trying to push the boundaries even further. 'Eleven.'

'No. I consider ten o'clock late enough for a thirteen-year-old, but if you want to raise it with your social worker when we see her on Monday, that's fine.'

'It's not fair,' she moaned. 'You always fucking win.'

'It's not about winning or losing,' I said. 'I care about what happens to you and I do what I think is best to protect you. And Joss, I've told you before about swearing and that you'd be sanctioned. There are other ways to express anger apart from swearing and stomping around. Tomorrow is pocket-money day and I'll be withholding some of yours.'

'You can't do that!' she snapped. 'It's my money. The social services give it to you to give to me.'

'I will be giving you half tomorrow, and then the rest on Sunday evening, assuming you haven't been swearing. If you do swear, I'll keep the money safe for you and you can earn it back through good behaviour.'

'Yeah, whatever,' she said, and, folding her arms, she turned her back on me.

I ignored her ill humour. 'Dinner will be ready in about fifteen minutes. I think Lucy wants to talk to you. Is that OK?'

'I guess.'

I went out of Joss's room, called to Lucy that Joss was free and then with a sigh went downstairs to finish making the dinner. I knew I'd have another anxious evening worrying about Joss, and I'd be lying if I said I didn't have doubts that I'd made the right decision in agreeing to foster her. I was especially concerned about the effect her behaviour could be having on my children. But I hadn't really had much choice. I was the only experienced foster carer available at the time, and the social services couldn't place Joss with an inexperienced carer, as they had done the first time. Joss had been that carer's first placement and she'd only lasted two weeks. I hoped she was given an easier child for her next placement, or she might lose hope and resign.

Once dinner was ready I called everyone to the table. Adrian had stayed in his room while Joss was erupting, and now greeted her with an easy 'Hi'. There wasn't an atmosphere at the meal table as there had been on Tuesday and Thursday when I'd stopped Joss from going out at all. Now she was happy at the prospect of a night out and ate quickly, gobbling down her food and finishing first.

'I'm going to get ready,' she said, standing and pushing back her chair.

'Wouldn't you like some pudding first?'

'Nah. I need to get ready.'

'All right. Off you go, then.' Normally I encouraged the children to remain at the table until everyone had finished, as it's polite. But with a child like Joss, who had so many issues, I had to be selective in choosing which ones I dealt with first. I couldn't change all her behaviour at once, and coming home at a reasonable time for her own safety and not swearing were more important than having exemplary table manners.

It was the beginning of June and therefore still daylight at seven o'clock when Joss yelled, 'Bye. See ya later!' from the hall and rushed out. I was in the living room drinking a cup of coffee, with the patio doors open and the warm summer air drifting in, thinking – worrying – about Joss. I'd thought about little else since she'd arrived. Although I'd been fostering for a long time, Joss was possibly my biggest challenge yet. I was also thinking about her mother, Linda, whom I would be meeting for the first time on Monday. Judging by what I knew from the social services, Linda had been a good mother and had done her best for Joss and her younger brother, Kevin, supporting them through the tragic loss of their father and then, more recently, gradually and sensitively introducing them to her new partner, Eric. I certainly didn't blame Linda for wanting to move on with her life and remarry. I was divorced, so I knew what it was like bringing up children alone, and it's not easy. Yet, sadly, it had all gone horribly wrong for Linda – by introducing Eric into her family she'd effectively lost her only daughter.

* * *

I never completely relaxed while Joss was out in the evening, but there was always something to do to occupy myself. I cleared up the kitchen, sorted the clean laundry and then returned to the living room and wrote up my fostering log. Foster carers are required to keep a daily record of the child or children they are looking after, which includes appointments, the child's health and well-being, significant events and any disclosures the child may make about their past. When the child leaves, this record is placed on file at the social services. Once I'd finished, I watched some television.

Lucy, Paula and Adrian were in their rooms for much of the evening; the girls were doing their homework so that it wasn't hanging over them all weekend, and then they chatted to their friends on the phone, and Adrian – who was in the middle of his GCSE examinations – was studying. By ten o'clock all three of them were getting ready for bed and I was listening out for Joss. I prayed she wouldn't let me down this time. If she hadn't returned by midnight I'd have to report her missing to the police, as I had done the previous Saturday. Then, doubtless, as before, she'd arrive home in the early hours, having wasted police time, and be angry with me for 'causing a fuss'. I hadn't given Joss a front-door key as I'd learnt my lesson from previous teenagers I'd fostered who'd abused the responsibility. My policy – the same as many other carers – was that once the young person had proved they were responsible, then they had a key, and it gave them something to work towards. But, of course, not having a key was another of Joss's grievances that she would be telling her social worker about on Monday. Joss wasn't open to reason; she felt victimized and believed she was invincible, which was a very dangerous combination.

At five minutes past ten the doorbell rang. I leapt from the sofa and nearly ran down the hall to answer it, grateful and relieved she'd returned more or less on time.

'Good girl,' I said as I opened the door. 'Well done.' I heard a car pull away.

'Well done,' she repeated, slurring her words. And I knew straight away she was drunk.

'Oh, Joss,' I said.

'Oh, Joss,' she mimicked.

Keeping her eyes down, she carefully navigated the front doorstep. 'I'm going to bed, see ya,' she said, and headed unsteadily towards the stairs.

As she passed me I smelt the mint she was sucking to try to mask the smell of alcohol, and also a sweet, musky smell lingering on her clothes, which was almost certainly cannabis – otherwise known as marijuana, weed or dope. I'd smelt it on her before. My heart sank, but there was no point in trying to discuss her behaviour with her while she was still under the influence. Greatly saddened yet again by her reckless behaviour, I watched her go upstairs.

I gave her five minutes to change and then went up to check on her. Her bedroom door was closed. I knocked but there was no answer, so I went in. She was lying on the bed, on her side, asleep, and fully clothed apart from her shoes. I eased the duvet over her legs, closed the curtains and then came out, leaving the door slightly open so I would hear her if she was sick or cried out. Joss often had dreadful nightmares and screamed and cried out in her sleep. On those nights I would immediately go to her room to comfort and resettle her, but that night – possibly because of the alcohol – she didn't wake.

She was still asleep when I got up the following morning. As it was Saturday and we didn't have to be anywhere I left her to sleep it off. She finally appeared downstairs in her dressing gown shortly after twelve. I was in the kitchen making lunch.

'Sorry,' she said, pouring a glass of water. Joss apologized easily, but it didn't mean that she wouldn't do it again.

'Joss, we need to talk,' I said.

I heard her sigh. 'Can't we make it later? After I've showered. I feel like crap.'

'I'm not surprised. Have a shower and get dressed, then, and we'll talk later. But we do need to talk.'

She returned upstairs to get ready and then half an hour later came down, and we all sat at the table for lunch. She looked fresher and chatted easily to Lucy, Adrian and Paula as though nothing untoward had happened, which for her it hadn't. Arriving home drunk and smelling of dope was a regular occurrence – at her parents', her aunt's, her previous foster carers', and now with me. She didn't talk to me, though, and after lunch kept well away from me all afternoon, although I heard her chatting and laughing with Lucy and Paula. Not for the first time, I hoped their good influence would rub off on Joss and not the other way around. The girls were a similar age to Joss and it was a worry that her risky behaviour could appear impressive and exciting. I'd talked to them already about the danger she placed herself in, and would do so again.

It was nearly five o'clock before Joss finally came to find me. I was on the patio watering the potted plants. I knew why she was presenting herself now, complicit and ready to hear my lecture: she would want to go out again soon.

'You wanted to talk?' she said, almost politely.

'Yes, sit down, love.'

I put the watering can to one side, pulled up a couple of garden chairs and in a calm and even voice began – the positive first. 'Joss, you did well to come home on time last night. I was pleased. Well done. But I am very worried that you are still drinking alcohol and smoking dope after everything I've said to you.'

She looked down and shrugged.

'I thought you understood the damage alcohol and drugs do to a young person's body.'

'I do,' she said.

'So why are you still doing it, Joss? You're not daft. Why abuse your body and mind when you know the harm it's doing?'

'Dunno,' she said, with another shrug.

'It's not only your physical and mental health that are being damaged by drink and drugs,' I continued. 'You're putting yourself in great danger in other ways too. When someone has a lot to drink or smokes dope, they feel as though they haven't a care in the world – that's why they do it. But their awareness has gone; they lose their sense of danger and are more at risk of coming to harm.' I was being careful to talk in the third person and not say 'you' so that she wouldn't feel I was getting at her – another complaint of Joss's. 'Joss, apart from your health, I'm worried something dreadful could happen to you. Do you understand?'

'Yes.' She glanced at me. 'So if I promise not to drink or smoke, can I go out tonight?'

'Where?'

'Chloe's.'

'Did Chloe's parents know you were drinking and smoking drugs last night?'

'We weren't,' Joss said.

I held her gaze. 'Joss, I'm not stupid.'

'No, they didn't know. They weren't in,' she admitted.

'So who brought you home last night?'

'Not sure,' Joss said easily. 'Her uncle, I think.'

'You think?' Joss could have just admitted to eating too many sweets for all her lack of concern. 'Joss, are you telling me that you were so off your head last night that you don't even know who drove you home?'

'I'm sure it was her uncle,' she said.

I looked at her carefully. 'Joss, I'm very worried about you.'

'I know, you said before. I'm sorry, but I can look after myself.'

I wish I had a pound for every teenager who's said that, I thought. 'Joss, I don't want to stop you from having fun and spending time with your friends, but I do need to keep you safe. Given what happened last night, and last weekend, the only way you're going out this evening is if I take and collect you in my car.'

'But that's not fair!' she cried, jumping up from her chair, all semblance of compliance gone. 'You treat me like a fucking baby. I hate you and this fucking family! I hate everyone.'

CHAPTER TWO

I THOUGHT YOU LOVED ME

I left Joss to calm down for a little longer than usual, allowing her time to reflect and me a chance to recharge my batteries. I found her outbursts exhausting and stressful. I was never sure what she might do or what she was capable of – the carers who'd looked after Joss before had reported that she'd hit one of them – and, although she hadn't physically threatened me (yet), I always put some distance between us when she was very angry.

I continued to water the plants on the patio, largely as a displacement for my anxious thoughts. How could I get through to Joss before it was too late and she came to real harm? Continue as I had been doing with firm boundaries, love, care and concern? It had worked in the past with other young people I'd fostered, but would it work now? Joss was coming close to being the most challenging child I'd ever looked after, and it wasn't something for her to be proud of.

Deep in thought, I set down the watering can and was about to go indoors to find Joss to talk to her, as I always did after one of her flare-ups, when she appeared on the patio.

'Sorry,' she said. 'You can take and collect me tonight if you want.'

'To Chloe's?' I asked, slightly surprised by the sudden turnaround.

'Nah. To the cinema. We've decided to see a film.'

'OK. That sounds good. Which film are you going to see?'

Joss rattled off the title of a film I knew was showing at the local cinema and then said, 'It starts at seven-thirty, so I'm meeting Chloe there at seven to give us time to buy our tickets and popcorn. The film finishes at nine-forty-five, so you can collect me at ten.'

It did cross my mind that this all sounded a bit pat, but I had to trust Joss, so I gave her the benefit of the doubt. 'All right. We'll leave here at six-forty,' I said. 'Lucy is seeing a friend this evening, so I'll drop her off on the way.'

'I'll tell her,' Joss said helpfully, and went back indoors.

We ate dinner at six and then, having explained to Adrian and Paula that I was dropping off Lucy and Joss and I'd be gone for no more than an hour, we left. Sometimes I feel I'm running a taxi service with all the driving I do, but I'd much rather that and know the children are safe than have them waiting for buses that don't always arrive, especially at night. Both girls sat in the rear of the car, and as I drove they chatted to each other, mainly about the film Joss was going to see. Lucy wanted to see it too and was hoping to go to the cinema with a friend the following weekend. I dropped Lucy off at her friend's house (her friend's mother was going to bring her home later) and then I continued to the cinema.

'Chloe will be here soon,' Joss said, opening her car door.

'You can wait in the car until she arrives if you like,' I suggested.

'Nah, it's OK. She might be waiting inside.'

Joss got out and closed the door. I lowered my window. 'I'll see you at ten o'clock, then,' I said. 'If Chloe doesn't arrive, phone me and I'll come back to collect you.'

'Sure,' Joss said. Then she spotted her waiting to cross the road. 'Hi, Chloe!' she yelled, waving hard.

'Hiya!' the girl yelled back.

I pulled away, pleased that I'd believed Joss. She'd come to me with a history of lying, so I found myself doubting everything she told me, which wasn't good, and not like me. Usually I trusted people and accepted what they said, unless experience proved I should do otherwise. I was so pleased I hadn't doubted Joss or questioned her further on her trip to the cinema with Chloe, as it could have undermined our already very fragile relationship.

At home, Paula and I watched some television together and then I suggested to Adrian that he left his studies for tonight and relaxed. The examinations he was revising for were important, as he needed good grades to continue to the sixth form, but I was concerned he was overdoing it. Half an hour later he joined us and we had a game of Scrabble before it was time for me to leave to collect Joss.

Although I was ten minutes early, Joss was already waiting outside the cinema with Chloe. They came over and I lowered my window.

'Can you give Chloe a lift home?' Joss asked. 'It's on the way.'

'Of course. Get in,' I said.

Both girls giggled, climbed into the back and giggled some more – possibly from teenage self-consciousness or embarrassment, I didn't know. Chloe was a largely built girl with jet-black, chin-length hair, heavily made-up eyes and a very short skirt. She looked older than Joss, but then Joss was so petite she looked younger than thirteen. Both girls reeked of cheap perfume, which I assumed was Chloe's, as Joss hadn't been wearing any perfume when she'd left. It was so strong I kept my window open a little.

'Was the film good?' I asked as I drove.

'Yeah,' they said, and giggled again.

'And you're in the same class at school?' I asked after a moment, trying to make conversation.

'Yeah,' Joss said, while Chloe remained silent.

'Where do you live?' I asked Chloe. 'I'll take you to your door.'

'We pass it,' she said. 'I'll shout when we're there.'

There was more giggling and then whispering as I drove, and finally Joss yelled, 'Stop! We're here!'

I checked in my mirrors and pulled over. We were outside a small parade of shops about five minutes from where I lived. 'I'll take you to your door,' I said to Chloe.

'You have!' Joss shouted, laughing. 'She lives here.'

'I live over the newsagents,' Chloe explained. 'Thanks for the lift.'

'You're welcome.'

There was more giggling as Chloe got out, and then before Joss closed the car door she yelled to her, 'See ya Monday!'

'Yeah, see ya, you old tart!' Chloe yelled back.

Joss shut the car door with more force than was necessary and I pulled away. As we passed Chloe walking along the pavement Joss banged on her window. Chloe grinned and put up her middle finger in an obscene gesture. I didn't comment. Chloe was the only friend of Joss's I'd met so far and I didn't want to criticize her, but she was so unlike Lucy's and Paula's friends that I had to stop myself making an instant judgement. If I felt Chloe might not be the best choice of friend for Joss, who was drawn to trouble, I didn't say so, and reminded myself that first impressions can be deceptive.

'How does Chloe get into her flat?' I asked out of interest, for there hadn't been an obvious front door.

'Round the back of the shops and up the fire escape,' Joss said.

'You've been to her flat?'

'Yeah, we hang out there sometimes.'

Now that the smell of perfume was starting to clear – with Chloe's departure and the window open – I was beginning to catch the smell of something else, which I thought could be dope, but I wasn't sure. I knew that just as mints are used to mask the smell of alcohol, dope, tobacco, glue and other substances on the breath, so perfume and cologne can be used to try to hide the smell from clothes, skin and hair. I wasn't going to accuse Joss unjustly, but I wanted her to know I was aware of the possibility that she may have been using again.

'What's the perfume?' I asked.

'It's Chloe's. I don't know what it's called.'

'It's very strong,' I said, and I glanced at her pointedly in the mirror.

Joss immediately looked away. 'I haven't been smoking, if that's what you think,' she said defensively.

'Good.'

I guessed that Joss would want to go out again on Sunday, as previous carers had complained that she went out as soon as she was dressed and didn't return until after midnight, and then she was too tired to get up for school on Monday morning. Joss had been out both Friday and Saturday evening, so I thought it was reasonable that she spent Sunday with us. I look upon Sundays as family time, as many others do, and I like us to try to spend most of it together, as a family, which obviously includes the child or children I am fostering. When my children were little I used to arrange an activity on a Sunday, visiting a park or place of interest, or seeing family or friends, but now they were older I accepted that they didn't always want to be organized every weekend and liked to spend time just chilling. However, we hadn't been out together the previous two Sundays, so I thought a family outing now would be nice for everyone, including Joss. Doing things together encourages bonding and helps improve family relationships – something Joss was a bit short on. I knew Adrian would want to do some exam revision first, so I would make it for the afternoon only. I racked my brains for an activity that wasn't too far away, preferable outdoors as the weather was good, and that they'd all enjoy. I came up with the Tree Top Adventure Park. It was an assault course set in the treetops of a forest about half an hour's drive away. It had zip wires, swing bridges and rope ladders, and was suitable for ages ten and above. I'd taken my children before but not for a while. I mentioned it to Lucy and Paula first, who liked the idea, and then to Adrian, who agreed that taking the afternoon off would be fine.

Then I knocked on Joss's door.

'Yeah? Come in!' she called from inside.

She was propped up on her bed using the headboard for support, earphones in, and flicking through a magazine. I motioned for her to take out an earphone so she could hear me, then I explained about the proposed outing, emphasizing how much fun it would be and that it was suitable for teenagers, girls and boys. 'You'll need to wear something a bit looser than those tight jeans,' I suggested, 'so you can climb. And trainers rather than sandals.'

'Nah, it's OK,' she said, returning her attention to the magazine. 'You can go. I'll stay here.'

'Joss, I'd like you to come with us, so would the girls and Adrian. While you're here you're part of this family and it's nice to do things together as a family sometimes.'

'Nah, thanks,' she said. 'I'm OK.'

'I want you to come, Joss,' I said.

She looked up. 'If you don't trust me here alone I can go out and meet up with my mates. That's what I did when the other carers went out.'

'But I won't do that,' I said more firmly. 'I would like you to come. It's just for the afternoon and I've chosen an activity you'll like.'

'What if I don't like it?' Joss said. She challenged me on everything if she had a mind to.

'Then you'll put it down to experience and won't ever go again. But at least you will have tried it.'

'Nah,' she said again. 'It's not my thing.' She went back to the magazine and flipped a couple of pages.

There was no way I was leaving Joss alone in the house having heard about the mischief she'd got up to at her previous carers' when she'd been left alone – underage drinking and smoking dope with friends, the house trashed and the police called. Neither was I agreeing to her going out and spending the afternoon on the streets, with the potential for getting into more trouble. Apart from which, I wanted Joss to come with us as part of the family and have a good time.

'I think you'll enjoy it,' I said.

'Nah. I won't,' she said.

I took a breath. It was hard work. 'OK, Joss, the bottom line is: you come with us, which is what I would like, or I can take you to another foster carer for the afternoon.' I knew carers who would help me out if necessary, as I would help them, but whether they were available at such short notice on a Sunday, I didn't know. I was hoping I wouldn't have to put it to the test.

'I don't want to go to another carer,' Joss moaned, her face setting.

'I don't want you to go either. I want you to come with us.' I smiled.

'Is it only for the afternoon?'

'Yes. We'll leave here around twelve-ish and we'll be back about six.'

'OK. You win. Again,' she said. 'But I won't enjoy myself. I'll be miserable all afternoon.'

'Joss, I bet you two pounds you do enjoy yourself. If you do, you'll win; if not, I win.'

It took her a moment to work this out and then she smiled.

Despite her appalling behaviour and bravado, I liked Joss. I felt that underneath there was a nice kid trying to get out. I appreciated that losing her father in such tragic circumstances and then not getting on with her stepfather was a bad deal, but I was hoping that coming to live with me would give her the chance to sort her life out.

Joss did thoroughly enjoy herself at the Tree Top Adventure Park, despite staying in the very tight jeans that pinched her legs when she climbed. She was confident and tackled even the very high walks, wires, swings and ladders fearlessly. So much so that the supervisors stationed throughout the park warned her a few times to take it more steadily or she could fall and injure herself. But then, of course, that was part of Joss's problem. She had no sense of danger. Paula and Lucy took the course together at a steadier pace, and Adrian met a friend from school and they went off together. I completed one circuit and then sat on a bench in the shade of the trees reading my book and also watching the young people having fun. By six o'clock they were all tired and hot and sitting with me in the shade eating ice creams. Our tickets allowed us to stay until the park closed at eight o'clock, but everyone agreed they were ready to go. As we left, Joss actually asked if we could come again.

'We could,' I said. 'But there are other fun places to go on a day out.'

'But I like it here. I've had a good time,' she said.

'Great. You win the bet,' I said. I handed her the two pounds.

On the way home we picked up a takeaway, and after we'd eaten Adrian resumed his studies, Lucy and Paula went up to Paula's room and Joss went to hers. I was just congratulating myself on a successful day when Joss appeared in the living room. I knew straight away from her expression she was in challenge mode. 'As I did what you wanted me to this afternoon, can I go out now?' she said.

'No, Joss. Not tonight, love. You were out Friday and Saturday, and you have school tomorrow. It's already seven-thirty.'

'I'll be back by ten. Just for a couple of hours.'

'No, not tonight. Two nights out over the weekend is plenty.'

'But that's not fair.'

'I think it is fair, but you can raise it with your social worker tomorrow if you wish.'

'I fucking will!' she said, stamping her foot. 'And you can't stop my pocket money now, because you've already given it to me! Cow!'

She stormed out of the living room and upstairs into her bedroom, slamming the door behind her. I felt my heart start racing. Another confrontation. It was so stressful. But I reminded myself that at least she was doing what I'd asked and was staying in, which was a huge improvement. At her previous carers' she'd come and gone as she'd liked, often defying them when they said she had to stay in. Foster carers (and care-home staff) are not allowed to lock a child in the house or physically prevent them from leaving, even if it is for the child's own good. It's considered imprisonment. With your own child you'd do anything within reason to keep them safe, and I think the whole area of what a carer can and can't do to keep a young person safe is something that needs to be looked into, with practical guidelines set up.

I tried not to take Joss's words personally. I knew she was angry – not only with me, but with life in general – and I was an easy target, especially when I put boundaries in place. Once she'd calmed down she usually reverted to being pleasant and often apologized. Sure enough, ten minutes later I heard her bedroom door open. She came down and said she was sorry. Then she joined Lucy and Paula in Paula's room, where the three of them sat chatting and listening to music until it was time to get ready for bed.

Joss had another nightmare that night. I heard her scream and was out of bed in a heartbeat, going round the landing to her room. As usual, she was sitting up in bed with her eyes closed, still half asleep. Normally she didn't say anything as I resettled her, and in the morning she would have no recollection of the nightmare, so I no longer mentioned it. But now, as I gently eased her down and her head touched the pillow, she said softly, 'Daddy used to take us on outings too.'

'That's a lovely memory,' I said quietly. Her eyes were still closed. I sat on the edge of the bed and began stroking her forehead to soothe and comfort her. I guessed the memory had been triggered by our day out.

Her eyes stayed shut, but then her face crumpled in pain. 'Why did you leave us, Daddy? Why? I thought you loved us.' A small tear escaped from the corner of her eye and ran down her cheek onto the pillow. I felt my own eyes fill. The poor child.

She didn't say anything further and appeared to be asleep. I continued to stroke her forehead and soothe her as she drifted into a deep sleep. Then I stood and quietly came out and returned to bed. Joss had never talked about her father to me, but I guessed the horrific memory of that day was probably as fresh as ever. There are so many feelings connected with the suicide of a loved one, apart from the immense sadness at losing them: regret and remorse at things that were said and unsaid; rejection because the person chose to go; guilt (was it something I did?) and anger – perhaps the most difficult to cope with – that the person has gone. Joss was clearly still hurting badly, and I didn't think her behaviour would improve until she had dealt with all the conflicting emotions she must still be wrestling with following her father's death.

The following morning Joss didn't mention her dream. I assumed that, as before, she hadn't remembered it, so I didn't say anything. She had her usual cereal and a glass of juice for breakfast, and then, as I saw her off at the door, I reminded her that she had to go straight to the council offices after school for the meeting with her social worker. I was going too, and so was her mother. I'd offered to collect Joss from school, which would have guaranteed that she arrived, and on time, but she'd refused, and I felt it wasn't something I needed to take a stand on.

'Make sure you catch the first bus as soon as you come out of school,' I emphasized to Joss as I said goodbye. 'No chatting with your friends tonight.'

'I know. I'll see you there,' Joss said. 'But if Mum brings *him* to the meeting, I'm leaving.'

As usual, *'him'* meant her stepfather, Eric, whom Joss so deeply resented. I hadn't met her mother or stepfather yet, and I didn't know if Eric would be there, but it wasn't for me to tell the social worker whom to invite to a meeting. She was aware of the animosity between Joss and her stepfather, so hopefully would have advised Joss's mother, Linda, accordingly.

During the morning, Jill, my supervising social worker, telephoned to see how the weekend had gone, so she had an update from me prior to the meeting. She would be there too. All foster carers in England have a support social worker, also known as a supervising social worker or link worker, supplied by the agency they foster for. Jill had met Joss a few times and was aware of her history. I gave Jill a brief résumé of our weekend, good and bad, but emphasizing that we'd had a good afternoon on Sunday, and Jill said she'd see me at four o'clock at the meeting.

CHAPTER THREE

CONTRACT OF BEHAVIOUR

I arrived in the meeting room that afternoon five minutes early; even so, Amelia, Joss's social worker, whom I'd met when she'd brought Joss to me, was already there, talking to another woman I took to be Joss's mother. I smiled as I sat down but Amelia didn't introduce me, so I said, 'I'm Cathy.'

'Sorry,' Amelia said. 'This is Cathy, Joss's current foster carer. Cathy, this is Linda, Joss's mother.'

'Nice to meet you,' I said. Linda managed a small smile. She looked anxious and a little intimidated. 'Joss is coming here on the bus, straight from school,' I clarified, and Linda nodded.

'You're Joss's third carer, aren't you?' Amelia now said, looking at me.

'Yes, and I need to be her last. She's had too many moves.'

'I'm pleased to hear you say that,' Linda said quietly. 'It's been an added worry for Eric and me.'

'I can imagine.' I sympathized.

'The social services were talking about putting Joss in a secure unit if her behaviour didn't improve,' Linda said.

This was news to me. I looked at Amelia.

'It's something that we might have to consider if Joss doesn't turn her behaviour around, to keep her safe,' she said.

No pressure then, I thought.

'But you know how to look after Joss, don't you?' Linda asked me, desperation in her voice. 'They said you were very experienced.'

'Yes, I am,' I said. 'And I'll do my very best. I think there are a lot of things we can do to help Joss.'

'Thank you so much,' Linda sighed gratefully.

I'd taken an immediate liking to Linda and felt sorry for her. Quietly spoken and unassuming, she was petite – I could see where Joss got it from – and in her early forties. She must have suffered dreadfully after her husband's suicide, and then her stab at happiness had ended in disaster with her daughter becoming out of control and leaving home. It's every parent's worst nightmare.

'Is Joss doing what you tell her?' Linda asked. 'Amelia says her behaviour has already improved.'

Since Joss had been placed with me Amelia had telephoned twice for updates and had obviously passed these on to Linda, although with a little embellishment by the sound of it.

'There haven't been any major incidents,' I said, 'although the first weekend I had to report her missing to the police. There have been a couple of instances of her drinking and, I believe, smoking dope when she's out with her friends, but no violence. I've sanctioned her and she's not happy with me, nor with the boundaries I'm putting in place. I know she wants to talk about these today, but it's early days yet, so I'm hopeful.'

'So you haven't had to call the police to her?' Linda asked. 'She hasn't hit you?'

27

'No. Joss obviously has a lot of anger and I wonder if counselling would help?'

'She won't go,' Linda said. 'Our doctor has offered it a number of times. When my first husband …' Linda paused and took a deep breath. 'When my first husband took his life, our doctor thought it would help Joss to come to terms with the bereavement, but she wouldn't go. I did. Then, more recently, after I married Eric and Joss's behaviour deteriorated badly, I went to our doctor again. But when I told Joss I'd been she got so angry. She accused me of betraying her father and even said that I'd made him so unhappy that he took his life.' Her eyes filled. 'It's not true. We were happy together. No one was more shocked than me. There was nothing in our lives that could have made him do that.' She stopped and looked away.

The room was quiet for a moment and my heart went out to her, then Amelia said, 'It's often the case that loved ones have no idea their partner is thinking of suicide.'

Linda gave a small nod and, taking a tissue from her handbag, blew her nose.

'I'll ask Joss if she will attend counselling at CAMHS [Child and Adolescent Mental Health Services],' Amelia said. 'I suggested it when she first came into care, but she refused. Maybe she's changed her mind.'

The door opened and Jill came in. 'Sorry I'm late – the traffic's heavy,' she said. Then to Linda, whom she hadn't met before: 'I'm Jill, Cathy's supervising social worker.'

'Hello,' she said.

Jill sat next to me. I glanced at the wall clock. It was now five minutes past four. 'I told Joss to come straight here,' I said, feeling responsible for her lateness.

'I hope she comes,' Amelia said, a little weakly. 'One of the items on my agenda is to draw up a contract of behaviour, and I can't do that without Joss.'

A contract of behaviour is a signed agreement between the young person and the adult(s) responsible for them, sometimes known as a home rules contract. It's a set of rules and expectations to modify the young person's unsafe or unacceptable behaviour, with rewards for improving it and consequences for not doing so. For example, the young person may have to be in at a certain time, or do their homework, or stop swearing, smoking or drinking. The consequence of breaking a rule is usually the loss of a privilege.

'What do you do if Joss doesn't do what you tell her?' Linda now asked me.

'I explain why I'm asking her to do – or not do – whatever it is, and if she still won't cooperate I warn her that I'll have to sanction her. Then I make sure I see it through.'

'What sort of sanction?' Linda asked.

'Sometimes I remove the television from her bedroom. All teenagers like to relax on their beds and watch television. It's just for a set period – for example, an hour – then I return it. It's a statement as much as anything, saying that she has to do as she's told. I've also withheld her pocket money and she earns it back through good behaviour. She's not happy with that and it's something else she wants to raise today.'

'Eric and I tried all sorts of things,' Linda said. 'But it just made Joss hate me and become more angry.'

'Joss doesn't hate you,' Jill said. 'She's upset by everything that's happened. It's coming out in her behaviour. We tend to hurt the ones we love.'

At that moment the door opened and Joss came in. 'Are you talking about me?' she asked confrontationally.

I saw Linda tense.

'Of course,' Jill said lightly. 'You're the most important person here.'

'We haven't really said much so far,' Amelia said timorously. 'We were waiting for you.'

Joss pulled out a chair at the far end of the table, away from us all, sat down and tucked her earphones into her bag. She hadn't said hello to her mother, nor had she looked at her, although Linda was looking at Joss very anxiously.

'Now we're all here, let's start by introducing ourselves,' Amelia said. 'I'm Amelia, Joss's social worker.' We took it in turns to state our name and role. When it was Joss's turn she gave a snort of embarrassed laughter and said, 'Joss, the foster kid.'

'Thank you,' Amelia said to Joss as she wrote in her notepad. 'I'll be taking a few notes of the meeting, although we will be keeping it very informal so there's nothing for you to worry about, Joss.'

I heard the patronizing edge in her comment, and so did Joss.

'Whatever,' Joss said with attitude and a dismissive shrug.

Linda looked at her daughter but didn't say anything, and I formed the impression that she was frightened to chastise her.

'This meeting gives us a chance to work together and plan how we can best help you,' Amelia said, addressing Joss. 'First, perhaps you'd like to tell us how you feel you are settling in at Cathy's. You've been there two weeks now.'

'OK, I guess,' Joss said with a shrug.

'Cathy has children of a similar age to you,' Amelia said. 'How are you getting on with them?'

'OK, I guess,' Joss said again.

'She's getting on well with everyone,' I said.

'I can confirm that,' Jill said. 'Joss has settled in well.' Although Joss's stay with me so far had been far from easy, it was important we stayed positive as well as addressing the negative issues so that Joss could hear good things said about her too.

'So you're happy to stay at Cathy's for the time being?' Amelia now asked Joss. This wasn't the right thing to say, and I saw Jill look at Amelia. The question suggested to Joss that she could leave whenever it suited her, which shouldn't have been an option. Every child in care needs to feel secure by putting down roots with their foster family and bonding with them.

I was half expecting Joss to reply with something like, 'For now, maybe,' but to her credit and my relief she said, 'Yeah. It's OK.'

'Good,' Amelia said, making a note. 'Is there anything you want to add about living at Cathy's? Anything you particularly like or dislike?'

'Not really,' Joss said, and shrugged again.

'All right,' Amelia said. 'Let's start by looking at the contact arrangements with your natural family. As you know, you're in care voluntarily, under what is known as a Section 20. That means you and your mother agreed it was best for you to come into care, so the department didn't have to go to court for an order. We can therefore decide on the level of contact, and at present you go home when you want. I think it would be a good idea to formalize the contact arrangements so that you have set days when you see your family. For example, you could spend all day Saturday with them so you can see more of your brother.'

'Yeah, I want to see more of Kevin,' Joss said. 'But not if *he's* gonna be there.' *He*, of course, was her stepfather.

Amelia looked at Linda for her response.

'I can't ask Eric to go out every Saturday,' Linda said quietly. 'It wouldn't be right. It's his home too.' Which was a fair comment.

'There! Told you!' Joss exclaimed. 'It's always him!'

'Perhaps Eric could go out for part of the day?' Amelia suggested. 'Or maybe you and the children could go out? To the cinema, shopping or to the park, or similar?'

'It's possible,' Linda said. 'I'd have to ask Eric. He likes to do things together as a family at the weekends.'

'That's right. You go and ask him! What about me?' Joss snapped.

The problem Linda was experiencing is one faced by many stepfamilies: trying to be fair to all family members and cater for everyone's needs. It's a juggling act and plenty of stepfamilies struggle in the early years. For some it never works out, and sadly either the children leave home as soon as they can or the parents end up separating.

'What do you think about going out with your mother and Kevin?' Jill asked Joss, who was now tapping her fingers on the table and looking very moody. 'Would you like to give it a try?'

'Yeah, OK,' Joss said.

'I'll talk to Eric and see what I can do,' Linda said. 'In the meantime, can we carry on as we have been, with Joss popping in when she's free? I only work part-time so I'm home after school. Even if it's only for a few minutes, it's nice to see her.'

Again I felt so sorry for Linda, who was caught in the middle and trying to please everyone.

'Or we could formalize it,' Amelia persisted. 'We could set some days when Joss definitely goes to you after school – say, Tuesdays and Thursdays, from four till six?'

'No, that won't work,' Joss said. 'I won't know if I'm seeing my mates until the day.' Joss liked to hang out with her friends after school, and that in itself was causing a problem, as she was getting into trouble with them.

'I think I'll leave it as it is,' Linda said. 'Then Joss can pop in when she wants to.'

Amelia accepted this and made a note. 'But you will ask Eric about Saturdays?'

'Yes,' Linda said.

'I need some more of my stuff from home,' Joss now said. 'I want my sound system.'

'I've told you, you can have it,' Linda said. 'It's yours. But I'm concerned it might get damaged if you take it on the bus.'

'Perhaps I could bring Joss in my car to collect what she needs?' I offered.

'Thank you,' Linda said. 'It was an expensive present and I don't want it broken.'

'Shall we set a date for that then?' Amelia asked.

'Wednesday,' Joss said.

'That's all right with me,' Linda said.

'And me,' I confirmed. 'What time?'

'Five,' Joss said.

I made a note in my diary. 'You'll need to come straight home after school, or I can pick you up in my car?' I said.

'I'll use the bus,' Joss said. 'But I'm not speaking to the creep.'

'Don't talk about him like that, please,' Linda said softly. 'It's very hurtful. He's my husband.'

'And I'm your daughter! Or was!' Joss snapped. Linda didn't respond, but I could see she was upset. It was the first time I'd seen mother and daughter together, and it was painful and pitiful to watch. Joss was clearly very angry with her mother and appeared to have the upper hand. I guessed Linda felt guilty that her marriage had resulted in Joss going into care and therefore she didn't like to speak more firmly to her.

'Is there anything else you need to make your stay at Cathy's more comfortable?' Amelia now asked Joss.

'A front-door key,' Joss said.

'I'm sure Cathy has a spare one she can let you have,' Amelia said, turning to me.

'I have a spare key,' I said. 'But I've explained to Joss that she won't be having it just yet. Not until she can show me she is responsible enough to own one – by coming home on time and improving her behaviour at school.'

Amelia and Linda looked slightly taken aback and glanced at Joss for her reaction.

'I think that's fair,' Jill said.

'So do I,' Linda said, emboldened by the stand I was taking. 'I made the mistake of giving Joss a key too young, and so did her other carers. I agree with Cathy. When Joss has proven she is adult enough, then she can have a key.'

'Is that all right with you?' Amelia asked Joss.

Of course it wasn't all right with Joss, and it wasn't wise to ask her. Young teenagers don't always know what is best for them, and sometimes the adults responsible for them have to take charge for their own good.

'No,' Joss predictably said. 'Supposing I get home before Cathy. I won't be able to get in.'

Amelia looked at me.

'I always make sure I'm home first,' I said. 'It hasn't been a problem yet, has it, Joss?'

'Supposing I get taken ill at school and have to come home on the bus and you're not in?' Joss said, ready with an answer as usual. 'I'll have to wait outside in the freezing cold and it'll make me even more ill.'

I didn't point out that it was summer. 'If you're taken sick at school then the school will telephone me,' I said. 'I will come and collect you. No school would ever send a sick child home on the bus. It would be irresponsible of them.' I'd had a lot of experience of looking after children, and if Joss thought she had an answer for everything, then so too did I. Amelia, on the other hand – in her twenties and, I guessed, newly qualified – didn't have the same experience.

'Is that all right, then?' she asked Joss.

Joss shrugged.

'I'm sure Joss will earn the right to a front-door key soon,' Jill said positively, then moving the meeting on she added: 'What's next on the agenda? Counselling?'

'Yes,' Amelia said, glancing at her notepad. 'Joss, you remember when you first came into care I explained about CAMHS and asked if you wanted to talk to someone? I was wondering if –'

'I'm not going,' Joss said adamantly before Amelia could get any further.

'Why not?' Amelia asked.

'I don't want to.'

'Anything you discuss with the counsellor would be confidential,' Jill said. 'It can help to talk to a professional.'

Joss hesitated briefly, but then said, 'No. I don't want to.'

'OK. Tell me if you change your mind,' Amelia said, and made another note on her pad. 'What's next?'

'I want to go out more,' Joss said. 'I want that discussed.'

'Good,' Amelia said, pleased Joss was engaging with the meeting. 'Tell us what you would like.'

I sighed inwardly and thought I heard Jill sigh too. Amelia was pleasant enough but so naïve.

'I want to go out with my mates every night,' Joss said.

Amelia nodded thoughtfully.

'What about your homework?' Jill asked.

'I'll do it before I go out,' Joss replied.

'I think you should stay in one evening,' Amelia said.

'All right. I'll stay in one,' Joss said. 'Monday. There's not much going on at the mall on Mondays.' Joss regularly congregated with her friends at the shopping centre in town, often after the shops had closed. It was one of the places where Joss had come to the attention of the police, and on at least one occasion they had tipped away the alcohol she and her friends were too young to have and sent them on their way.

'I think Joss should be at home with us more than just one night a week,' I said. 'She's only thirteen and she's behind with her school work. Also, we'd like to see more of her.' That being at home would also reduce the number of opportunities for Joss to get into trouble I left unsaid, as Amelia, Linda and Jill would be aware of this, and I wanted to stay as positive as possible.

'I'll make sure I'm back on time,' Joss said.

Amelia didn't respond.

'Most teenagers I know just go out at the weekend,' Jill said.

'Not the ones I know,' Joss said. 'My friend Chloe can see her mates whenever she likes. I go to her place sometimes, so I'm not always on the streets. I can sleep at Chloe's if I like.'

'Joss is welcome to bring her friends home,' I said. 'I always encourage the children I foster to invite their friends back.'

'I'd rather go to her place,' Joss said.

'How would you feel about staying in two nights a week?' Amelia now asked her. 'Would that be all right?'

'I guess,' Joss said.

'I don't think that's enough,' I said. 'I would suggest she goes out on Friday and Saturday only during term time, unless there is a special occasion.'

'No,' Joss said forcefully, jutting out her chin. 'That's not enough. I'm not a kid. And I want to stay out later than nine. That's ridiculous.'

The discussion about how often Joss could go out and when she had to come home continued for another ten minutes, until Joss and Amelia decided between them that Joss would stay in two nights, Sunday and Wednesday, but could go out the other nights as long as she did her homework first. It was agreed, though not by Joss, that she had to be back by 9.30 p.m. on a weekday and 10.30 p.m. on Friday and Saturday, unless there was something special on, when she would negotiate a later time with me. Even so, I felt this was too much for a girl of thirteen with a history of getting into trouble. While Joss was out of the house it was impossible for me to protect her, but I could see that Amelia hadn't wanted to sour her relationship with Joss by going against her. As a foster carer you have to do what the social services decide, unlike in parenting when you can make whatever decisions you deem appropriate for the good of your own child.

'We'll include all of this in the contract of behaviour,' Amelia said as she wrote. 'And that you will stop smoking and drinking alcohol.'

'I can't,' Joss said.

'You can try,' Jill said.

'Can we include that Joss needs to improve her behaviour and grades at school?' Linda asked.

'Yes, of course,' Amelia said, and Joss sighed.

Smoking dope wasn't included in the contract of behaviour, as there was no conclusive evidence that Joss had been smoking illegal substances, although her mother, aunt, previous carers and I had all smelt it on her. The sanctions for not complying with the rules of the contract were loss of privileges: not being allowed out and loss of television time. Jill also said that it should be included that if Joss arrived home more than an hour late then, following current fostering practice, I should report her missing to the police.

'Do you understand that?' Amelia asked Joss.

'Fine with me, but I don't want my pocket money stopped. It's not fair. It's my money and I need it.'

'I understand,' Amelia said.

'It's withheld, not stopped,' Jill said. 'Foster carers are very limited in the sanctions they can use, and withholding pocket money for negative behaviour is something our agency approves of, especially for teenagers. They can and usually do earn it back through good behaviour, and if they don't then it goes into a savings account for them. They don't lose it.'

'We tried stopping her pocket money,' Linda said, 'but Joss said she'd steal what she needed.'

Joss glared at her mother.

'I'm sure you wouldn't be that silly,' Jill said to Joss. Although we all knew that Joss had been caught twice stealing alcohol from small corner shops.

'So shall I include stopping your pocket money in the contract?' Amelia asked Joss ineffectually. 'Is that all right?'

'No. But you'll do it anyway,' Joss moaned.

I saw Amelia hesitate. 'How would you feel if I put that only half of your pocket money could be withheld? Then you'd always have some.'

'Whatever,' Joss said.

'Don't be rude, love,' Linda said gently.

'Why not?' Joss snapped. 'You can't tell me what to do. You lost that right when you married *him*.'

Joss's anger was vehement and I felt for Linda, just as I'm sure Jill did. Without counselling I couldn't see how Joss was ever going to move on with her life or accept that her mother had a right to another chance of happiness, and that remarrying didn't mean she loved her any less.

Amelia glanced at the clock on the wall. It was now 5.40 p.m. We'd been here over an hour and a half. 'Is there anything else you want to discuss, Joss?' she asked.

Joss shrugged.

'Well, in that case I think it would be a good idea to finish now,' Amelia said. 'I'll have the contract typed up and printed, and then I'll arrange for us to sign it. I'm so pleased you were able to come to this meeting, Joss. I think it's been very positive.'

The silence from the rest of us spoke volumes.

CHAPTER FOUR

NO DADDY DOLL

Because Amelia was inexperienced she was trying to be Joss's friend, and it didn't work. Parents, carers, teachers, social workers and others responsible for a child can't ingratiate themselves with the young person and still hope to have the authority necessary to put boundaries in place for their safety and acceptable behaviour. Once the child is a responsible adult it's different – parents often become their friend – but while they are growing up, especially if they are angry and rebellious, as Joss was, then the adults responsible have to take control and accept that sometimes the child won't like them. I'd seen some very good contracts of behaviour that had worked well, but I thought Joss's was simply a licence to do whatever she wanted. It wasn't long before I was proven right.

On the way home in the car Joss lost no time in telling me that, as it was Monday, she was allowed out until 9.30 p.m.

'After you've done your homework,' I said.

'I haven't got any,' she replied.

I doubted this and I'd asked for a meeting with her teacher to discuss Joss's education, but for now I had to accept what Joss told me, so she could go out. Once home, she quickly changed out of her school uniform into leggings and a T-shirt, gobbled down her dinner and then left, shouting goodbye as she went. Although Adrian, Lucy and Paula didn't comment, I knew they felt as I did that it wasn't good for Joss to be out so much, and they would have liked her to stay in more. Their friends' parents had similar rules to me, so they generally accepted the boundaries I put in place.

They were upstairs getting ready for bed when Joss returned at ten o'clock. When I let her in I could smell alcohol on her, although she didn't appear drunk. I was worried more than annoyed.

'Joss, why do you keep drinking when you know how bad it is for your health?' I asked wearily.

'To forget,' she said, kicking off her shoes.

This was far more revealing than any of her previous responses of 'dunno' or 'none of your business' or 'I like it', so I felt she might want to talk.

'Joss, I understand you don't want to see a counsellor, but can you try to share with me what exactly you are trying to forget?'

'You know already,' she said. 'My dad and *him*.'

'Do you want to talk about your dad?' I asked.

'No.'

'Do you want to talk about your stepfather?' I tried.

'No.'

She began upstairs.

'Joss, do you talk to anyone – Chloe maybe? – about the things that worry you? We all need someone to talk to.'

She shrugged and continued upstairs. 'Are you going to stop my pocket money because I was late?'

'Not if you are back on time tomorrow.'

She paused on the stairs and turned to look at me. 'Why do you foster? It can't be much fun.'

I smiled as I met her gaze. 'Because I like fostering. I like to try to help young people, and if I can make even a small difference I feel very pleased.'

'But what if you can't help them?' she said.

'It hasn't happened yet. I always find a way to help a little.'

'Not with me, you won't,' she said bitterly and, turning, continued upstairs.

'Even with you, Joss,' I called after her.

'No. I'm beyond your help.'

Joss cried out in the night, and as usual I went round and resettled her. She wasn't awake, but I stayed with her until she was in a deep sleep again. It was indicative of the high level of her inner turmoil that she had so many nightmares, but until she opened up and started talking about her profound unhappiness the nightmares would continue – and so too, I thought, would her angry and self-destructive behaviour.

She had breakfast with us as usual on Tuesday morning and I saw her off to school at the door. Then at 9.30 a.m. her school's secretary telephoned to say that Joss hadn't arrived. It was school policy to notify the parents or carers if a young person hadn't arrived by 9.30, and it had happened before. I assumed that, as before, Joss would arrive late, and sure enough at 9.50 the secretary telephoned again to say that Joss had just arrived – an hour late – and that she would be kept in a sixty-minute detention after school to make up the work she'd missed. This was also school policy. I thanked the secretary for letting me know and asked if she'd remind her form

42

teacher that I would like a meeting with her to discuss Joss as soon as possible. She said she'd pass on my message.

School finished at 3.30 p.m., so, allowing for the sixty-minute detention and half an hour on the bus, I was expecting Joss home at about five o'clock. In fact, she arrived home at 5.30, which wasn't too bad, so I let that go, but I did ask her why she'd been an hour late for school that morning when she'd left the house on time.

'I went home first,' she said.

'What for?'

'To get a book I needed for school. I thought I might have left it there. They give you a detention if you keep forgetting your books.'

'And did you find the book?'

'No. I think I've lost it. I tried to tell my teacher the reason I was late, but she didn't believe me.'

I was suspicious too, but I didn't say so.

'Joss, in future it's better to forget a book than arrive an hour late for school. I was worried where you might have got to.'

'OK. I did my homework in detention, so can I go straight out? It's Tuesday and I'm allowed out.'

'I know, but you're having your dinner first, and really, Joss, I'd like it if you stayed in. We could watch some television together, or you could spend some time with Lucy and Paula. They'd like that.'

'I'll see them tomorrow evening instead,' Joss said, ready as always with a reply. 'It's Wednesday so I'm not allowed out. And you're taking me to get my sound system from home.'

'I hadn't forgotten. If you go out tonight, where will you be going?'

'To Chloe's.'

'I can take you in the car.'

'No, thanks.'

'I'll collect you, then.'

'No, thanks.'

I couldn't insist on this as a condition of her going, as I had done with her trip to the cinema, because the contract of behaviour had overridden me.

'Make sure you're back by half past nine, then,' I reminded her. 'No later.'

She nodded.

Joss arrived back at ten minutes past ten – forty minutes late – and smelling of alcohol, so I told her I was stopping half her pocket money and that she could earn it back through good behaviour: by coming home on time and not drinking for the rest of the week.

'That's not fair!' she yelled angrily.

'It is fair, Joss. I warned you last night when you were late back that I would stop your pocket money if the same happened again tonight.'

'I hate you!' she yelled, and stomped upstairs. 'I fucking hate you!'

Lucy suddenly appeared from her bedroom in her pyjamas. I could see she was angry.

'Don't you dare yell at my mother like that!' she shouted at Joss as she arrived on the landing. 'Who the hell do you think you are? You want to be bloody grateful my mum took you in. No one else would!'

'Lucy!' I cried, running up the stairs. 'Calm down.' I'd never seen her so angry before.

'You can shut your face too!' Joss shouted at Lucy.

Lucy raised her hand as if she was about to slap Joss as I arrived on the landing and moved her away. 'No, Lucy,' I said firmly. 'Don't.'

She lowered her hand and Joss grinned provocatively.

'Go to your room, now!' I said to Joss.

She hesitated.

'I said now!'

Smirking, she went round the landing to her room, slamming the door behind her with such force that the whole house shook.

Lucy was still fuming and looked as though she might go after Joss. I took her arm. 'Come on, let's go and sit in your room and talk.'

She came with me into her bedroom and we sat side by side on the bed. We could hear Joss stomping around in her room, nosily opening and closing drawers.

'Who does she think she is?' Lucy said. 'I'm not having her talk to you like that.'

I slipped my arm around her waist and held her close.

'It's all right, love.'

'I'm going to really hit her hard one day,' Lucy said, clenching her fists in her lap. 'I just know it. I won't be able to stop myself.'

I took her hand in mine. While I was touched by Lucy's loyalty, we both knew that physical violence was never right in any circumstances and if she ever did hit Joss, it would put an end to our fostering forever.

I held her close and gently stroked her hand as she slowly calmed down.

'I know I shouldn't have threatened her,' she said at last. 'But she gets to me.'

'That's what she's aiming for,' I said. 'Joss thinks that if she pushes us too far then I'll ask for her to be moved, as the other carers did. And that will confirm to her that she really is as bad and unlovable as she believes.'

'But why?' Lucy asked, raising her head from my shoulder. 'She doesn't have to behave like this. My life was hell for a long time before I came into care. I just wanted to die, so I know how she feels. But she's safe here, and at some point you have to let go of your anger and move on. You can't feel sorry for yourself forever.' Lucy had been through a lot before she came to me two years previously – I tell her story in *Will You Love Me?*

'That's true, but Joss hasn't reached that stage yet; far from it. She's harbouring a whole lot of unresolved feelings around her father's death and her mother remarrying. She feels very rejected.'

Lucy sighed. 'I know, but how long is this going to go on for?'

A knock sounded on Lucy's door, and we both looked over as it slowly opened and Adrian poked his head round. 'Are you two all right?' he asked, concerned.

'Yes, thanks, love. We're OK.' It was all quiet in Joss's room now.

'Paula wants to talk to you when you're free,' Adrian said.

'Please tell her I'll be with her in a few minutes.'

'Will do,' Adrian said, and went out.

'Joss's behaviour upsets Paula at lot,' Lucy said.

I felt even more worried. 'I'll talk to her in a moment, but other than keep going as we have been, I'm not sure what else we can do for Joss right now. You're the same age as her. Have you got any suggestions of how I can help her more?'

'Not really. I know I was angry about everything that had happened to me, but it came out in different ways. I stopped eating, for one.'

I nodded thoughtfully. Lucy had been anorexic when she'd come to me, but she had recovered now.

'Could I have done anything differently with you?' I asked.

'I don't think so. You gave me the space and time I needed. I felt safe here, and you were always ready to listen to me when I wanted to talk. You still are.' She kissed my cheek and I hugged her. 'Mum, I'll try to be more patient with Joss, but it's difficult. Paula and I have welcomed her like a sister, so it makes us really cross when she is horrible to you.'

'I understand.'

Fostering changes the social dynamics within the family, and the foster child's age, experience before coming into care, disposition and coping mechanisms all have an effect and create an individual whom the fostering family have to adjust to and accommodate – quickly. Although Lucy was the same age as Joss and knew what it was like to be a foster child, they were very different personalities and at different stages in their lives. I thought it would be best if, for the time being, Lucy put some distance between her and Joss to avoid another flare-up. Lucy certainly wasn't a violent child, but she was protective of me, and I could see how Joss would wind her up.

'Lucy, I don't want you to worry about me, love,' I said. 'I appreciate all you've done to welcome Joss and help her settle in, but you have your own life to lead, and you're doing very well. Leave her to me until she's calmer. I'll call you if I need your help.'

Lucy threw me a small smile. 'I think that's a good idea, or I might do something I later regret.'

'Good girl. Now you'd better get into bed. It's late and you've got school tomorrow.'

Lucy nodded. 'I *was* in bed when I heard Joss kick off.'

I waited until she was back under the covers and then hugged and kissed her goodnight. Reassuring her again that she mustn't worry about me, I came out and closed her door. I went to Paula's room next. She was sitting up in bed, using the headboard as a backrest, with her lamp on, and gazing pensively across the room. I went over and she made room for me on the bed, resting her head on my shoulder. We often sat like this for our bedtime chats, but it was getting late – nearly eleven o'clock.

'You won't be able to get up in the morning,' I said gently.

'I'm not really tired now,' she said.

'Try not to let Joss's behaviour upset you. She's angry. I don't take her words personally.'

'But what I don't understand is how she can be nice one minute, wanting to play with my doll's house, and then stomp around and be revolting the next.' Paula had a really nice doll's house that she was given as a special present when she was four. Since then she'd bought beautiful furniture for it, so it was really a collector's piece now. Although she no longer played with it as such, given that she was twelve, it still stood majestically on a small table in the corner of her bedroom where she could see and admire it. I knew Joss liked to play with it, role-playing the family as a much younger child would. She always asked Paula first if she could play with it and Paula always let her.

'Joss is very confused,' I said. 'I'm afraid you're going to have to try to ignore her mood swings. Don't take it to heart. She's had a rough time.'

'I know. Her dad died and she hates her stepfather,' Paula said.

'Does Joss ever talk to you about it?'

'Not really. But I've noticed she never plays with the daddy doll in the house. She hides him in the garage and then plays with the mummy doll and the two children. I almost understand why she hides the daddy, and yet I don't. My dad doesn't live with us, but when I used to play with my doll's house I always included him. I mean, it's OK to pretend, isn't it?'

'Of course it is, love, but then you still see your dad, even though he doesn't live with us. Joss can't ever see her dad again, can she? Perhaps that's why she hides the daddy doll. Perhaps it's too painful for her to even pretend.'

Paula nodded. 'That makes sense. I think I might be a child psychologist when I leave school and help children who've suffered. It's interesting the way the mind works.'

'It is,' I agreed. 'And a child psychologist is a very good career,' I added, although I knew, of course, that Paula was young and could easily change her mind before she decided on a career.

'Will Joss see a psychologist?' Paula now asked.

'Hopefully, or a counsellor, when she feels ready.'

'I think it could help her, don't you?'

'I do,' I said.

'I don't like it when she's so angry.'

'I know, love, it's frightening to watch, but you know I'll always protect you.'

She hugged me hard.

'Was there anything else you wanted to talk about?'

'Not really. I just wanted to make sure you were all right, and tell you I love you.'

'I love you too,' I said. 'I'm fine, so don't you worry about me. And, Paula, it's nice that you let Joss into your room whenever she wants, but you know you don't have to. If you want time alone, you can just tell her politely that you'll see her later.' I wondered if perhaps Paula was intimidated by Joss's angry outbursts and felt she had to do whatever she asked.

'I usually let her in because I feel sorry for her, and she's OK to be with sometimes.'

'That's fine. But remember you don't have to. It's your room.'

We hugged and then I kissed her goodnight and came out. Thankfully, Paula and Lucy could talk about their worries. It was all quiet in Joss's room, but I wanted to make sure she was OK too, so I went round and, giving a small knock, quietly opened her bedroom door. She always slept with the light on low, so I could easily see from the door that she was in bed and fast asleep. I closed the door again. There was no sound coming from Adrian's room either, so I lightly knocked on his door and then slowly opened it. His room was in darkness, so I knew he was in bed asleep.

'Night, love,' I whispered.

'Night, Mum,' came his muffled, sleepy reply.

I closed his door and went downstairs. Thankfully, Adrian had taken the last of his GCSE examinations that day, so I no longer had the added worry that Joss's rages might be disturbing his studies. Downstairs I settled Toscha in her bed for the night and then locked up. By the time I climbed into bed it was nearly midnight and I was exhausted. Despite my concerns about Joss and the impact her behaviour was having on the rest of the family, I soon fell asleep. Joss must have been exhausted too, for she slept through without a nightmare and I had to wake her in the morning.

'A new day, a fresh start' is my motto, but there was an atmosphere at breakfast between the girls. No one was usually very talkative at breakfast anyway, but this morning there was a frosty silence, broken only by the sound of cutlery on china. When Joss stood to take her empty cereal bowl into the kitchen she caught the table and it jolted against Lucy, who was sitting opposite. Possibly it was an accident, although Lucy clearly didn't think so.

'It's not clever,' she hissed at Joss.

'Touchy!' Joss retaliated with a sneer.

I motioned for Lucy not to say anything further, and Joss put her bowl in the sink and then went upstairs to get ready.

'Sorry,' Lucy said after she'd left the room.

I nodded and let it go. Joss had provoked Lucy – intentionally or by accident – and Lucy had retaliated instead of ignoring it. She'd apologized, so that was the end of the matter.

When Joss was ready I saw her off at the door, reminding her to come straight home, as we had to be at her parents' house at five o'clock.

'Mum's house,' she corrected. 'It's not *his.*'

'OK. See you later,' I said.

Adrian, Lucy and Paula left soon after. Although Adrian had taken his exams, he was still expected to attend school until the end of the summer term, in six weeks' time. Jill telephoned mid-morning and, having asked how we all were, she said she'd raised concerns about the behaviour contract with Amelia. She'd pointed out that it was too lax to be of any use, but Amelia had said she felt that if the rules were any stricter Joss would rebel against it and not cooperate at all.

'She's barely cooperating now,' I said. 'I hope Amelia appreciates that while Joss is out of the house I cannot be held responsible for her safety or what trouble she might get into.'

'I made that clear,' Jill said. 'Sadly, Amelia thinks a secure unit might be the only option for Joss in the end. You can only do your best.'

CHAPTER FIVE

ERIC

Because there were so few opportunities to praise Joss, I tended to go over the top when one arose. So on Wednesday afternoon, when she came home straight from school as I'd asked, I was very effusive in my praise and told her she'd earned back one pound of her pocket money. This led to Lucy taking me to one side and remarking a little sarcastically, 'What's the occasion? Have I missed something here? I thought I came home on time every day.'

'I know you do, love,' I said. 'I'd assumed you knew how grateful I was that I don't have to worry about you, or Adrian and Paula, as I'm having to do with Joss. It's very stressful.'

Lucy looked suitably embarrassed and went quietly into the garden to join Paula, who was sitting on the bench in the shade of the tree. Adrian had stayed behind at school with some of his friends to use the gym. I'd made quiche for our evening meal, which we could heat up quickly later when I returned from taking Joss to collect her sound system from home. I told the girls that if they and Adrian were hungry they could eat before I got back, and do some new potatoes and peas to go with the quiche.

Once Joss had changed out of her school uniform, I said goodbye to the girls, and Joss and I got into the car. She was wearing a very short skirt and a tiny little T-shirt that didn't cover her middle. While this was just about acceptable for a hot afternoon and riding in the car, it wouldn't have been acceptable for going out in the evening with her friends and using public transport. The way Joss dressed was something else I needed to advise her on one day, but not yet. There were other, more pressing matters to address first; for example, her drinking and drug-taking.

Joss hadn't said hello or goodbye to Lucy and Paula, and as I drove she kept her earphones in so she didn't have to talk or listen to me. She didn't remove them until I pulled onto the estate where she lived – as I slowed the car, uncertain of where her house was, she finally took them out and gave me directions. The small, well-maintained estate had been built about fifteen years before, and was a mixture of social and private housing. Joss's house was semi-detached in a street of similar houses, each with an integral garage and a neat, open-plan front garden.

'Perfect timing,' I said as I parked by the kerb and cut the engine. 'It's exactly five o'clock.'

'Sod it, I've forgotten my front-door key,' Joss said. 'I've left it in my school bag.'

'Your mother will be in, won't she?'

'Yeah, I guess,' Joss said.

We got out and I followed her up the short path to the front door. 'Will your stepfather be in too?' I asked.

'No,' she said, pressing the bell. 'He doesn't finish work until six.'

Linda opened the door and Joss said a frosty 'Hi'.

'Come on in, love,' Linda said, smiling and welcoming her. 'Hello, Cathy.'

As we entered, a young boy ran down the hall, yelling 'Joss!' at the top of his voice.

'Kevin!' Joss cried. 'How's my little brother?' She spread her arms wide and he ran into them, laughing. 'Good to see you, mate,' she said, and hugged him hard.

Joss's sulky ill humour, which had dominated the last couple of days, immediately lifted. Now I saw a loving older sister, as pleased to see her little brother as he was to see her. Her tenderness gave me a glimpse of another, much warmer side to Joss that she usually kept well hidden under a tough exterior.

'Come through to the living room, Cathy,' Linda said. 'Can I get you a drink?'

'Could I have a glass of water, please?'

'Sure.'

She showed me into a tidy and tastefully furnished living room at the rear of the house that overlooked a garden with recently mown grass and borders of shrubs and flowers. I sat in one of the armchairs as Joss and Kevin appeared in the garden from the back door, laughing and throwing a ball to each other. Linda returned with two glasses of water and set them on the coffee table. 'You're not in a rush, are you?' she said. 'It's nice if they spend some time together. I've already packed Joss's sound system and some other things she might need.'

'Thanks. I can stay for a while. It's lovely to see them playing together. I expect Kevin misses Joss a lot.'

'He does,' Linda said. 'For all Joss's bad ways, she's always been a good sister to Kevin.' I nodded. 'We had to wait a while for Kevin,' Linda said. 'There's an age gap of five years, but right from the start Joss adored him. She liked to help me feed and change him when he was a baby, and she's always looked out for him and protected him. Even now, big as she is, she's still happy to have a rough and tumble with him.'

The patio doors were slightly open and through the gap the sound of Joss and Kevin laughing drifted in. I smiled and took a sip of my water.

'How has Joss been?' Linda asked, concerned.

'About the same,' I said. 'She has been late back the last two evenings, so I've stopped half her pocket money, as was agreed at the meeting. Joss wasn't happy, but she can earn it back.'

'I didn't think much of that behaviour contract,' Linda said. 'Neither did Eric when I told him. He wanted to put in a formal complaint. He's never liked that social worker.'

I wasn't going to be drawn into a discussion about Amelia; clearly she'd thought she was doing what was right, so I steered the conversation in a different direction and now asked Linda something that had been on my mind for a while.

'Joss has a lot of nightmares. Did she have them here?'

'Yes, and at her other carers'.'

'When did they start?'

'A few days after her dad died, but they got a lot worse about a year ago. I don't know why. Eric says it's the drink and drugs affecting her brain.'

'They certainly won't help,' I said. 'But I suppose Joss still carries the memory of her father's death with her. It must have been very traumatic for you all.'

'Yes, it was. Although it was over four years ago now, if I think about it I can still see it as clearly as though it were yesterday – and I had bereavement counselling for two years. Joss would never talk to anyone about what happened. She began bed-wetting and having nightmares a few days after her father died. The bed-wetting stopped as she got older, but the nightmares continued on and off. Thankfully Kevin didn't witness the horror as Joss did. You don't forget it.'

She took a deep breath and swallowed hard before continuing.

'I'd collected Joss and Kevin from school that afternoon. Kevin had just started nursery. Steven, their father, had taken the day off work sick. He said he had a stomach ache, that was all, and then he'd spent most of the afternoon tinkering in the garage. The car wouldn't always start and he thought he knew what was wrong with it. He seemed fine, normal, when I left. There was nothing to say he was about to take his life. I called goodbye as I left the house, and when he didn't reply I assumed he couldn't hear me because he had the radio on. He usually had the radio on when he was working in the garage. I now know he could have already been dead.' Linda paused and took another breath. My heart went out to her. 'The coroner put the time of his death at around three o'clock, which was the time I left the house. If Steven wasn't already dead then he was about to kill himself. Of course, I've tormented myself with what if, instead of calling goodbye, I'd gone into the garage to say goodbye – could I have saved him? I'll never know.

'When I returned from school with the children,' Linda continued, 'Joss – always a daddy's girl – wanted to be with him in the garage. She liked to be with him, helping him, passing him a spanner or a rag to wipe his hands on when they were oily. She was by my side as I opened the door, that door in the hall.' Linda nodded in the direction of the hall. 'It goes straight into the garage. Joss ran in slightly ahead of me and screamed. He'd tied a rope to a rafter in the roof of the garage and hanged himself by stepping off the car roof. I grabbed Joss and pushed her out of the garage, but it was too late. She'd seen what I had. I knew straight away he was dead.

'I closed the door and phoned for an ambulance. They played the call in the coroner's court and you can hear Joss screaming in the background. It's blood curdling. The paramedics and police arrived, and my parents came over and looked after Joss and Kevin while I gave a statement to the police. Mum and Dad were as devastated as we were – they loved Steven like a son. No one had expected it, absolutely no one. The police notified Steven's parents as I couldn't make that call. After they'd got over the initial shock, they blamed me for not noticing Steven was depressed. But he wasn't. Perhaps I should have seen something, but try as I might I don't know what it could have been. His parents don't see us any more.' Linda stopped.

'I'm so very sorry,' I said.

'Thank you, Cathy. You never forget something like that, but I told myself that Joss was young and in time she would get over it. I was going to move us away, but this house was our home and it had seen happy times too. The counselling helped me. I never dreamed I'd marry again, but then eighteen months ago I met Eric and he proposed five months later. Joss was cold towards him from the start, but I assumed it was just a matter of time. Eric has been very understanding, but it hasn't helped. Joss has said some awful things to him – that she wishes he'd hang himself.' I grimaced. 'I know, awful, isn't it? Kevin has been far more accepting, but then, of course, he's younger and didn't see what Joss and I saw. To be honest, Cathy, if I could have foreseen how this would turn out, I wouldn't have remarried. I thought we'd all be happy, but we're not.' Linda's eyes filled and she reached for a tissue. I felt so sorry for her, but it was difficult to know what to say. Sometimes a tragedy is so great that words are completely inadequate.

We were both quiet for some moments. My gaze went to the garden where Joss and Kevin were now playing badminton, laughing and shouting as they hit or missed the shuttlecock. In their play I saw the happy, carefree family that had lived here before tragedy struck.

'Joss is only thirteen,' I said. 'Perhaps in time, and with her living away from home, she might start to see things differently.'

'That's what I thought when she first went to stay with my sister. I thought, give her time and she'll mend her ways and come back. But it hasn't happened. As you know, her behaviour was so bad at my sister's that we had to ask the social services for help. Then the first two carers weren't able to cope, and now I'm so worried they'll put her in a secure unit before long. Imagine your thirteen-year-old daughter in prison ... although they don't call it that.' Linda's brow furrowed.

'I'm doing all I can to try to stop that from happening,' I said.

'I know you are. And I am grateful. It just gets to me sometimes.'

'Is Eric supportive?' I asked.

'Yes. Very. He couldn't do more for us.'

We both looked down the garden as Joss screamed, having narrowly missed a shot. 'Beat you!' Kevin shouted, also laughing.

Then another noise came from the hall – a key going into the lock of the front door. Linda visibly tensed. 'It must be Eric home early,' she said anxiously. Standing, she left the room.

I heard the front door open and Linda say, 'Hi, love, you're home early.'

'I left work early so I could meet Cathy and see Joss,' Eric said.

'Cathy is in the living room and the kids are in the garden,' Linda told him.

A moment later Eric strode into the living room and I stood to shake his hand. 'Eric, Joss's stepfather,' he said. 'Lovely to meet you at last.'

'And you,' I said.

Of average height and build, I guessed he was at least ten years older than Linda – in his mid-fifties. He was dressed in grey trousers with a light-grey open-neck shirt and was clearly very hot – beads of perspiration glistened on his forehead.

'Would you like a cold drink, love?' Linda asked him.

'I'll get it. You stay here and talk to Cathy. I'll join you when I've said hello to the kids.'

Linda still looked very tense and waited until Eric had left the room before she spoke again, and then it was in a lowered tone. 'In some ways I think it would be better if he stopped trying to be friends with Joss and just left her alone. He keeps trying in the hope that one day he'll get through to her, but it's having the opposite effect.'

I nodded. 'It must be very difficult.'

'It is,' she said.

A few moments later Eric appeared in the garden and we heard him call 'Hello' to Joss and Kevin. Joss let the shuttlecock fall to the ground and threw her racket after it. I could see the anger on her face. She stormed up the garden, past Kevin and Eric and into the house. She came into the living room looking like thunder.

'What the fuck is he doing here?' she demanded.

'Joss, don't, please,' Linda said. Standing, she went over to her daughter. 'He just wanted to see you and meet Cathy. He was trying to do the right thing.'

'Right thing my arse! I'm going to my room,' Joss said. She went out of the living room as Kevin and Eric could be heard coming in from the garden. 'Kev!' she called. 'Come with me to my room. But make sure that creep doesn't come or I'll kick him where it hurts.'

Linda looked so embarrassed. 'I'm sorry, Cathy.'

'Don't worry. I've heard worse. I'll speak to Joss later about her language and behaviour.'

'Thank you. I'm afraid we just let her get away with it now, as nothing we say makes any difference.'

Eric came into the living room with a glass of water, mopping his brow with a piece of kitchen towel. He sat on the sofa beside Linda and patted her arm. 'Try not to worry, pet,' he said.

Linda shrugged despondently. Easier said than done, I thought.

'Linda tells me you've been fostering a long time,' Eric said, making conversation.

'Yes, over fifteen years.' I smiled.

'That's marvellous. It's something I'd like to do, or adopt. I understand there's a shortage of foster carers.'

'Yes, there is,' I said.

'Linda and I have talked about it, haven't we, pet?' Eric said, turning towards her.

'I think we need to sort out Joss's problems first,' Linda sensibly said. 'I'll go up and see her.'

Linda stood and left the living room. Eric drank some of his water and then set the glass carefully on the table. 'At least Kevin likes me,' he said awkwardly.

'It can be very difficult raising stepchildren,' I offered.

He gave a small laugh. 'You can say that again. I'm sure it would be much easier raising our own child.'

I nodded politely. Footsteps sounded on the stairs and then Joss's voice called from the hall. 'Cathy! We're going!'

I smiled at him and stood. 'It was nice meeting you,' I said.

'And you,' he said, also standing.

He followed me down the hall. Joss stood at the front door with Kevin and her mother, holding a bag each.

'What do you want?' Joss said to Eric as soon as she saw him.

'Joss!' Linda chastised.

'I just wanted to say goodbye,' Eric said.

'Well, you've said it, so bugger off.'

Linda sighed. Given Joss's animosity towards Eric, I felt it would have been wiser if he'd stayed in the living room and had called goodbye from there, but it wasn't for me to say.

Joss opened the front door and went out first, carrying the largest of the bags, followed by her mother and brother. Eric followed me out and we went down the path. He stood with the others on the pavement as I unlocked the car and lifted the boot lid.

'Do you want some help, pet?' he asked me, stepping forward.

'Not from you!' Joss snapped. And again I felt Eric would have done better keeping his distance (as Linda had suggested), for clearly anything he did or said antagonized Joss.

'It's OK, thank you,' I said to him.

I helped lift the bags into the boot, checked that the bag containing the sound system was secure and couldn't fall over, and then closed the boot lid. Joss hugged and kissed Kevin, said a stiff 'Goodbye' to her mother and blanked Eric.

I said goodbye to the three of them, and Joss and I got into the car.

'Creep,' Joss said, loud enough for Eric to hear, before she closed her car door.

I started the engine, gave them a brief wave and drove away. I couldn't ignore Joss's bad language and behaviour, for to do so would suggest I was condoning it.

'Joss, you obviously love your brother a lot. Don't you think you should set him a good example? I'm sure you would be appalled if he started behaving as you do.'

'*He*', meaning Eric, 'shouldn't have come home,' Joss said, still angry. 'He only did it to annoy me.'

'Why would he do that?' I asked.

'Because he knows I hate him. He never leaves work early. He always comes in at the same time – that's why I call in at Mum's on the way home from school. I know he won't be there. He did it to upset me.'

'But why would he want to upset or annoy you?' I asked.

Joss shrugged.

I glanced at her as I drove. 'Joss, there could be another reason why Eric came home early, a nicer reason: that he's trying to build a relationship with you.'

'Bullshit,' Joss said. 'He's a wanker. I hate him and he knows why.'

'Whatever you may think of him, I don't want you using that language. Not to me, your parents or anyone, and certainly not in front of your younger brother. Swear again and I'll remove your television from your bedroom for the rest of this evening.'

'Whatever!' Joss said, and she put in her earphones and turned up her music.

CHAPTER SIX

DECEIVED

The following afternoon I received a telephone call from Joss's form teacher, Miss Pryce. She apologized for not being in touch sooner, she'd been very busy, and she invited me to go into school to meet her the next day at 12.30 p.m.

'I'm afraid my lunch hour is the only time I have free,' she said.

I thanked her, confirmed I'd be there and felt marginally guilty for taking up her lunch break.

When Joss arrived home from school that afternoon I told her I was seeing her teacher the following day. 'So I hope she's going to tell me lots of good things about how well you've been doing,' I said. 'And that all your homework is up to date.'

'I doubt it,' Joss said with her usual shrug.

'Well, in that case you need to do your homework before you go out this evening. That's what the contract of behaviour says.'

'I haven't signed the contract yet,' Joss said, ready with a retort as always. 'Anyway, my homework is up to date.'

I wasn't convinced this was true, but I would wait until I'd heard what Miss Pryce had to say before I said anything further to Joss about her school work.

The atmosphere at dinner that evening was less strained than it had been during the last few meals, after Lucy and Joss's set-to – they made an effort to speak to each other, while Paula and Adrian kept a low profile and concentrated on eating. As soon as Joss had finished her pudding she stood to leave.

'Joss, would you remain at the table, please, until everyone has finished,' I said. 'It's polite.'

'Do I have to?' she grumbled. 'You sound like my mum.'

'Yes, please. It's only six-twenty; you've still got plenty of time to go out.'

She pulled a face but did as I asked, and sat down and waited until we'd all finished.

'Done?' she asked as Paula, the last to finish, set her spoon in her bowl.

'Yes, thank you,' I said. 'You can go now.'

Joss took her dishes to the kitchen sink, then went into the hall, put on her shoes and called goodbye as she left.

I am sorry to say that I always felt more relaxed when Joss was out of the house, as I never knew when she would erupt in another angry outburst or confrontation. Although, of course, when she was out I also worried – about the mischief she could be getting up to and whether she was safe. I was expecting her to return home late – she hadn't managed to return on time after an evening out with her friends yet – and if she did I would be stopping one pound from her pocket money (the one pound she'd earned back for coming home on time the previous afternoon). She would still have half her allowance, as Amelia had stipulated she should. However, to my surprise and delight, she returned at exactly 9.30 p.m.

'Well done, good girl,' I said. 'I am pleased.'

'Can I have a door key now, as I'm back on time?' she asked.

'Not yet, love. "One swallow doesn't make a summer."'

She looked at me slightly oddly, and slipped off her shoes.

'You're working towards it,' I said. 'A couple of weeks of coming home on time and then we'll see.'

'What's a couple?' she asked.

'Two.'

She pulled a face. 'I can't do that,' she said. 'Two weeks is far too long. I'm not an angel.'

I had to smile. She had a dry sense of humour sometimes. 'Joss, you've come home on time tonight, as you did yesterday afternoon, so there is no reason why you can't do it again, and again.'

'I had a lift tonight,' she said.

'From Chloe's mother?'

'Her uncle.'

'I trust he hasn't been drinking too?' I could smell alcohol on Joss's breath, although she wasn't drunk.

'Only one. He's sensible,' she said.

She said she wanted a glass of water and went into the kitchen. I wandered in too.

'Was Chloe in the car with you as well?' I asked casually.

'I think so,' she said as she took a glass from the cabinet.

'You must know, love.'

'Yeah, she was.' Joss concentrated on filling her glass from the cold-water tap.

I looked at her carefully. 'Joss, I'm only trying to protect you and keep you safe. I care about you, and while you're with me I'm responsible for you.'

'Yeah, I know, you said. Thanks. It's much appreciated,' she said dismissively.

She switched off the tap, said goodnight and went upstairs to bed. Joss's hostility and constant rebuffs were without doubt a defence mechanism – to stop others from getting close. The logic behind this is that if you don't form an attachment, with the possibility of losing that person, then you won't be hurt again. Only, of course, it doesn't work like that, and one of the scariest places to be is a teenager isolated, alone and suffering in silence.

The following day, at 12.15 p.m., I parked my car in a side road close to Joss's school and made my way round to the main front entrance. The weather was warm and the students were allowed off the school premises during lunch break. I passed small groups of kids chatting and laughing and also smoking quite openly, although out of sight of the main building. I thought it was a great pity that so many young people still thought smoking was cool and hadn't got the message that it was damaging their health. The school was in the older part of town and didn't have the best reputation. From what I'd heard and read in the local newspaper, the standard of teaching was reasonable, but there were ongoing concerns about discipline and the students' behaviour, both inside and outside the school. Shopkeepers in the area complained about pilfering, and residents said that gangs of students roamed the streets after school, graffitiing fences and walls, throwing rubbish into gardens and bad-mouthing anyone who came out to complain.

I went in through the main doors and gave my name to the receptionist, explaining that I had an appointment with Miss Pryce at 12.30. She said she'd let her know I was here and asked me to sign in the visitors' book and take a seat in the waiting area, which was over to the left. The corridors were noisy at lunchtime with students milling around. They wandered past me in pairs and small groups on their way outside. Many of the girls wore their skirts very short, as Joss did, with knee-length socks, which were fashionable. Both girls and boys had their ties loosened, or weren't wearing them at all, and some had multiple ear piercings, as Joss did. Presently, Miss Pryce appeared. She introduced herself – 'Lisa Pryce' – and then led the way down a corridor and into a room on the right.

'We shouldn't be disturbed in here. Do sit down,' she said, waving to the four chairs that stood around a small table in the centre of the room. A photocopier, filing cabinets and cupboards stood against the walls.

'Thank you for making the time to see me,' I said.

'Not at all. It's important we meet. I'm very worried about Joss, and all the moves haven't helped. She won't be moved again, will she?'

'I hope not. But ultimately it will be for the social services to decide what is best for her in the long term.'

Miss Pryce tutted. I guessed she was in her mid-thirties, about five feet six inches tall, and her brown hair was cut in a neat bob. She was wearing a pale-blue summer dress. She would be aware of Joss's past.

'I feel very sorry for Joss,' she said. 'But that's not going to help her achieve or get back on course. She's like a runaway train at present, heading for disaster. Up until a year ago she was a grade-A pupil, but now she's barely achieving Ds. Much of her work is unfinished or completely missing, so it is ungraded. Worryingly, Joss doesn't seem to care. I have to treat all my students the same, and it's no help to Joss if I just keep letting her off.'

'No, indeed,' I said. I'd immediately warmed to Miss Pryce's direct, no-nonsense approach, and I formed the impression that she would be firm but fair with her pupils.

'We've offered Joss counselling,' she continued. 'The school may not have the best academic results in the county, but we are a very caring school. Joss knows she can talk to the school counsellor, or me, or any other member of staff at any time, but she's never taken up this offer. She's often late for school, especially after lunch. As you probably saw, pupils are allowed off the premises during the lunch break, as long as they return on time. We've had instances of Joss returning late, with another girl, smelling of smoke and possibly under the influence of something – perhaps cannabis. She's had one exclusion and she's heading for another. If she continues like this she'll be excluded permanently, which will mean more uncertainty for her and a move to a new school, possibly miles away. I know Joss's mother, Linda, and I've met one of Joss's previous foster carers, so I'm aware that her behaviour at home is causing great concern too. Joss is on a path of self-destruction and, to be honest, I'm at a loss to know how to help her. I'm sorry this all sounds so negative, but you need to know.'

I felt utterly deflated. 'I knew things weren't good at school,' I said. 'But I hadn't realized they were this bad. Some children I've fostered have misbehaved at home but tried their best at school.'

'Not with Joss, I'm afraid,' Miss Pryce said. 'She's a capable girl, but she's destroying any chance she has of achieving academically. I'm also worried about her on a personal level. I'm a mother and I'd be devastated if this was happening to my daughter. Who are the two men who collect her from school sometimes? Do you know?'

'No, I don't.'

'They've been seen a number of times, waiting further up the road, at lunchtime and also after school. Members of staff have spotted Joss and Chelsea getting into their car.'

'I didn't know about any of this. Do the social services know?'

'We informed them, but as far as I know no action has been taken. Although in fairness to them, what can they do? The car is parked on a public highway and they are not committing any offence. Both Joss and Chelsea were spoken to by a member of staff, but the girls were blasé and couldn't see any danger. They insisted the lads were old friends. Perhaps they are.'

'I don't know,' I said. 'I'll try to talk to Joss about this, but she's not very communicative with me yet. I sanction her if she's late in, and now I know she's behind with her school work I'll make sure she does it before she goes out.'

'Thank you. It's a pity she can't find another friend. Chelsea has so many problems of her own.'

'Who's Chelsea?' I asked. 'I haven't heard Joss mention her.'

Miss Pryce looked slightly surprised. 'They spend all their time together. Chelsea is two years older than Joss, but they're inseparable. If there's trouble, you can be sure they're in it together. A biggish girl with long black hair.' I realized this sounded like Chloe.

'And Chloe?' I asked. 'Is she part of their group?'

Miss Pryce frowned, puzzled. 'No. Chloe who?'

'I don't know her surname. She's in Joss's class?'

'There is a girl called Chloe in the class, but she and Joss aren't friends. They don't have anything to do with one another. Chloe is a quiet, shy child, very studious and hard-working. Her parents would never let her out to wander the streets with Joss or Chelsea.'

I felt the criticism personally. 'You appreciate that, as a foster carer, I'm very limited in the sanctions I can impose on Joss. For example, I can't stop her from going out if she wants to.'

'I know. It's ridiculous. We have other children in school who are in care, so I am aware of what foster carers can and can't do. If these were our own kids, we'd lock them in the house if necessary to keep them safe.'

'Exactly. I'm doing all I can to try to get Joss back on track, but it may take time. If you could inform me of any incidents at school, I'd be grateful. Joss needs to see we are all working together in this.'

'Of course. As I said, Joss is an intelligent girl, but she's throwing it all away.' Miss Pryce glanced at her watch. 'I'll show you some of Joss's work and then I'm afraid I'll have to go. I've got to see a pupil at one o'clock. But do phone me if you have any concerns.'

'Thank you. One last thing: does Joss ever talk about her father or stepfather in school, do you know?'

'Not as far as I know.'

'Thank you.'

Miss Pryce showed me Joss's English, Maths and Science folders, which as she'd said held poor-quality or incomplete work, together with a list of work that was entirely missing. I thanked her for her time, said again that I would do all I could to help Joss and then she saw me to reception where we said goodbye. I signed out of the visitors' book and returned to my car with a heavy heart. While I wasn't wholly surprised by what Miss Pryce had told me in respect of Joss's school work, I was surprised and hurt by the level of Joss's lying about Chloe/Chelsea. I thought back to the time I'd met Chelsea, whom I'd been led to believe was Chloe, when I'd given her a lift home from the cinema. I remembered the girls laughing and sniggering in the back of the car, which I'd put down to self-conscious teenage giggling, but now I guessed they'd been laughing at the deception they'd played on me. I could see the logic in choosing Chloe – an exemplary, hard-working, well-behaved student – for if I did make enquiries at school I'd be told what a good girl she was, which would reflect well on Joss, as opposed to Chelsea, who appeared to attract as much, if not more, trouble than Joss.

But as a parent or foster carer, you can't afford to stay hurt for long, and by the time I arrived home I was trying to work out the best way to approach Joss without damaging our already frail and rocky relationship. It would have been very easy to make Joss squirm and look small by not telling her I knew of her deception and asking her about Chloe, and then hearing more of her lies before I told her I knew the truth. However, that wouldn't have given me any satisfaction and certainly wouldn't have helped my relationship with Joss, so I decided that honesty was the best policy and that I needed to tackle the matter head-on.

'I'm hot,' Joss moaned as I opened the door to her that afternoon when she returned home from school. 'And Miss wouldn't let me leave the class for a drink of water. It's against my human rights.'

It was a constant gripe of Joss's that 'Miss' (read: most teachers) had contravened her human rights by not allowing

73

her to leave the class during a lesson – to get a drink, go to the toilet, find a missing book, and so on. But had Joss been allowed to leave, she would have spent more time out of lessons than in them.

'It's summer,' I said. 'That's why you feel hot. Fetch yourself a glass of water and then come into the living room, please. I need to talk to you.'

'Tell me now,' she said, dumping her school bag in the hall. 'I'm tired. I need to lie down before I get ready to go out later.'

'You won't be going out until we've had a chat,' I said firmly. 'Do as I ask, please.'

Joss looked at me, slightly taken aback. 'I don't want a drink. I'll come with you now and get it over with.'

'All right.' I led the way down the hall and into the living room. The patio doors were slightly open and the fragrant summer air wafted in. Adrian wasn't home yet, and Lucy and Paula were both in their rooms chilling out.

'What is it?' Joss demanded as we sat down – me on the sofa and Joss choosing the chair furthest away from me.

'I saw Miss Pryce today,' I said.

'Yeah, I know. What's the old bat been saying about me?'

'She was very pleasant and said you were a clever girl but you'd slipped behind with your work. She said you were capable and had been doing well, but now you had a lot of catching up to do. She wants to help you achieve, as I do, but Joss, why did you lie to me about Chloe?'

'I didn't!' she snapped defiantly, as a reflex action.

'You did, love,' I said evenly. 'Surely you must have known you'd be found out at some point.' I held her gaze.

'OK. I did then. Sorry.' But there was no sincerity in her apology.

'I was hurt that you took me for such a fool and persuaded Chelsea to lie too.'

'I didn't. It was her idea,' Joss said vehemently, jutting out her chin. 'She thought it would look better if you checked up at the school.'

'I realize that was the reason behind it, but it would never have worked long term.'

'I won't be here long term,' Joss said tartly. 'Did you tell Miss Pryce?'

'No. There were more important issues to discuss.'

'Like what?'

'Your school work.'

Joss shrugged.

'Miss Pryce said you were very able and had been getting good grades, but over the last year you'd fallen a long way behind. I'm hoping that now you are settled with me you will be able to catch up. We both want to see you do well.'

'I don't really care,' Joss said.

'I do. Education is important.'

'I don't have to do my school work. You can't force me to, and I don't see any point in doing it. It's boring and it's not going to do me any good.'

'It might not seem so now,' I said, 'but a good education will help you to get a good job, so you can have a comfortable lifestyle and feel fulfilled in your work. It's also interesting to learn new things.'

'I don't think so,' Joss said moodily.

'Maybe not, but from now on you'll be doing an hour's school work every evening before you go out, and at the weekend, so you can catch up.'

'What!' Her eyes blazed as she stared at me, defiant and

annoyed. 'You can't do that. I'll tell my social worker,' she threatened.

'That's all right with me. I'm sure Amelia will agree. It says in your behaviour contract that you can go out after you've done your homework. I'm helping you by setting the guideline of an hour.'

'I won't do it!' Joss said, folding her arms across her chest. 'I'll sit in my bedroom for an hour and listen to music and paint my toenails.'

'No. You'll be down here for the hour so I can help you with your work if necessary.'

Joss stood to leave.

'Sit down now, Joss,' I said forcefully. 'I haven't finished yet.'

'What?' she demanded. I waited for her to return to her chair.

'The young men in the car you and Chelsea have been seen getting into. Miss Pryce is concerned and so am I. Who are they?'

Joss opened and closed her mouth, clearly trying to find the best-fit answer. 'Chloe's – I mean Chelsea's – uncles,' she said.

'Both men are Chelsea's uncles?'

'No. One is, and the other is his friend.'

'The uncle who brought you home last night?'

She nodded but couldn't meet my gaze.

'Does your mother know them?'

'No. I met them after I left home.'

'So they're not old friends?'

'Not really. Sort of.'

'How old are they, Joss?'

'Twenties, I guess.' She shrugged.

'Do they work?'

'I think so.'

'What do you do when you are out with them?'

'Hang out and have a good time.'

'You've been arriving back at school very late for afternoon lessons.'

'I won't again,' Joss said.

I looked at her carefully. 'Joss, I really don't think it's a good idea for two young girls to be joyriding in a car with much older lads.'

'Why? What have you got against them?' she demanded.

'Nothing personally. But I think you and Chelsea are placing yourselves in an unsafe position. One thing can lead to another, especially when drink and drugs are involved. Do they give you the alcohol and cannabis?'

'No. Sometimes,' Joss said. 'Is that all? Have you finished now?'

'Joss, I can't stop you from seeing them. If I tried, you'd go behind my back. But you are sensible, and I'm asking you to think about what I've said and make the right decision.'

'Yeah, OK, I will,' she said, eager to be away. 'I'll do my hour's homework now and then I can go out straight after dinner.'

CHAPTER SEVEN

LETTER FROM THE POLICE

Joss couldn't see the danger as I could. Having been a foster carer for a long time, I was aware of what could – and did – happen to vulnerable girls like Joss who were hurting, needy, had their guard down and desperately wanted to be loved. They were easy prey for unscrupulous older lads, and although Miss Pryce hadn't said much about Chelsea, I'd formed the impression that she was as vulnerable and open to exploitation as Joss. However, as Joss's foster carer I was limited in what I could do to keep her safe, so I hoped that with firm and consistent boundaries, praise, love and concern, and using what few sanctions I had, Joss would start to listen to reason and turn a corner before it was too late.

On a positive note, Joss did do her school work that evening as I'd asked her to – not graciously or happily, but she did it. I told her I wanted her to work at the table in the kitchen-cum-dining-room while I made dinner, and after some moaning, scowling and muttering she fetched her school bag, plonked it on the table. She asked for a Biro and then took out some books and began writing while I peeled the potatoes. As we both worked, every so often I praised her and asked her if she needed any help, but she didn't. She sighed theatrically from time to time, looked pointedly at the wall clock, sighed some more and then continued writing. When Paula and Lucy came down to get a drink and ask what was for dinner, they looked surprised to see Joss sitting at the table, studiously poring over her books.

'You got homework?' Lucy asked her.

'Yeah. Your mum's making me do it,' Joss said, putting down her pen and sitting back in her chair, ready for a chat.

'Cool,' Lucy said.

'No, it isn't. Have you done yours?'

'Most of it,' Lucy said.

'What subjects did you have?'

'Maths and English.'

'Yuk,' Joss said. 'Are you good at them?'

It was clear that Joss would much rather chat than do her homework, so once Lucy had her drink I asked her to leave Joss alone until she'd finished her school work.

'Yeah, that's right,' Joss said, ready with one of her smart-alec retorts. 'Do what your mum tells you. I can't concentrate if you keep talking to me.'

Thankfully, Lucy didn't rise to the bait.

At 5.45 p.m., exactly one hour after Joss had started her home-work, she packed away her books with another theatrical sigh, stood and handed the Biro to me.

'Keep it. You need a pen for school,' I said. 'Would you like me to check your work?'

'No, thanks. Can I go out now?'

'After dinner.'

'I'll get changed, then. As I've done my homework can I stay out later tonight?'

I looked up from what I was doing. 'You can anyway,' I said. 'It's Friday and you're allowed out until ten-thirty, although I'd be very pleased if you came home before then. I think it's far too late.'

'As I've done my homework, can I stay out until eleven?' Joss said, trying to push the boundaries as always.

'No. Ten-thirty is late enough. How are you getting home? Shall I come and meet you?'

'No. I'll get a lift back.'

Which I had to accept. 'Well done for doing your school work,' I added. 'I'm pleased.'

She shrugged and sauntered away to change as though she didn't care, but I knew she probably did. Everyone likes to receive praise and hear good things about themselves; it gives us a warm glow and increases our self-esteem, although we may not show it.

Joss ate her dinner quickly and as soon as we'd all finished she went out, wearing tight jeans and a not-too-skimpy top, which I was pleased about. While she was out I wrote up my log notes, including the details of the appointment I'd had with Miss Pryce and the concerns she'd raised about Joss's school work and behaviour, and the fact that she'd been seen getting into a car with two men, one of whom Joss had told me was Chelsea's uncle. I would also telephone Amelia on Monday and make sure she was aware of this latest worry. Miss Pryce had said the social services had been informed but that she hadn't heard anything further. Perhaps it was inno-cent, but I had concerns and I felt it needed to be followed up.

As 10.30 p.m. approached I went up to my bedroom, which is at the front of the house, and watched out for Joss's return.

If Joss was brought home by car I'd make a note of the registration number and model, so that if she went missing again I would have more information to give the police to help find her. Although it was dark outside, the street lamps were on and with my bedroom light off I could see a good way up the street. The road on which I live is reasonably quiet, and the few cars that passed continued along without stopping. Then, at 10.40 p.m., I saw Joss walking down the street, alone; if she had been given a lift then she must have been dropped off out of sight at the end of the road. She made a sorrowful figure: small, by herself in the dark, and without her usual armour of couldn't-care-less bravado. I thought she looked sad too, so when I opened the door I said, 'Hello, love. Is everything all right?'

'I guess.' She stepped in.

'Are you sure? You seem a bit low.'

'No more than usual,' she said.

I looked at her and my heart clenched. 'Oh, Joss, I wish you could talk to me, love. I'm sure it would help.'

'And tell you what?' she said, her defences going up.

'About what's making you so unhappy.'

'That's easy,' she said, turning to go upstairs. 'My dad hanged himself and my mum married a creep. Goodnight – I'm going to bed.'

'Joss,' I called after her, but she continued upstairs.

I tried to talk to her again when I said goodnight, but she didn't want to know.

She had another nightmare in the early hours, and as usual I was out of bed as soon as I heard her first scream. By the glow of the dimmed light in her room I could see she was sitting up in bed clutching the duvet to her chest. 'Don't touch me! Get away!' she said. For a moment I thought she was talking to me, but her eyes were closed and it seemed she was still asleep and this was part of her nightmare.

'Joss, it's all right,' I soothed, going over. 'You're safe. There's nothing to worry about. It was just a bad dream.'

'Bad dream,' she repeated groggily in her sleep.

'Yes, you're safe now. Snuggle down and get some rest.'

I eased her down onto the bed and she curled onto her side. I waited until she was in a deep sleep again before I came out and returned to my bed. Although Joss always went back to sleep quite quickly after a nightmare, it took me much longer. That night I lay in the darkness, my thoughts wrestling with Joss's pain and trying to work out what on earth I could do to help her. The last time I looked at the bedside clock it was nearly 3.30 a.m. and when I woke it was 8.15. Thankfully, it was Saturday, so I didn't have to be up early.

When I'm fostering younger children I'm always up, showered and dressed before them, even at weekends, but with Joss and my family being that much older and all of them liking a lie-in, it was nearly nine o'clock before I went downstairs. I fed Toscha and made a cup of tea, which I took into the living room. It was another lovely morning, so I opened the patio doors and then sat on the sofa, sipping my tea with birdsong and the early morning air drifting in. Five minutes later the telephone rang. I reached out and picked up the handset from the corner table. 'Hello?'

'Cathy, it's Linda, Joss's mum. I hope I haven't woken you – I waited until nine o'clock.' I was surprised to hear from her. Although we had each other's telephone numbers, we hadn't used them before.

'I'm up,' I said. 'Is everything all right?'

'No. Eric said I should phone you. I've received a letter from the police. Joss is in trouble again and it happened after she came to you.' My heart sank. 'Joss has been warned before about underage drinking, and this time she swore at a police officer. It says this is her final warning. Next time she'll be prosecuted in court.' Linda's voice shook.

'I'm so sorry,' I said, immediately feeling responsible. 'When did this happen?'

'The letter says Saturday, 5 June, at approximately 8.45 p.m. at Maple Park. She must have given the police this address.'

'Linda, can you hold on a moment, please? I want to check my diary to see where Joss was supposed to be that evening.'

'Yes, go ahead. I'm so upset, and angry that she's allowed out so much.'

'I'm sorry,' I said again. 'Just a minute.'

I set down the phone and my cup of tea and went into the front room where I kept my fostering folder and other important documents in a locked drawer. I took out my log and turned to the date Linda had given. My heart sank further as I realized it was the Saturday I'd taken Joss to the cinema to meet Chelsea (then known as Chloe).

I returned the folder to the drawer and went back into the living room where I picked up the handset. 'Linda, Joss was supposed to have been in the cinema that evening with a friend. I took her there myself, and collected her after.'

'They couldn't have gone in,' Linda said. 'The park where they were found drinking isn't far from the cinema. Joss is a very silly girl. She won't be given another chance. She's had so many warnings. I really thought she might change when she came to you.'

I shared Linda's depressing disappointment. 'I'll talk to her,' I said.

'Yes, as soon as she is awake, please. And also, can you tell her that Eric is out this morning until one o'clock, so she can come and see Kevin and me if she wants to.'

'I will. Linda, I'm sorry this has happened, but hopefully I can talk some sense into Joss. The letter from the police may give her the shock she needs.'

'It may,' Linda said without any conviction.

I didn't wait for Joss to wake up. Leaving my tea half drunk, I went upstairs to Joss's bedroom where I gave a loud knock on her door and went in.

'What time is it?' Joss groaned, turning over.

'Time you woke up,' I said. 'I need to talk to you.'

'Can't it wait? I'm tired.' She pulled the duvet over her head.

'No, it can't wait.' I sat on the chair a little way from her bed. 'Your mother has just telephoned me. She's very upset, understandably.'

Joss groaned. 'What now?'

'She's received a letter from the police, a final warning. Can you think what it might be about?'

'No,' came the muffled reply from beneath the duvet.

'Maple Park on Saturday, 5 June,' I said, 'when you were supposed to be at the cinema with Chelsea. Joss, you must have known you'd be found out!'

Another groan. 'Don't care,' she said.

'Well, I do. Pull the duvet down and look at me when I'm talking to you, please.'

I waited. There was no movement at first, but then she gradually lowered the duvet, although she didn't look at me.

'Apart from the fact that you lied to me – you didn't go into the cinema at all – you were drinking alcohol in a public place and then swore at a police officer! How stupid was that? Your mother will show you the letter when you go home this morning, but it's your final warning, Joss. Make no mistake. You've run out of chances. Any further instances and you will be prosecuted in a court of law and very likely sent to a young offenders' institution. Then you certainly won't be drinking in the park or joyriding in a car with young men. In fact, you won't be allowed out at all without an escort.' My voice had risen with the passion of what I was saying. How could she have been so stupid? Joss knew I was annoyed.

'Sorry,' she said.

'Joss, you've said sorry many times before, but you haven't changed your behaviour! Perhaps you think it's funny, a joke, to behave like this, but I guarantee you won't be laughing when you're in court and then locked up. How do you buy alcohol, anyway? You don't look eighteen.' It is illegal in the UK to sell alcohol to anyone under eighteen and shopkeepers are obliged by law to ask for ID if there is any doubt.

'I don't buy it,' Joss said. 'My friends do.'

'What friends? The men in the car? Chelsea's uncle?'

'Yeah.'

'What a good influence they are!' I said caustically. 'Do they give you cigarettes too?'

'Yeah, I guess.'

'And drugs?'

'No.'

'Do they take drugs?'

'Dunno.'

85

I sighed. 'Can't you find some better friends, Joss? You're worth more than this.'

'I like them,' she said defensively. 'We have a laugh. I won't get into trouble again, I promise.'

What more could I say? 'I just hope you've taken on board what I've said this time, Joss, I really do. Because you won't get another chance.'

'I know. I'll stay out of trouble; really, I will.'

'I hope so. Now, your mother also said that Eric is going out this morning, so you can go home and see her and your brother. But I want you to come straight back here afterwards. You've homework to do this afternoon. I'll be stopping your pocket money for the incident in the park.'

'But that's not fair!' Joss cried indignantly, sitting up in bed. 'That happened weeks ago. You can't stop my pocket money for that now.'

What wonderful logic, I thought. 'I am stopping it, Joss. Your mother and I have only just found out about it. But you can earn it back as usual.' I would have liked to have stopped Joss from going out that night too, but that wasn't an option. 'Now get dressed so you can go and see your mother and brother. You'd better apologize to your mum, and tell her it won't ever happen again. I feel sorry for your mother, I really do. She doesn't need all this worry.' Neither do I, I thought.

I left Joss to wash and dress, and when she came downstairs for breakfast she was subdued. She apologized again and promised she would do her best to behave in future, and also find some better friends who were more her age. Ever optimistic, I began to allow myself to hope that maybe she meant what she said this time and her behaviour would improve in future.

* * *

Linda had said that Eric would be out of the house until one o'clock, so I assumed Joss would leave when he arrived. Allowing time for her to walk to the bus stop plus the thirty-minute journey home, I was expecting her to return to me by two o'clock. When she hadn't arrived by three o'clock, I telephoned Linda.

'Joss left two hours ago,' Linda said. 'As soon as Eric walked in. She said she was going to see Chelsea. I asked her if that was all right with you and she told me you'd said it was, as long as she was back by ten-thirty tonight.'

'What!' I cried. 'That isn't what I said at all. Just the opposite, in fact. I told her she had to come straight home after she'd seen you. She knows she has homework to do.'

'Sorry,' Linda said. 'I should have checked with you first.'

'It's not your fault. I should have collected her in the car. I didn't think it would be necessary. She promised me she'd mend her ways.'

'She always does,' Linda said despondently. 'I don't think she can help herself. Do you know Chelsea?'

'I've met her once, although I do know where she lives.'

'I got the impression Joss was going to her place. She said they had to keep off the streets and not get into more trouble with the police.'

'At least she listened to that part of my lecture,' I said. 'Pity she didn't listen to the rest. I think I might go to Chelsea's flat and bring Joss home. She needs to understand she can't do whatever she wants whenever she pleases.'

'That's good of you,' Linda said. Then I heard a man's voice in the background and, lowering her voice, Linda said, 'Eric says Joss needs a damn good smack. But I've never hit my children. Steven and I were against it.'

'So am I,' I said. 'There are better ways to discipline a child. And foster carers aren't allowed to smack children. I'll go now and see if Joss is at Chelsea's flat. Shall I phone you when I return?'

'Yes, please. I am grateful. Thank you so much, Cathy.'

I felt there was little to thank me for.

CHAPTER EIGHT

OUT OF PATIENCE

Adrian and Lucy were both out that Saturday afternoon; Adrian was playing tennis and Lucy was shopping with some friends. I explained to Paula that I was going out to try to find Joss. I asked her if she wanted to come with me and wait in the car or stay at home. She said she'd stay at home, so I left her sitting on the bench in the garden reading a book with Toscha curled up beside her.

I knew where Chelsea's flat was from when I'd given her a lift home from the cinema – assuming she and Joss had told me the truth as to where Chelsea lived. To be honest, Joss had told me so many lies I now doubted much of what she said, and I thought that as they'd given me a false name for Chelsea, perhaps they'd also given me a false address. But I would try it. Joss needed to see I was serious about the boundaries I was putting in place and that when I said something, I meant it. The worse that could happen was that Chelsea didn't live in the flat, in which case I'd apologize to the occupants for disturbing them, and then perhaps I'd drive around some of Joss's favourite haunts – Maple Park and outside the shopping centre, for example – and see if I could spot her.

I pulled in to the kerb and parked where there was a space a little way from the parade of shops. The night I'd dropped off Chelsea I hadn't seen a front entrance to the flat, but Joss had told me it was at the rear, up a fire escape. I got out of the car, walked round the end of the building and immediately saw the flight of stairs she meant. Taking the handrail, I made my way up, my shoes echoing on the metal steps. At the top of the stairs there was a landing, which ran the length of the seven flats. The landing was south facing and a few old dining chairs were outside for residents to sit in the sun, although they were unoccupied now. There was also washing hanging on a makeshift line strewn between the railings, drying in the sun. The newsagents below was the third shop in, so I went to the third door. It was number 79. A small window was open in a room overhead and from it I could hear a television.

Now that I'd arrived I was apprehensive, and I felt my heart step up a beat. The plan I'd hatched for bringing Joss home seemed flawed. Even if Joss was here, supposing she made a big scene and refused to come with me – what could I do? Not a lot, and my credibility as a foster carer in her eyes would suffer even more. But I was here so, taking a deep breath and summoning my courage, I lifted the small rusty knocker and gave the door a sharp tap. I waited. No one answered and the television above continued. I knocked again, harder this time, and waited some more.

I was about to knock a third time when a noise came from the other side of the door – a lock being turned – and then the door slowly opened. Chelsea looked at me, astonished.

'Hi, love,' I said non-confrontationally, throwing her a smile. 'Nice to see you again. Is Joss here?'

She gave a small, anxious nod.

'Good. I've come to give her a lift home.'

There was no sign of Joss, but Chelsea looked at me, very worried, clearly not knowing what to do.

'Could you tell her I'm here, please, or perhaps I could come in?'

I took a step forward and Chelsea opened the door wider to let me in. I found myself in a kitchen, cluttered and dirty. The sink and draining board were overflowing with used pans, dishes and cutlery, and a Formica table was littered with empty takeaway boxes, beer cans, drink bottles and anything else the occupants couldn't be bothered to take out to the rubbish bins. The place reeked of stale food and smoke. I followed Chelsea from the kitchen into the main room.

'Joss, your foster carer is here,' Chelsea said as we entered.

The air was thick with cannabis smoke. I blinked as my gaze went to an old sofa up against one wall where Joss was scrabbling to straighten her clothes and move away from the man she was with. More empty beer cans and spirit bottles were strewn around and grey net curtains hung at the window that overlooked the street. On the floor up against the other wall was a mattress, and the guy lying on it looked me up and down.

'Yeah? What do you want?' he said rudely.

'I've come to give Joss a lift home,' I said evenly. I turned to Joss, who had the decency to look embarrassed. Both guys laughed. I guessed they were in their early twenties and both wore jeans and short-sleeved T-shirts that showed heavily tattooed arms.

'Hi, I'm Zach, nice to meet you,' the guy who'd been with Joss said sarcastically.

I nodded. 'Are you ready?' I asked Joss, wanting to get out of there as soon as possible.

She glanced anxiously at Zach.

'Go home with your carer,' he said mockingly. 'But give us a kiss first.'

Joss leant over him and gave him a quick kiss on the lips. He laughed and squeezed her bottom, then reached down for the beer can and took a swig.

'Go on, run along,' he said to her.

'Will I see you later?' Chelsea asked Joss.

Joss shrugged.

Chelsea came with us to the door and said a very quiet goodbye to Joss before closing the door behind us. I breathed in the fresh air, grateful to be out of there with Joss and without a scene. I was as shocked by the state of the flat as I was by finding Joss and Chelsea with the two men. Joss knew she was in trouble and walked with me in silence to my car. Once in the car, I put the key into the ignition but didn't start the engine. I turned in my seat to look at her.

'What?' she asked defiantly. 'We weren't doing anything.' Meaning, I supposed, that they weren't having sex.

'Joss, you went to your mother's. You were supposed to come straight home after, not go to Chelsea's flat.'

'But I wanted to see Zach. He's my boyfriend. I knew you wouldn't let me.'

'For good reason. How old is he – twenty-three?'

'Twenty-two. He's Chelsea's uncle,' Joss said, as though that made it all right.

'And you are thirteen, Joss. Who was the other man?'

'Zach's friend. Chelsea's boyfriend.'

'Does he have a name?'

'Carl,' Joss said.

'And their surnames?' I wanted to find out as much as possible about them.

'Don't know.'

'Are these the men you've been seen with at school?' I asked.

Joss gave a reluctant nod. I continued to look at her, trying to work out how I could begin to make her see the danger she was placing herself in.

'We weren't doing anything,' she said again. 'Zach respects me. He treats me nice.'

'Joss, it didn't look like that to me. The place reeked of cannabis and clearly you were all drinking. When I came in he was groping you on the sofa – I don't call that respectful.'

She shrugged dismissively.

'Does Chelsea really live in that flat?'

'Yeah. Can we go now? I've got to do my homework before I can go out tonight.'

I looked at her aghast. 'You're not going out tonight.'

'I'm allowed to! It's Saturday!' she shouted.

I started the engine and pulled away.

'Joss, it would be completely irresponsible of me to let you go out this evening now that I've seen what's going on at Chelsea's flat with those two men. I want to speak to your social worker first, on Monday.'

'Why?'

'To see how best to keep you safe. Who else lives in that flat?'

'Dunno. Chelsea's dad, and some of his friends, I guess.'

'And Zach?' I asked as I drove.

'Sometimes.'

'Where's Chelsea's mother? Do you know?' I navigated the traffic.

'She left years ago.'

'I'm sorry to hear that. Who was upstairs with the television on?'

'Her dad. He never gets up until evening. He's a lazy sod.' Joss gave a little laugh.

I didn't think it was funny. 'So he knew that you and Chelsea – two underage girls, one of whom is his daughter – were downstairs smoking drugs and drinking alcohol?'

'He doesn't mind,' Joss said. 'He's cool. He smokes and drinks too.' As if that made it all right!

'It's not cool, Joss,' I said, pulling up to the traffic lights. 'It's completely irresponsible. I appreciate you and Chelsea can't see the danger, but he should be able to. He's an adult and her father.'

'I don't care what you think,' she said. 'I like him. He's my friend.'

I was even more worried now than I had been before when I'd believed Joss had been on the streets with friends more her own age. She'd got into trouble with them, but what I'd discovered this afternoon raised my concerns to a whole new level. Not only was Joss placing herself in an unsafe situation by going to that flat with those men and smoking and drinking, but also Chelsea appeared to be living with it on a daily basis. I would telephone Amelia first thing on Monday to inform her of what I'd found and discuss what could be done to better protect Joss (and Chelsea). I would be pushing for Joss to stay in more.

The rest of the journey continued in silence, with Joss staring straight ahead, clearly very annoyed with me. Once home she stomped up to her bedroom, and then she stomped back down again a few minutes later and joined Paula in the garden. I took the opportunity to telephone Linda as I'd promised. Eric answered and said that Linda had popped to the local shops and would be back in about half an hour.

'Could you tell Linda I've found Joss,' I said. 'She was at Chelsea's.'

'That is good news,' Eric said. 'Our Joss can be a little minx sometimes. I hope you punish her.'

'She'll be staying in tonight,' I said. 'Please tell Linda that too, and that I've spoken to Joss. She can phone me if she wants to, but Joss is safe.' I didn't go into all the details, as it would worry Linda. If she telephoned me and wanted to know more, I'd tell her. Eric said he'd pass on the message and we said goodbye.

When I went into the garden Joss had a school book open on her lap. I guessed why.

'As I'm doing my homework, can I go out tonight?' she said.

'No. Not tonight, love.'

'What if I don't see Chelsea?'

'I want you to stay in with us tonight. We'll have dinner and then we can play some board games or watch a film together. Adrian's out tonight so it'll be a girls' night in.'

Joss pulled a face, but didn't argue further. I think even she knew she'd overstepped the boundaries enough for one day, and she read her school book for a while. After dinner Adrian went to a friend's house and the girls and I watched a film and shared a bowl of microwave popcorn, then we ate ice cream from the freezer. Joss relaxed, got over her pique and appeared to be enjoying herself, although she didn't admit it. The film was a romantic comedy and we all laughed together. I hoped that, once I'd spoken to Amelia, Joss would be staying in more and we could all enjoy further family evenings together.

Joss slept well that night and was up and dressed early the next morning, and in a very good mood. I'd invited my parents to lunch and I was looking forward to seeing them, as were Adrian, Lucy and Paula. Joss had met them briefly once, a few days after she'd arrived, when they came for dinner, but she'd been on her way out. Today would give her and my parents the opportunity to get to know each other better. Mum and Dad are the classic grandparents: loving and doting, they welcome the children I foster with open hearts, and the children very quickly call them Nana and Grandpa. But it soon became clear that Joss had different plans.

'Pity I'll miss them again,' she said as we finished breakfast.

'You won't. They're coming here today, at twelve,' I said.

'Yeah, but I'm going out soon.'

'No, you're not. It's Sunday. You stay in on Sundays.'

'You're wrong,' Joss said. 'I'm not allowed out in the evening, but I can go out during the day. That's what the behaviour contract says.' I felt the atmosphere around the breakfast table shift as Adrian concentrated on his food and Paula and Lucy looked at Joss.

'It was agreed you'd stay with us on Sundays,' I said. 'I remember distinctly.' We hadn't been sent a copy of the contract yet, but I felt sure I was right. 'I'll ask Amelia on Monday when I phone her, but until I've checked I want you to stay in today. You'll enjoy it.'

'No, I won't,' Joss said, her face setting. 'I was in all last night.'

'Nana and Grandpa are lovely,' Paula tried.

'Good for you,' Joss snapped, 'but they're not my fucking

grandparents.' She jumped up from the table, stamped upstairs to her room and slammed the door.

'I don't know why you bother,' Lucy exclaimed, annoyed.

'Because I care.'

We finished our breakfast in silence.

I went up to see Joss a couple of times during the morning, but she refused to even look at me and kept her earphones in and her eyes down while I tried to talk to her. I knew it would be impossible for my children and I to enjoy my parents' visit if Joss stayed in her room, angry and upset, so half an hour before they were due to arrive I went up to her room and tried again. She was no longer listening to music but was flicking through some magazines. I began talking to her gently, again explaining why I put in place boundaries and why I wanted her to come down and join us, but she continued to ignore me and eventually I ran out of patience.

'Joss, it would be very rude of you and discourteous to my parents if you didn't come down, so I want you downstairs in five minutes or I'll ground you for the whole of next week.'

Joss suddenly found her voice. 'You can't do that!' she cried, turning to face me, her eyes blazing.

'Watch me,' I said. 'Five minutes. Understand? I've had enough. It's bad enough you're rude to me, but I'm not having you being disrespectful to my parents.' I came out and closed her bedroom door.

My heart was racing. I was annoyed and stressed. I'm a patient person, but I wasn't going to have my parents hurt and another day ruined because of Joss. I knew what I'd said was a gamble. If Joss didn't come down or ran out of the house, my authority would be severely damaged and Joss would see my ineffectiveness as a passport to do whatever she wanted in the future.

An anxious five minutes passed, and then ten. Paula and I were in the kitchen preparing the meat and vegetables for lunch. Adrian and Lucy were setting up the garden chairs and the sun umbrella so we could all sit outside. Another five minutes passed and then I heard Joss's bedroom door open above, followed by her footsteps on the stairs. Paula and I both paused as she neared the bottom of the stairs. To my utter relief Joss didn't go out the front door but went down the hall and into the sitting room. Paula and I continued with the preparations for lunch. I didn't rush in and praise Joss – she should have done as I'd asked in the first place instead of creating a scene. It doesn't do young people any harm to feel a parent's or carer's disapproval for a short while after they've done something wrong.

Ten minutes later the doorbell rang, signalling my parents' arrival. Joss was still in the sitting room and she didn't come to the front door to greet them as the rest of us did. But as soon as they were in the living room, saying hello and asking her how she was, she dropped her grumpiness and began to answer them politely. From then on the day went as I'd hoped. It was a pleasant and relaxing family day, with Joss eventually joining in unreservedly. Perhaps she didn't want to lose face in front of my parents, or perhaps she had simply reflected on what I'd said, but whatever the reason I was pleased. She helped me serve dinner, played badminton in the garden after we'd eaten and when it was time to say goodbye to my parents she came with us to the front door to see them off. Once they'd gone, I told her I was pleased she'd joined in.

'So am I,' she said with a small smile.

CHAPTER NINE
ON REPORT

Amelia was out of the office when I telephoned her on Monday morning, so I left a message with a colleague asking her to telephone me when she returned. She did so later that afternoon.

'Did you have a nice weekend?' she began.

'Mixed,' I said. 'We had a nice day yesterday with my parents, but there are a number of matters I need to talk to you about.'

'Yes?' she asked, concerned.

'I'm not sure if you're aware of this, but Joss and her friend Chelsea have been spending a lot of time with two men in their early twenties. I saw Miss Pryce, Joss's teacher, on Friday and she said that the school had raised concerns, as members of staff have seen Joss and Chelsea getting into a car at lunchtimes with some men. Miss Pryce said the social services had been informed, but the school hadn't heard anything further.'

'That's possible,' Amelia said a little guardedly.

'Then on Saturday Joss went to her mother's in the morning, but instead of coming straight back here she went to Chelsea's flat. I went to the flat to collect her. Chelsea's father was upstairs while Chelsea and Joss were downstairs with the same two men, smoking cannabis, drinking alcohol and cuddled up on the sofa and an old mattress. Joss said they're called Zach and Carl. She said she didn't know their surnames.'

'Did you see Chelsea's father at the flat?' Amelia asked.

'No. He stayed up in his bedroom. I was shocked by the state of the flat and that Chelsea was living there.' I then continued with a description of what I'd seen.

'The social services are aware of Chelsea,' Amelia said, 'although she's not one of my cases. I'll tell her social worker what you've said and she may want to talk to you.'

'Thank you. I'm very concerned. Also, Linda telephoned me on Saturday morning,' I continued. 'She's received a final warning letter from the police in respect of an incident a few weeks ago. Joss was found drinking alcohol again in a public place and then she swore at a police officer.'

'I'll need a copy of that letter,' Amelia said, taking it in her stride. 'I've got to phone Linda soon; I'll ask her for it then.'

'I'd like to keep Joss at home with me more,' I said. 'Her teacher said that Joss is a capable student, but she is very behind with her work. Staying in more would allow her to catch up and also give me a better chance of keeping her safe. Joss calls Zach her boyfriend, but he's a man and appears to be leading her into bad ways. She's so vulnerable and I fear she could easily be taken advantage of and exploited.'

'You can't keep Joss in all the time,' Amelia said. 'Have you spoken to her about contraception?'

I was shocked. 'No! She's thirteen. She's a child. At her age I will be telling her not to have a sexual relationship, not encouraging her.'

'It's not encouraging her,' Amelia said. 'But it would be more responsible for her to go on the Pill than to have a baby. Can you talk to her about choices, please?'

'Yes – but she may not have a choice. If she's plied with drink and drugs she may be coerced or forced into having sex.' I felt Amelia and I were coming from very different places. 'I want to keep Joss in more to protect her,' I said bluntly. 'Is that all right with you?'

'What does Joss say?'

'She obviously wants to go out. It's fun to her. But at her age she doesn't necessarily know what is best for her and she can't see the danger. The schools break up in three weeks' time for the summer holidays. There'll be even more opportunity for her to get into trouble if she's out all day, every day.'

'Perhaps we could renegotiate the contract of behaviour with Joss,' Amelia said.

Stuff the contract, I thought but didn't say. 'Sundays,' I said, coming to my next point. 'My understanding is that Joss is with me all day on Sunday. She seems to think she can go out during the day as long as she is in for the evening.'

'I can't remember what we agreed,' Amelia said. 'Just a minute, I have Joss's file here.' I waited and then Amelia said, 'It's not clear. We agreed at the meeting that she'd stay in Sunday and Wednesday evenings, but there is no mention of during the day on Sundays.'

'So I can assume she's in with me? She enjoyed the last two Sundays when we've all been together.'

There was a small pause before Amelia replied. 'I think this is something we need to discuss at Joss's review. She's due a review and I was going to suggest a week on Wednesday. Four o'clock so Joss can be present.'

'Joss doesn't get home from school until four-thirty at the earliest.'

'We'll make if four-thirty, then. Can you tell her? I'll send out invitations to all parties. Is it all right to hold the review at your house?'

This was usual practice when a child was in care under a Section 20.

'Yes,' I said. 'And until the review, I can keep her in more during the week and also next Sunday?'

'If Joss agrees, yes.'

As I said before, Amelia was pleasant but naïve.

Children in care have regular reviews. The child's parent(s), teacher, social worker, foster carer, the foster carer's support social worker and any other adults closely connected with the child meet to ensure that everything is being done to help the child, and that the care plan (drawn up by the social services) is up to date. The reviews are chaired by an independent reviewing officer (IRO), who also minutes the meeting. Very young children don't usually attend their reviews, but older children are expected to, as it is about them.

I made a note of the date of Joss's review in my diary, and when Joss came home from school, just before five o'clock, I told her.

'Not another review!' she exclaimed. 'What a waste of effing time. Nothing ever happens and no one listens to me.' Which I knew to be the view of many teenagers in care.

It was Monday, so Joss was expecting to go out in the evening, and given that she'd spent all of Sunday at home I didn't feel I could protest. Parenting a teenager with challenging behaviour often requires give and take, and of course at present the contract of behaviour stipulated that Joss could go out, although I wondered how many other thirteen-year-olds were out on the streets in the evening. Certainly none I knew.

I asked Joss where she was planning to go and she shrugged.

'To the park, maybe.'

'Not to Chelsea's?' I asked.

'Nah.'

Clearly I didn't know if she was telling me the truth, but because Joss knew going out relied on her doing an hour's homework first, she immediately took her school bag to the dining table and worked while I made dinner. I felt this part of Joss's routine was going well, and as usual I praised her and asked if she needed any help, which she didn't. As soon as the hour was up, she packed away her books.

'Have you finished your homework?' I asked.

'I've done the hour,' Joss said, which wasn't the same thing, but I left it at that. She'd done an hour and I knew that, with only three weeks before the end of term and the academic year, the schools were reducing homework – Adrian, Lucy and Paula had less. 'Miss says I'm doing well,' Joss added.

'Excellent. Good girl. You've earned back the pocket money you lost for swearing.'

'Wow,' Joss exclaimed a little sarcastically. But I could see she was pleased. It was part of Joss's armour to reject praise and compliments as though she didn't care: a defence mechanism to stop others getting close to her, in the belief that this would protect her from being hurt again.

* * *

Joss went out as soon as we'd finished dinner, but to my surprise she returned at 9.20 p.m., ten minutes early.

'Are you all right?' I asked, fearing she might be ill or that something bad had happened to her.

'Zach said I should get back on time and do as I'm told more.' Which stopped me in my tracks. I was amazed, although I wasn't about to revise my opinion of Zach yet, for Joss had come in sucking a mint.

'Did he give you alcohol?' I asked.

'Only a little cider. But we didn't go to Chelsea's flat,' she added, as though this made it all right.

'How much is a little?' I asked.

'One small bottle.'

'Joss, we need to talk,' I said. I closed the front door.

'I'm not drunk!' she exclaimed. 'Not on one small bottle. And you've already told me how bad alcohol is for me so let's skip the lecture. I'm tired, I need to go to bed.'

'It's not about alcohol,' I said. 'Although you shouldn't be drinking at all. Your social worker has asked me to have a chat with you about sex and relationships.'

Joss groaned and pulled a face. 'Must we? I'm not doing it, if that's what you think.'

'I don't, and I'm pleased to hear it, but I want to have that chat with you anyway. It's not late and it won't take too long.'

Joss groaned again but came with me into the living room where we sat in the easy chairs. During the evening I'd given much thought to what I wanted to say, so I had my words ready.

'Joss, I'm going to speak to you frankly and honestly. Please listen to what I have to say, as it is important. Stop me if you have any questions or comments. All right?'

She gave a small nod but looked down at her hands in her lap.

'Sometimes us girls have to make difficult decisions in respect of boys – or, as in Zach's case, young men. They may want a physical relationship before we are ready or old enough. I was a teenager once and I can remember the conflicting emotions I felt. Attitudes have changed since then, but I think it is still true today that sex is much better in a loving and committed relationship. This is what I've told Adrian, Lucy and Paula and all the teenagers I've fostered. But I know girls can feel pressurized into agreeing to have sex and then later regret it. They might not like to say no, because they want to please the boy and keep him as their boyfriend. Any boy or man who says they will leave a girl if they don't have sex with them isn't worth hanging onto. I've even heard of boys telling girls that if they don't have sex and ejaculate regularly it makes them ill.'

Joss smiled, or rather smirked, but didn't look up.

'That's nonsense, of course,' I said. 'And in this country, as in many others, it is illegal for an adult to have sex with a young person – under the age of sixteen. There is a good reason for this, Joss. It's because the law recognizes that young people don't have the maturity to deal with a sexual relationship and can be easily taken advantage of. The law protects them, as I am trying to protect you. Although a girl always has the right to say no, I am concerned that by drinking alcohol and smoking cannabis you are putting yourself in a position where you could agree to something you later regret, or be coerced or forced into it.'

'Zach's not like that,' Joss protested, finally looking up. 'He respects me. He wouldn't do anything I didn't want to. I know him. We're going to wait.'

'Good, but Amelia has asked me to talk to you about contraception. Contraception is free and the service is confidential. You can go to the doctors or the family planning clinic if you need to. Do you know where they are?'

'Yes, but I don't need them. I'm not doing anything.'

I looked at her carefully. 'Joss, when I collected you from Chelsea's flat on Saturday you were on the sofa with Zach and your clothes were all ruffled.'

'Yeah, but we were only kissing and cuddling,' she said. 'Honestly. Tell Amelia I don't need contraception. I'm not like that, and Zach isn't either.'

'I'll tell her,' I said. 'Does Zach know how old you are?'

'Yes, and he said he's happy to wait until I'm older. He's not what you and Amelia think. He's polite and thoughtful. He's interested in me as a person, not my body. He treats me like an adult and listens to what I have to say. He's so kind and sympathetic about what happened to me when I was little, about my dad. He cares about me and looks out for me. He brings me home in his car to keep me safe. He loves me, Cathy, and we're going to get married as soon as I'm old enough.' Joss stopped. Her eyes glistened with passion and adoration for Zach.

'Why doesn't he have a girlfriend his own age?' I asked.

'He doesn't like them. He says most of them are self-opinionated tarts. He likes me because I'm fresh and innocent.'

Which did nothing to lessen my concerns.

'How did you meet him?'

'At Chelsea's flat. I told you, he's one of her uncles. She has lots of uncles, of all ages.'

'On her father's side of the family or her mother's?'

'I don't know,' Joss said with a shrug. 'But Zack is a real gentleman. He looks after me, not like that creep Eric.'

I could see that, having lost her own father so young and in such tragic circumstances and then not getting on with her stepfather, Joss could be attracted to a father figure in a partner, but from what I'd seen of Zach he certainly wasn't that.

'Does Zach work?' I asked.

She nodded. 'Sort of. He's in business. He's doing well. He always pays for everything.'

Including drink and drugs, I thought but didn't say. 'What sort of business? Do you know?'

'No. Zach doesn't like talking about work or himself when he's with me. He says he'd rather talk about me. I'm more interesting.' She smiled. 'He's not like the boys at school, Cathy. They're so immature and silly. All they can talk about is themselves and football. Zach is very mature and not at all silly. He's responsible.'

I think at thirteen and in Joss's position I might have fallen for Zach's charm too, but with maturity and the insight that came from fostering, I wasn't swayed by what Joss had told me. Indeed, I was more concerned than ever. I was pleased that Joss had opened up, but from what she'd said it sounded to me like sweet-talking Zach was slowly, carefully and very cleverly grooming her. However, I knew that any more warnings or negativity from me would drive Joss further into his 'understanding' arms. It was back to the same old problem: if Joss had been my daughter I would have done whatever it took to keep her safe and away from Zach, but as a foster carer I was very limited in what I could do.

'Joss, rather than you keep going to Chelsea's flat, why not bring Zach here?' I suggested.

She laughed out loud.

'What's the matter? It seems reasonable to me. This is your home for now, so why not invite him here? When Adrian, Paula and Lucy have partners I'm sure they'll bring them home.'

I could see Joss's thought processes working. 'Zack wouldn't like it,' she said at last.

'Why not? I'd make him feel welcome.'

'We – I mean he – couldn't drink or smoke here.'

'No, but at thirteen you shouldn't be anyway. I'm sure Zach would understand that if he's as mature as you say.'

'Nah. He wouldn't come,' Joss said.

'Why? If he's planning on marrying you, surely he will want to meet your family, and we're part of your family. We could ask your mother and brother to come too.'

'No. It's not his scene,' Joss said.

I bet it's not, I thought. That would really cramp his style. 'Ask him,' I suggested. 'You might be surprised by his reply.' Although not as surprised as I would be if he accepted the invitation and came to meet us all.

'OK, I'll ask him,' Joss agreed. 'But don't get your hopes up.'

I nodded. Joss said goodnight and went to bed. I believed her when she'd said she wasn't having a sexual relationship with Zach, or 'doing anything', as she'd put it. But my concerns for what could happen remained. He was a grown man, and although I'd only met him briefly, and despite all Joss's reassurances that he respected her, I didn't trust him.

* * *

The following day Miss Pryce telephoned me during her lunch hour. 'I thought you should know Joss is on report,' she said.

'Oh, no. What is it for this time?' I said. 'She told me yesterday you said she was doing well.'

'Yes, I did, in the morning, but then in the afternoon Joss swore at a member of staff. The head was going to exclude Joss – and it would have been a permanent exclusion, as she's already had one fixed-term exclusion and multiple warnings. But I persuaded her that now Joss is settled with you, she deserves another chance.'

'Thank you so much,' I said gratefully.

'Let's hope she doesn't let us down,' Miss Pryce sighed. 'In case you don't know what being on report involves, the student carries a card with them to each lesson. At the end of the lesson the teacher signs the card and writes a comment about the student's behaviour during the lesson. The head reviews the comments with the student at the end of every week.'

'Thank you. How long will Joss be on report?'

'Until the end of term – two-and-a-half weeks. Then hopefully Joss can start the new term afresh in September. I'm optimistic that having spent the summer with you, she will return a new person.'

'I'll do my best,' I said. 'What was the situation that gave rise to Joss swearing?'

'She went out with Chelsea at lunchtime and was late back again. A member of staff told her she was in detention for being late, and also warned her against joyriding in a car with two young men. Joss got angry and told her it was none of her effing business.'

'I'm so sorry,' I said. 'I'll speak to her, and also sanction her.'

'Thank you. We'd like to keep her and a few others we have concerns about in at lunchtimes for their own protection, but we've been advised we can't do that regularly, as everyone else is allowed out.'

'I understand,' I said. I thanked her again and we said goodbye.

It seemed that the school was in a similar position to me when it came to taking steps to keep Joss safe. There was only so much we were allowed to do, and it simply wasn't enough.

CHAPTER TEN

A POSITIVE SIGN?

Joss had a detention after school that Tuesday, so she didn't return home until 5.30 p.m.

'You know what happened, so don't ask!' she thundered as she came in. 'Miss said she'd phoned you.'

'She did phone,' I said.

I closed the front door as Joss kicked off her shoes. She was clearly angry, so there was no point in trying to talk to her now. She marched upstairs to her room and I went into the kitchen to continue making dinner. A few minutes later she came down again, holding her school bag, which she plonked unceremoniously on the dining table. 'I suppose I'll have to do my effing homework before I go out.'

I turned to look at her. 'You won't be going out tonight, love,' I said. 'Not after the way you behaved at school today.'

'But that's not fair! I'm allowed out on a Tuesday. I'm not doing my homework, then. You can stuff it!'

Here we go again, I thought. Grabbing her bag, she stormed back upstairs. I heard her bedroom door slam and then her moving nosily around in her room, which was directly above the kitchen.

How much easier it would be, I thought, in the short term at least, if I let Joss do as she wanted instead of trying to put in place guidelines for good and safe behaviour. Here I was, at the start of yet another evening, tense and anxious, with my stomach tied in a knot. But letting Joss continue unchecked would do her no good and would have been irresponsible of me as a parent and carer. Someone needed to make Joss understand that there would be consequences if she kept behaving as she was, and who else was there to do that but me? Her mother and stepfather had tried and failed, so had an aunt and two previous foster carers, and it looked as though I was going the same way. I knew Joss and I were heading for a showdown – her will against mine – but it was essential she learnt to behave in a safe and acceptable manner.

Joss stayed in her room for the next fifteen minutes, until six o'clock when I called everyone to dinner. She came immediately and was no longer angry or even sulking; she took her seat at the table and spoke pleasantly to Lucy and Paula – Adrian wasn't home yet. Naïvely I assumed that, alone in her room, she'd had time to reflect on her behaviour, had realized she was in the wrong and now accepted she wasn't going out. She ate her main course, didn't want any pudding, but remained seated at the table until we'd all finished. Then we took our dishes through to the kitchen and Joss returned upstairs to her room. I'd go up shortly and encourage her to come down, as I didn't want her sitting alone all evening. However, a minute later, while I was clearing up, I heard her bedroom door open and then her footsteps on the stairs. I was expecting her to go into the front room where Paula and Lucy were, or possibly to come and find me, but a few moments later I heard the front door open and then close. I went straight into the hall to find it empty.

'She's gone out,' Lucy called from the front room.

'I don't believe it! She wasn't allowed out tonight. I'm going after her.' I quickly pushed my feet into my sandals and opened the front door.

'Be careful,' Paula said, appearing in the hall.

'Don't worry, I won't be long.'

I went out, down the front path and onto the pavement just in time to see Joss disappearing around the bend further up the road. I assumed she was heading for the bus stop on the high road, in which case I'd need to reach her before she got on the bus. It was a fine evening and still light. I walked quickly, but as I turned the bend I saw her standing on the pavement further up. She was looking away from me, concentrating on the top of the road, watching and waiting for someone to arrive, I guessed. I continued towards her and only at the last moment, when I was pretty close, did she turn and look at me, shocked and surprised.

'What do you want?' she demanded.

'I told you to stay in tonight,' I said none too quietly. 'How dare you disobey me and go out.'

'Go away,' she hissed, glancing anxiously around. 'You can't make me stay in.'

'I'm not going home without you. Who are you waiting for?'

'No one. Leave me alone. I can do what I like.'

'No, you can't,' I said. 'No one can do as they like all the time, and certainly not at thirteen!'

Joss looked around, clearly embarrassed. It was a warm summer's evening and people were out, on their way home from work and the shops, and of course I was making a scene.

'I want you to come home with me now, Joss,' I said quite loudly. 'Then we can talk about this.'

'I'm not coming. I'm waiting for my friends,' she hissed.

'Who? Zach?'

She nodded.

'I'll wait with you then and explain what's happened.'

'You can't do that. Go home,' she hissed again.

'Not unless you come with me.'

'He'll be annoyed if he finds you here,' she said, and it sounded like a threat.

'Don't worry. I'll handle it. Is this where he usually picks you up and drops you off?' I asked.

'Yeah. Now go away, will you?' She looked anxiously up the street.

'I'm not going anywhere, Joss, without you,' I confirmed, and remained standing beside her.

'Oh, shit!' she suddenly said.

I followed her gaze to the shiny black BMW that was now turning onto the road.

'He's here. Go away!' She tried to elbow me away and a passer-by looked at us.

Clearly the driver of the BMW must have seen us, and for a moment I thought he was going to drive straight past, but then the car slowed and pulled in to the kerb, level with us. I could see Zach at the wheel, Carl in the passenger seat and Chelsea in the rear. The front windows stayed up, but Chelsea lowered her window and looked out.

'What's up?' she asked Joss.

'*She* says I can't go out tonight,' Joss said.

'Aww,' I heard Carl sneer from the front.

'Come on,' Chelsea said. 'Don't take any notice of her. Get in.'

Much to Chelsea's surprise, I opened the rear door. 'Hello, everyone,' I said, looking in.

'Hello,' Zach said sombrely, while Carl gave a snort of derisive laughter. Both lads continued to look straight ahead.

'Are you getting in or what?' Chelsea asked Joss.

'No, she's not,' I said. Joss stood beside me, embarrassed, agitated and not knowing what to do.

'She's not coming out tonight,' I confirmed.

'Do what your carer says,' Carl sniggered. Then to Zach he said: 'Come on, man, let's go. We don't want any trouble.' Zach revved the engine.

'You coming? Last chance,' Chelsea said to Joss.

'No, she's not,' I said.

'Close the fucking door, man,' Carl snarled from the front.

'Bye then,' Chelsea said, annoyed, and slammed the door. Immediately the car sped away, tyres screeching.

'Now look what you've done!' Joss cried, turning to me, close to tears.

My heart was pounding and my legs were like jelly. I hate confrontations, but this one had been essential.

'I've done what is right to keep you safe,' I said. 'If I tell you you're not going out, I mean it.'

'They'll all be laughing at me,' Joss moaned. 'And why didn't Zach stick up for me?'

'Because he's not the friend you thought he was?' I offered gently.

'Yes, he is,' Joss snapped. 'It's you. You're ruining my life. I want to see my friends and have fun.' We turned and began back down the street.

'I'm not trying to stop you from having fun, Joss, but I'm very concerned that the type of fun you're having at present

115

isn't safe. Why not invite a friend of your own age home? You could watch a film and eat takeaway pizza.' This was the type of fun a thirteen-year-old should be having – innocent, age-appropriate fun – but Joss, with all her problems, was missing out on that and trying to bury her sorrow in drink and drugs.

'Chelsea wouldn't come,' Joss said moodily as we walked.

'Well, invite another friend, then. Perhaps someone from your class?'

'I haven't got any other friends,' Joss said gloomily. 'Chelsea is my only mate.'

'I'm sure that isn't true,' I said. 'You're a nice person – when you're not angry,' I added with a smile.

'No one wants to be my friend,' Joss said, sadness now replacing anger. 'They think I'm bad news because I'm always in trouble. Their parents tell them to keep away from me.'

Which I could understand. 'There is a very obvious solution, Joss,' I said. 'Stop getting into trouble, behave yourself and then make some new friends. You don't have to keep breaking all the rules. It's not big and it's not clever. You can change if you want to. Miss Pryce said she's hoping that after the six-week summer holiday you'll go back to school and start afresh.'

Joss shrugged despondently. I felt sorry for her now. 'If I'm still there,' she said. 'They might have put me in lock-up by then.'

'Not if you stop your unsafe behaviour,' I said. 'I'm trying to help you do that.' I pushed open the front garden gate and Joss followed me through. I paused on the doorstep and looked at her. 'I know you've suffered, love, but don't keep punishing yourself. You can start afresh and have a great life.'

'What's the point?' she said. 'We all end up dead anyway.'

'Oh, Joss.' I touched her arm reassuringly. 'Let's go indoors and have a talk. You shouldn't be feeling like this.'

I unlocked the front door and we went in. I thought Joss might want to talk now and open up a little, but once inside she said, 'Are Lucy and Paula in?'

'Yes, they're in the front room on the computer.'

'You can come and join us if you like,' Lucy called, having heard.

'Yeah, OK.' Joss disappeared into the front room, all animosity gone.

She spent most of the evening with Paula and Lucy, so it wasn't until bedtime that I had a chance to talk to her again. Although Joss never wanted a hug or a kiss goodnight, I always looked in on her to make sure she was all right. She was propped up in bed, flipping through a magazine. She loved her girly magazines and seemed to be spending most of her pocket money on them.

'You had a pleasant evening in the end,' I said, standing near her bed.

'It wasn't bad,' she returned, concentrating on the magazine. 'You know what you said about friends?'

'Yes.'

'Well, Paula and Lucy are your friends.'

'Yeah, good,' she said without looking up.

'Can we talk?' I asked.

'What about?' She turned a page.

'Anything you like. I was worried by your comment earlier about not seeing any point in life. It sounded as though you might be depressed.'

She glanced up briefly. 'Nah. I'm OK.'

'Are you sure?'

'Yeah.'

I hesitated. 'You would tell me if you were feeling very low, wouldn't you?'

'Yeah, I guess.'

I hesitated. What else could I say? She didn't want to talk to me. I couldn't force her. 'Well, goodnight then, love. You know where I am if you want me.'

'Yeah.'

'See you in the morning.'

'Yeah.'

I came out and closed her bedroom door, but I was worried. Being a teenager can be difficult enough with all the confusing emotions and decisions that have to be made, without the baggage Joss carried. However, I couldn't make her talk or seek counselling if she didn't want to. She knew it was on offer, so, frustratingly, all I could do was be on hand, ready for if and when she needed me.

The following day was Wednesday, and the contract of behaviour, which we still hadn't received a copy of or signed, and which Amelia said may now need updating, stipulated that Joss had to stay in on Wednesdays. Joss accepted this without argument and appeared a little relieved that the decision had been made for her. She did an hour's homework and then after dinner she spent some time in Paula's room playing with her doll's house, while Paula sat on her bed reading Joss's magazines. Wonderful, domestic harmony, I thought, and hoped we'd enjoy more evenings like this. Teenagers often appear grown up and in control of their lives, but inside they are children trying to find a way into adult life. It's a bit like buying a new outfit: you try on different clothes until eventually you find something that suits you and feels comfortable. So teenagers try different personas until they find the one that fits them best, but during the process they need a lot of direction. It's not cramping their style; it's helping them choose a good outcome.

Unfortunately, the glimpse of domestic harmony I'd seen earlier, when Joss had been playing with Paula's doll's house, hid a more sinister picture, one that served as a harrowing reminder of just how disturbed Joss really was.

It was nearly nine o'clock. Joss was in the bath and I was downstairs talking to Lucy, who'd just returned from a friend's house where she'd been working on an end-of-year presentation for school, which they could do in pairs. Paula was in her bedroom getting ready for bed when suddenly I heard her footsteps running down the stairs.

'Mum, come quickly!' she cried, arriving in the living room, her face pale from shock. 'Come and see what Joss has done. It's horrible.'

'Whatever is it?' I asked, immediately on my feet.

'You need to see. Come.'

Lucy and I ran down the hall behind Paula and upstairs to her room.

'Go and look,' Paula said, standing just inside the door and pointing to her doll's house.

Lucy was there before me. 'Oh, my God!' she gasped. 'That's horrible.'

I joined her at the front of the doll's house and my heart lurched. Like many doll's houses, the front of this one opened to show all the rooms with their furniture and doll people inside. The garage was at the bottom to the right, and the daddy doll, which Paula had previously told me Joss never played with, was now hanging by its neck with a piece of string from the roof of the garage. Its head had been bent grotesquely to one side in a parody of a broken neck, and the corpse dangled beside the car as though it had jumped off the bonnet. This was obviously a grizzly reproduction of what Joss had seen when her father had committed suicide in the garage, and it was truly disturbing.

'Why would Joss do that with the doll?' Lucy asked, still staring at the corpse.

My family knew that Joss's father had died in distressing circumstances, but they didn't know the details.

'Joss's father committed suicide,' I said.

'By hanging himself in the garage?' Lucy asked, clamping her hand over her mouth in horror.

'Yes,' I said.

I reached in and unpinned the doll from the ceiling and then untied the string from its neck. Paula was still by the door, watching from a distance, and I returned the daddy doll to the miniature sofa in the living room. 'That's better,' I said, hiding my shock and trying to restore normality.

'I'm not letting Joss play with the doll's house again,' Paula said, clearly upset.

'No, I wouldn't,' Lucy agreed.

'I'll talk to Joss when she's finished in the bath,' I said, closing the front of the house. 'But you know, girls, perhaps this is a positive sign that Joss is getting ready to talk about what happened, which would be a very good thing.' Although I wished she hadn't used Paula's doll's house to express it. The atrocity had sullied its childlike innocence, and I knew the taint would remain for some time.

* * *

When Joss had finished her bath and was in her bedroom, I knocked on her door and went in.

'What?' she asked, already on the defensive. I guessed she knew what I wanted.

'Paula is upset by what she found in her doll's house,' I said gently.

'Not half as upset as I was!' Joss snapped, referring, I assumed, to her father's actual death.

'I appreciate that, love. It must have been absolutely horrendous for you. I can't imagine how you coped.'

'I didn't,' she said, climbing into bed. 'But shit happens. There's nothing you or anyone can do about it. And before you ask me, no, I don't want to talk about it.' She picked up a magazine and pulled it open.

I waited. 'Are you sure?'

'Yes.'

'All right, I'll leave you to it, then, but you know where I am if you need me.'

Joss gave a small nod and I said goodnight and came out of her room.

That night she had a nightmare. It was about her father. As I soothed her back to sleep, she whispered, 'Daddy. Daddy gone. Dead.' And a tear slipped from the corner of her eye. It was heartbreaking. I knew she had all that hurt buried deep inside her and it was trying to find a way out. Interestingly, the following morning she remembered some of her dream, which she didn't usually.

'I had a really bad dream last night,' she told me.

'Do you remember what it was about?' I asked carefully, aware I needed to handle this sensitively.

'It was about my daddy,' she said quietly. 'I think, the day he died.'

'Do you remember anything else?'

'Not sure. Were you there?'

'I heard you call out and came into your room to make sure you were all right. I always check if I hear one of you call out in the night. You went back to sleep quite quickly.'

She shrugged. 'I don't really remember. It's a blur.'

Joss didn't offer any more and I left it at that, but my amateur psychology told me that Joss hanging the doll and then starting to remember her dreams could mean that the shocking memories of her father's suicide were starting to work their way to the surface to be dealt with.

That afternoon Jill came for one of her scheduled four-weekly visits – to make sure I was fostering Joss to the required standard, to give support and advice as necessary and to sign off my log notes. I updated her on events since the last time we'd spoken on the phone, finishing with the incident of the doll and Joss's most recent nightmare.

'I'm no psychiatrist,' Jill said, 'but it could certainly be a positive sign. Keep doing what you have been doing – providing a safe and supportive environment – and Joss may feel able to start counselling before long and address her demons. Once she comes to terms with what happened and stops blaming herself, she'll be less angry and her behaviour should start to improve.'

I greatly valued Jill's opinion, so I was pleased to hear this, but what happened next showed Joss still had a very long way to go.

CHAPTER ELEVEN

NO PROGRESS

It was Friday morning, and at 9.30 a.m. I received the now familiar telephone call from the secretary at Joss's school, informing me that Joss hadn't arrived and that when she did she would be given an hour's detention at the end of the day. I apologized for her lateness, confirmed that she'd left for school on time and thanked the secretary for letting me know. If a child who usually arrived at school on time suddenly went missing I would be very worried, but Joss arriving late for school was a regular occurrence, so I knew from previous experience that it wouldn't be long before the school secretary telephoned again to say Joss had arrived. Sure enough, fifteen minutes later the telephone rang – however, it wasn't the secretary, but a man with an accent whose voice I didn't recognize. 'Is that Mrs Glass?' he asked.

'Yes.' I assumed it was a telesales canvasser, but what he said next scared me rigid.

'I have your daughter, Mrs Glass.'

'What? What do you mean?' My heart began drumming loudly in my chest.

'I have your daughter, Joss, here with me. You need to come and collect her. She is a very naughty girl.'

'Who are you? What are you talking about? Where is Joss? Put her on at once, please.'

There was a muffled sound as the handset was passed over and then Joss's voice came on, subdued and without her usual bravado. 'Cathy, please come and get me – he's scaring me.'

'Where are you? Who is he? What's going on?' My concerns grew.

'He's making me stay here with him until you come. He wants to see you.'

'Where are you?'

'The paper shop on the corner of South Road.'

'The newsagents there?'

'Yes.'

I knew where it was, although I'd never been in. It wasn't the newsagents below the flat where Chelsea lived, but one close to Joss's school.

'And he won't let you leave?'

'No.'

'Why?'

Joss didn't answer.

'I'll call the police,' I said.

'No! Don't do that! Please, Cathy,' Joss pleaded. 'I'm in enough trouble already. Don't get the police involved.'

'What's going on, Joss? He can't keep you there against your will. It's illegal. Are you hurt?'

'No. Just come and collect me, please. I'm in his sitting room at the back of the shop.'

'And you can't tell me what's happened?'

'He wants to tell you when you come for me.'

'Put him back on, please.'

124

His voice came on the line again. 'Mrs Glass, I was going to call the police, but your daughter begged me not to, so I insisted I call you instead. She's done wrong and I'm not just going to let her get away with it. Are you coming or shall I call the police?'

'I'm coming,' I said. 'I'll be there in ten minutes.'

'Very well. My wife will sit with her while I return to the shop. I will see you soon. Goodbye.' The line went dead.

I had my shoes on and was out of the door and in the car in an instant, still thinking I should call the police. Joss had pleaded with me not to and she'd said she wasn't hurt, but then perhaps he was standing over her with a knife and forcing her to say that? I'd been fostering for long enough to know that anything was possible, and that unbelievable and horrific events did occur. I was sick with fear and drove faster than I should have done. All teenagers can be volatile and reckless at times, but when it's your own child whom you know well, you have a fair idea of what they are capable of – good and bad. Joss was another matter entirely, and try as I had I still didn't have a clue what she was capable of. All manner of thoughts crossed my mind, including that the man might be a dangerous psychopath who was planning to hold me hostage too.

I parked in the side street next to the shop, got out and walked swiftly round to the front door, my stomach churning. A large handwritten notice in the shop window stated: *Only two school children allowed in together.* I opened the door and a bell clanged from inside, and then again as the door closed behind me. A woman customer left the shop and another was looking at a stand containing a display of greeting cards. With my mouth dry and my heart pounding,

I went up to the counter at the far end of the shop. A smartly dressed middle-aged Asian man was standing behind the counter, looking at me as I approached. I realized then that I hadn't asked the man who'd telephoned for his name. 'Are you the person who telephoned me about Joss?' I asked. 'I'm Mrs Glass.'

'Yes, I am,' he said sternly. 'This way, please.' He lifted the counter top to allow me to pass through. 'Your daughter is in here,' he said, lowering the counter again behind me.

I followed him down a short, dimly lit hall, which led into a small, cramped sitting room. The curtains were closed and the room was lit by a single bare bulb hanging from the centre of the ceiling. Cardboard boxes were stacked around the edges and the room smelt musty, so I guessed it was usually only used for storage. Joss sat in one of two old-fashioned armchairs, the only furniture, and a middle-aged woman dressed in a sari, whom I took to be the man's wife, sat opposite her. She stood as we entered, said something to her husband in another language and then went into the shop, closing the door behind her.

Joss stood. 'Can I go now?' she asked the man.

'Not yet. I need to talk to your mother first.' He turned to me. 'Do you know how much stock I lose every week from stealing? It's robbing me of my livelihood. I struggle to support my family as it is. It is not easy, owning a shop. I work all the hours God sends me and then I have the little I earn taken away from me by people like your daughter.'

I now had a good idea what this was all about.

'I telephone the school and tell them that their pupils are stealing,' he continued. 'I've even been in to see the headmistress, but nothing happens. She tells me she can't be held responsible for what their pupils do once they've left the school premises. If I call the police, they come eventually, take a statement, and then I see the same kids in here again the next day, and they're laughing at me. They think stealing from under my nose is a joke. I blame the parents. I have two children of my own and they would never steal. I have brought them up properly. They are trustworthy and polite teenagers. If they are naughty, they know what's coming. I have taught them respect and honesty, Mrs Glass. Something you need to teach your daughter.'

I remained silent, for I could see he wasn't finished yet.

'I've even had expensive CCTV fitted in my shop,' he continued. 'But the kids get around that by standing in a group and shielding the one stealing from the camera, hence the notice outside about only two being allowed in the shop. What a sad state of affairs that children can't be trusted to come in and buy a few sweets! I've had my suspicions about your daughter for some time – she comes in here a lot – but now I have the proof. She's not as clever as she thinks. The camera will show her putting a magazine into her bag and trying to leave the shop without paying for it. That's when I stopped her.'

Joss, who'd remained sitting silently and staring moodily straight ahead of her, now stood.

'If you've finished, can we go now?' she said disrespectfully.

'Not yet,' I said firmly. 'And you'd better take that silly look off your face and start listening to what this gentleman has to say or I'll be calling the police.'

The man straightened, clearly a little surprised that I was taking this firm line. Joss had the decency to look slightly abashed.

'I'm appalled and shocked at your behaviour, Joss,' I said. 'I don't know what you thought you were doing. You know it's wrong to steal. You can start by apologizing to this gentleman for what you have done, and then we'll ask him what we can do to compensate him.'

'I am pleased to hear you say that, Mrs Glass,' he said. 'Some parents take the side of their children and make excuses for them. They blame me and call me racist names. I hope you understand, I am only trying to protect my livelihood. I am sure you would do the same.'

'Yes, indeed,' I said. 'I'm sorry. Joss's behaviour is completely unacceptable. She will be saying sorry too.' I wasn't going to play the sympathy card and tell him Joss was in care and that she'd had a rough time as a child. He didn't need to know that, and Joss knew it was wrong to steal. 'I will punish Joss,' I said. 'But I would also like to pay for the goods she has stolen. Does she still have the magazine in her school bag?'

'No, my wife took it from her. But she has stolen many other magazines in the past. I just couldn't prove it until now.' My thoughts went to the stack of magazines Joss had in her bedroom, and the ones strewn across our living room; she was always coming home with a new magazine. I'd assumed she'd bought them with her pocket money, and my heart sank.

'Do you have any idea how many she may have taken?' I asked him.

He shook his head. 'I wouldn't like to guess.'

I looked at Joss. 'You must know how many magazines you've taken?'

'Dunno. Can't remember,' she said belligerently.

'Do you have any money on you?' I asked her.

'No.'

I began rummaging in my shoulder bag for my purse. I thought we should offer something towards the cost of the goods she'd stolen, even if we didn't know the full amount.

'There is no need for that,' he said.

'Yes, there is,' I said. 'Joss needs to learn that her actions have consequences. I shall be stopping the money from her allowance.' I took a ten-pound note from my purse and began to remove another, unsure of how much to offer him.

'No, Mrs Glass,' he said, covering my purse with his hand. 'I cannot take your money. But thank you for offering. It's appreciated. Perhaps you would like to make a small donation to the charity I support instead? There's a collecting tin on the counter in the shop.'

'Yes, of course, if that is what you'd prefer. Thank you. I'm sorry, I don't know your name.'

'Mr Chanda.'

'I apologize again, Mr Chanda, for Joss's behaviour. I'll make a donation on the way out and I'll be speaking to Joss very firmly when we get home. I'll make it clear to her that she's not to come into your shop again.' He nodded. 'If she does, telephone me and I will come and collect her straight away. Now, I hope you will accept the apology that she is going to make.'

We both looked at Joss, and either she didn't understand what was required of her or she was reluctant to say sorry, for she remained stubbornly silent.

'Joss,' I said sharply. 'Say sorry to Mr Chanda and then we'll go.'

'Sorry,' she said quietly.

Mr Chanda nodded.

'On the way out we will apologize to Mrs Chanda too,' I told Joss. 'I assume that was your wife?' I said to Mr Chanda, and he nodded.

Mr and Mrs Chanda were clearly decent, hard-working people who were doing their best to make a living, and it was appalling that Joss – and, from the sound of it, others from her school – was causing them so much trouble.

'Thank you,' he said.

I made to leave and he went ahead and courteously held the door open for Joss and me. We went down the short hall and into the shop, where Mrs Chanda was serving behind the counter. We waited until she'd finished and then her husband said, 'The girl is going to apologize to you.'

I looked at Joss. 'I'm sorry,' she said.

Mrs Chanda nodded coldly, and who could blame her? She must have been as fed up as her husband with having to deal with thieving.

'I'm dreadfully sorry,' I said to her. 'Joss will not come in here any more.'

She nodded again. Mr Chanda then raised the counter and Joss and I went through. I put the ten-pound note into the collecting tin and we left the shop.

As soon as we were outside, Joss relaxed. 'Phew, that was close,' she said, all humility gone.

I was furious. 'I can't believe how stupid you've been!' I said. 'Do you realize that if Mr Chanda had called the police you would have been sent to a secure unit for sure? Whatever were you thinking of? You know it's wrong to steal.'

She gave a nonchalant, couldn't-care-less shrug.

'How dare you treat those people like that!'

I unlocked the car and we got in. Before I started the engine I turned to Joss. 'Don't ever go in that shop again. Do you understand?'

'Yes,' she said.

'And don't be tempted to steal from anywhere else either. If you want a magazine, buy one. That's what your allowance is for.'

'But you keep stopping my allowance,' she said accusingly, as if this was forcing her to steal and therefore it was my fault.

'Yes, as a sanction for when your behaviour is unacceptable. It's a punishment, Joss. You go without something, although you know you can always earn it back. So don't blame me for your stupidity. You need to take responsibility for your actions. Who was in the shop with you?'

'No one,' she said moodily.

'Chelsea wasn't with you?'

'No. She waited outside. She can't afford to get caught any more.'

'And neither can you!' I said, my voice rising. 'And whether you get caught is not the issue. It's wrong to steal. You don't do it! That poor Mr and Mrs Chanda. Think of them. They have children too.'

'He shouldn't have kept me there against my will,' Joss said defiantly. 'He can't do that. He hasn't got the right. It's against the law.' Which was choice, considering she'd just been stealing.

'That's where you're wrong,' I said. 'A shopkeeper has the right in law to detain a shoplifter and call the police. You want to be damn grateful he called me instead. And when you get home tonight you're going to put all those magazines you stole in the bin.'

'No! You can't do that. They're mine!'

'They're not yours, Joss. You didn't pay for them. You stole them. I'm not having you enjoy something you've stolen. If Mr Chanda could sell them we'd take them back to the shop, but they're crumpled and out of date now, so you're going to throw them away.'

'Fucking hell,' she muttered. 'What a waste.'

'And don't swear.'

She turned her back on me and stared out of her side window. 'Fasten your seatbelt,' I said. 'I'll take you to school now.'

We both fastened our belts. I started the engine and then drove the couple of minutes to Joss's school, where I parked on the road outside.

'You don't have to come in with me,' Joss said, one hand on the door, ready to get out.

'I know, but I will, to save the secretary having to phone to tell me you've arrived.'

'You won't tell the school what happened, will you?' Joss said, turning to me, worried.

'No, but I will need to tell your social worker.' I held her gaze and my tone softened. 'Joss, please make this the last incident, for both our sakes. You can't keep going on like this. I hate to see you get into more and more trouble. You're an intelligent girl. Save yourself and make the right choices, please. You must.'

'I'll try,' she said too easily. 'Can I go out tonight? I've only been out once this week.'

'We'll see how the rest of the day goes,' I said. I knew I couldn't rein her in too much all at once or there would be a backlash and I'd achieve nothing, and of course the behaviour

132

contract was still running. But I thought it was positive that she was at least asking me if she could go out, rather than simply assuming she would be.

We got out of the car, went up the path and into the reception, where the school secretary sat at her computer behind the open-plan counter. She recognized me from when I'd had the appointment with Miss Pryce. 'You're very late, Joss,' she said, placing the late book on the counter ready for Joss to sign in. It was now nearly 10.30 a.m. 'She'll be kept in for an hour's detention tonight,' she confirmed to me.

I nodded.

'Can I go to my lessons now?' Joss asked, slightly subdued.

'Do you know where you're supposed to be?' the secretary asked.

'Maths, room twelve M,' Joss said, and she turned and sauntered off down the corridor.

'Goodbye,' I called after her. 'See you at five o'clock.'

She didn't reply, and the secretary looked at me questioningly. 'She's not very happy with me at present,' I said.

'She was very late. Where's she been?' she asked.

'She got lost,' I said, rolling my eyes in exasperation. Then, saying goodbye, I left the building. The secretary didn't need to know what had happened.

Joss arrived home after the detention at exactly five o'clock, as she was supposed to, and when I asked her she said she'd had a good day. Before she began her homework, and without being reminded to, she gathered together all the (stolen) magazines and put them in the bin. We ate at 6.30 and as we finished Joss asked if she could go out.

'Yes, but I want you back by eight-thirty,' I said.

'That's not fair!' she exclaimed. Adrian, Paula and Lucy tensed, sensing another confrontation.

'It's very fair,' I said firmly. 'Given what happened this morning, you're lucky to be going out at all. Where are you going?'

'Dunno yet,' she said, standing, eager to be away. 'All right, I'll be back by eight-thirty. See ya later.'

Everyone relaxed and we called goodbye.

Would she be back by 8.30? It was anyone's guess, although I felt that maybe she was starting to accept my authority. Going after her on Tuesday evening when she'd disobeyed me and left to meet Zach at the end of the road had possibly helped. It had proved that I meant what I said and the lengths I would go to. I hoped she realized I was doing it for her own good, because I cared about her and wanted to keep her safe. I'd said it enough times.

Joss did arrive home at 8.30. 'Well done,' I said. 'You've earned back your allowance.'

I fetched my purse straight away and gave her the money to reinforce the benefit of doing what she was supposed to. But the following day and over that weekend, a new problem came to light that made me realize we'd made no progress at all.

CHAPTER TWELVE

NOT MY FATHER

On Friday evening, while Joss was out, Paula came to me looking worried.

'Mum,' she said. 'I've lost my pocket money and I need it for tomorrow.'

'That's not like you,' I said. 'Where did you lose it? In the street?'

'No. I'm not sure. I thought I left it on my bedside cabinet, but it's not there now. I've searched my room.'

'It can't have gone far if it's in the house,' I said. 'Don't worry. I'm sure it will turn up. I'll give you the money and when you find it you can repay me. OK?'

She smiled. 'Yes, thanks. I'll go and have another look now.'

I thought nothing more of this. Paula was usually good with money, as were Adrian and Lucy, and I thought the five-pound note must simply have fallen out of view in her room and she'd find it before long. But the next day, Saturday, while Joss was out seeing her mother and brother, Lucy came to me.

'I'm not accusing anyone,' she began with a mixture of anger and concern, 'but ten pounds is missing from my money box.'

'Are you sure?' I asked her. 'You haven't spent it?'

'No. Definitely not. I was saving up for something. I know for sure I had thirty-five pounds in there and now I only have twenty-five.'

All three of my children each had an ornate silver money box given to them as a present from my parents: Adrian and Paula for their first birthdays, and Lucy when she had a birthday after she'd arrived. None of the money boxes had a lock.

I looked at Lucy and, of course, thought of the unexplained disappearance of Paula's money.

'I hate to say it,' Lucy continued, 'but there is only one person who could have taken it.' Which was true, for I trusted my own children unreservedly.

'Assuming it has been taken,' I said. 'I'm not doubting what you're telling me, but I'll need to be a hundred per cent certain. I'll give you the money, and if the ten pounds reappears, tell me at once. And obviously don't accuse Joss. There may be another explanation.'

'I won't,' Lucy said quietly. 'Although I can't think what else it could be.' I could see that she felt as wretched as I did at the possibility of Joss stealing from us.

It's a horrible feeling, suspecting a child of dishonesty, and it creates an uncomfortable atmosphere in the house, with everyone on their guard. Sadly, I'd been in this position before with children I'd fostered. Some children are very honest, but others are not, having been allowed to thieve by their parents or even encouraged to do so. Some children, aware that their parents are poor, steal money on their behalf for food and heating, and give them their pocket money too, which is pitiful. But whatever the reason, if Joss was stealing from us, I needed to handle it carefully. My relationship with her was already very delicate, and while I didn't doubt what Paula and Lucy had told me, the only way I would feel confident approaching Joss was if I caught her red-handed.

On Sunday Joss was going to be with me all day – until her social worker told me otherwise, this was how I was interpreting the contract of behaviour. Joss moaned and groaned, said it wasn't fair and then settled down to a relaxing day. I'd already told Lucy and Paula to keep their money boxes in a drawer in their rooms for the time being, and Adrian always kept his in a drawer anyway, as he felt the cute sliver-bear box wasn't quite his style now he was sixteen. My purse was in my handbag in the hall where I usually left it, but today I knew exactly how much money it contained. It was possible Joss had been stealing from me; if she'd only taken small amounts I wouldn't have noticed, as I only kept a rough tally of the cash I had so I knew when to draw out more. But today, much as I hated doing it, I'd counted my money and knew there were three ten-pound notes, a five-pound note, two one-pound coins and some coppers.

I checked my purse just before lunch and to my relief all the money was still there, but when I checked it again in the afternoon the five-pound note and a one-pound coin were missing. I felt sick. I was so hoping my suspicions were wrong and that no money would go missing, and Paula and Lucy would find theirs. But now I had the proof I needed, I couldn't put off any longer approaching Joss, although I would do it in private.

Ten minutes later I had the opportunity I needed. Joss went up to her room and I went after her, hating what I was about to do. She'd left her bedroom door open and I knocked on it and went in. 'Hi,' she said, rummaging in her wardrobe.

'Joss, leave that for a moment, please,' I said. 'I need to talk to you about something serious.'

'What is it?' she asked, turning to face me. Her expression was completely innocent and I felt so guilty for believing she was capable of stealing.

'Joss, this is very difficult, but it needs to be dealt with. I'll come straight to the point. Some money has gone missing in the house. Do you know where it might be?'

'No!' she said indignantly. 'Are you accusing me?'

'No. I trust everyone in this family. But I want you to think very carefully about whether you know where the money might be. If so, it's best if you say so now, so we can find a way of putting it right.' I hoped my non-accusatory approach would encourage her to be honest.

'How do you know the money has been stolen?' she asked. 'Perhaps it's been spent.'

'I know exactly how much money I had in my purse this morning, and I haven't been shopping. A five-pound note and one-pound coin is missing.'

Joss looked shocked and then, quickly recovering, said nonchalantly, 'Oh, that. I didn't think you'd mind if I borrowed some money. I used to help myself from Mum's purse when I was at home.'

'Did she know?'

Joss shrugged and turned to fiddle with something in her wardrobe. 'Sometimes. She didn't mind.'

'And what about your brother, Kevin? Did he let you help yourself to his money too?'

'No, of course not,' Joss said, spinning round again to face me. 'That's not –' She stopped, realizing the connection.

'Exactly. That wouldn't have been right, would it? To take money from Kevin. But you felt it was OK to take money from Paula and Lucy. Joss, everyone in this house treats you like family and trusts you. As I hope you do us. Families have to trust each other in order to function. You wouldn't dream of stealing from Kevin, but it's equally wrong to steal from Paula, Lucy, Adrian or me. If your mother allowed you to take money without asking her then that was her decision. I don't agree with it, and you don't do it here. Adrian, Paula and Lucy always ask me if they need to borrow money and I expect you to do the same. Do you understand?'

She nodded in a desultory, half-hearted way.

'I hope you do, Joss. Now, we'll start with the money you've taken from me today – six pounds. I'd like it back, please.' I knew she must still have it, as she hadn't left the house.

Joss hesitated and then went to the chest of drawers, opened the middle one, delved under some clothes and pulled out the five-pound note and one-pound coin. She closed the drawer and handed me the money.

'Thank you. Do you have Paula's and Lucy's money in there too?'

'No. I spent it.' Which I thought seemed very likely, as the money had probably been taken during the week.

'So how do you think you can best pay it back?' I asked.

'Stop it out of my allowance,' Joss said. 'That's what Mum did.'

I didn't point out that she'd just told me her mother didn't mind her taking money from her purse. 'That's acceptable,' I said. 'I'll stop one pound a week from your allowance until it's all paid back. But Joss, why are you stealing? You always have at least half your allowance and you usually earn back the rest through good behaviour. I buy all your clothes, toiletries and everything else you need. And you told me Zach's very generous and always pays for you when you're out with him. You don't need to steal.'

'Zach doesn't pay when it's just Chelsea and me out together,' Joss said as though that justified it. 'And Chelsea's dad is always broke, so he doesn't give her any money.'

'It's greed then, Joss,' I said. 'We all have to budget, so choose an activity that doesn't cost money. I've told you before you can always invite a friend here. That would be a low-cost evening. But alcohol, cigarettes and whatever else you may be smoking cost a lot of money, don't they? As well as being very bad for your health.' I wondered how many times I would have to say this before I finally got through to Joss.

'I know,' she agreed too easily, and I sighed inwardly.

I thought I would try to shame her to make her see sense. 'Joss, money has other uses apart from spending it on ourselves. Lucy saves a lot of her allowance. She likes to buy birthday and Christmas presents for friends and family. She's very generous – too generous, sometimes. She still sees her birth mother a couple of times a year and she always gives her a present, even when it's not her birthday. That's why she was saving up – to give her mother a nice present – and you've taken that from her.' I stopped and waited.

'I'm sorry,' she said.

'I hope you are, Joss, because you can't go on like this.'

'What will you do?' she asked. 'Send me away like the others did.'

'No. Absolutely not. But if you continue like this, the decision on where you live will be made for us. And we both know where that will be.' I paused to let the message sink in. Whether it did or not, I couldn't tell, but I'd said what I wanted to for now, so it was time to move on.

'OK, Joss, come downstairs when you're ready. I thought we'd all go out somewhere later and I'm not spoiling it for the others by not going.'

She didn't reply, so I left her room and went downstairs. I knew part of Joss's challenging behaviour was to test my commitment to her – hence her comment about sending her away – but there was more to it than that. Until she addressed the demons from her past that haunted her, there was little more I could do, other than support and guide her in the hope that eventually there would be a breakthrough – but it needed to come soon.

I told Lucy and Paula that the matter of the missing money had been sorted and left it at that. There was then a discussion on where we should go and everyone agreed on ice skating. Joss had been a few times before with her mother and brother, but that had been some years ago. However, she quickly proved a proficient and fearless skater. While the rest of us went round at a steady, slightly tentative pace – me especially – Joss whizzed round, overtaking other skaters with the same reckless determination with which she approached life in general. When she fell, which she did a couple of times, she picked herself up, brushed herself down and continued undaunted. It was a fun afternoon, and I was pleased Joss had been able to enjoy it with us. All the bad feeling about the missing money had gone, and of course the outing hadn't cost Joss a penny, as I always paid for everyone when we were out together as a family.

On Monday Joss stopped by her home on the way back from school – to see her mum and Kevin, and also check that her mother was coming to the review on Wednesday and wouldn't be bringing Eric. Her mother told her Eric would be looking after Kevin while she attended the review, so that was all right. That evening and Tuesday evening Joss was only ten minutes late back after going out, but came in sucking a mint. I again expressed my concern that she'd been drinking and smoking.

'Don't worry,' she said. 'Zach and Carl were with us the whole evening and brought me home in the car.' How that made it all right I didn't know!

On Tuesday, during the day, Jill and Amelia had both telephoned for updates on how Joss was doing in preparation for the review the following day. We were on the phone for quite a long time and although I always tried to be positive in what I said about Joss, it was proving more and more difficult. 'We had a nice day on Sunday,' I said. 'And she's doing homework most days.'

To her credit, though, Joss came straight home from school on Wednesday, as I'd told her to, so we were able to start her review on time – at 4.30 p.m. Amelia, Jill, Linda, Miss Pryce, Joss, the independent reviewing officer – Mark – and I were all in the living room, while Adrian, Lucy, Paula and Toscha amused themselves elsewhere in the house. My family were used to meetings connected with fostering taking place in the house and knew they weren't to disturb us unless there was an emergency.

Mark, the IRO who was also chairing and minuting the review, thanked us all for coming and then officially opened the meeting by asking us to introduce ourselves, which is usual practice. We went round one at a time, stating our names and our role in Joss's life, while Mark made a note of who was present. When it was Joss's turn she was only a little self-conscious, having attended previous reviews, and said clearly, 'Joss, foster child.'

'Thank you,' Mark said with a reassuring smile. Then he asked Amelia if we were expecting anyone else at the review and she confirmed we were not. Mark, who would be an experienced social worker, was in his late forties, smartly but casually dressed and had a quietly confident manner. Having met Joss at her previous reviews, he said he was pleased to see her and her mother again. Linda and Joss were sitting next to each other on the sofa and Linda returned a polite smile.

'So, Joss,' Mark now said, looking at her, 'perhaps you'd like to start by telling us how you're settling in here.'

'It's OK,' Joss said, with a small shrug.

'Cathy's children are a similar age to you. How is that working out?' Mark asked her.

'OK.' Joss said.

'So you are all getting along and talking to each other?'

'Yes,' Joss said.

I've found before at reviews that children who usually have plenty to say can become self-conscious and lost for words in the formality of a review, when all eyes are on them.

'And what do you like to do in your spare time?' Mark now asked Joss.

'Go out,' Joss said.

'And when you're not out, what do you do when you're in – with Cathy and her family, in the evening, for example?'

'My homework,' Joss said.

'Anything else?'

'Listen to music, watch television and talk to Lucy and Paula.'

'Excellent,' Mark said and made a note. 'So you are all getting on?'

Joss nodded.

'And are you receiving your allowance?' As the IRO, Mark would have a checklist of points he needed to cover in the review.

'Sometimes,' Joss said.

'Why only sometimes?' Mark queried.

'Cathy stops my money if I'm very late home or I swear,' Joss said.

'Quite right,' Linda put in.

'Joss usually earns back the money,' I clarified. 'The little she doesn't earn back I save for her. I've kept a record.'

'Thank you,' Mark said, making another note. Then to Joss: 'And how is school going? Miss Pryce will give us a report later, but how do *you* feel you're doing at school? You were having some problems before.' He would know this from Joss's last review.

'School's OK,' Joss said with a shrug.

'Joss is in detention a lot,' Linda said.

'What for?' Mark asked.

'Lateness,' Linda said.

'So you arrive late for school in the morning?' Mark asked Joss.

Joss nodded but looked away.

'She leaves home in plenty of time,' I said. 'But doesn't always go straight to school. I've offered to take her in my car, but she doesn't want that. I also understand that she's late back after lunch, although she doesn't come home.' I needed to state the reasons for Joss's lateness, otherwise it would reflect badly on me – as if I were allowing her to regularly leave the house late.

'It's worse than you told me,' Linda said, turning to her daughter.

Joss shrugged and kept her gaze down.

'I'm assuming you'll cover this later?' Mark said to Miss Pryce.

'Yes, I can do,' she confirmed.

'So tell us what is going right for you at school,' Mark now asked Joss.

Joss was silent and then shrugged. 'Dunno.'

'She's doing her homework regularly,' I said. 'An hour most evenings, so she's catching up.'

'Well, that's a great improvement,' Mark said to Joss. 'Well done. Whose idea was that?'

'Cathy's,' Joss said a little moodily and finally looking up. 'I have to do it before I'm allowed out.'

Mark threw me an approving look. 'It sounds a good routine to me, and Miss Pryce will no doubt tell us more later. Have you given any more thought to the offer of counselling?' Mark now asked Joss, moving on.

'I don't want it,' Joss said.

'All right. You know you can tell your social worker if you change your mind.'

Joss nodded and Mark wrote. Jill and Amelia also had notepads open on their laps and were taking notes.

'Is there anything else you want to tell this review before we move on and hear from your mother?' Mark asked Joss.

'No,' Joss said.

'Well, if you think of anything or have any questions, tell me as we go. This is your review, so your opinion is very important. All right?'

Joss nodded.

Mark now looked at Linda. 'After Joss, you are the next most important person in this meeting,' he said. 'Joss is in care under a Section 20 – or accommodated, as we sometimes call it – so you maintain parental responsibility for Joss and have a big say in planning your daughter's future. Do you have an up-to-date copy of the care plan?'

'Yes,' Linda said.

'So how do you think things are going for Joss now?'

With all eyes now on Linda, she was clearly nervous and she flushed. 'I know Cathy is doing her best, but we feel so guilty that Joss isn't with us. Eric, her stepfather, and I have been talking about it and we feel that maybe we should try again and have Joss home. Perhaps it would be different this time?'

There was silence. This wasn't what anyone was expecting, but Mark handled it well. 'Linda, as Joss is in care under a Section 20 you have the right to remove her from care and take her home. This should be a planned move, though, after discussion with Joss's social workers. However, if Joss did go home and the social services felt there were safeguarding issues that meant Joss could come to harm, they could then apply to court for a Care Order. This would mean that Joss would have to return into care, although not necessarily to Cathy's.'

Linda gave a deep sigh and looked worried. 'I know, but Eric and I feel we should try. She is my daughter, after all.'

'But I'm not his daughter!' Joss snapped, turning angrily to her mother and suddenly finding her tongue. 'So don't include him in this. I'm not interested in what that creep wants! And I've told you hundreds of times already: I'm not coming home while he's there. No way! I'd rather be sent to lock-up than live with him. He's not my father and won't ever be. Why don't you listen to what I'm saying?'

CHAPTER THIRTEEN

END IT ALL

It was obvious from Joss's outburst that going home wasn't an option. After some discussion Linda said she accepted this and would tell Eric. Whereas with a younger child he or she could be moved against their will, if necessary, with someone Joss's age she would simply 'vote with her feet' and walk out. Mark said that if the situation changed and Joss decided she'd like to go home then she and Linda could discuss this with Amelia at any time – they didn't have to wait for the next review, which wouldn't be for another six months.

'I won't change my mind,' Joss said.

'But it's nice to know you have the option of going home,' Jill said. 'Not many children in care can go home when they want to.'

Joss didn't reply but stared moodily straight ahead. Mark moved the meeting on by asking Linda if she was happy with the contact arrangements or if she wanted them formalized.

'I'd like the contact left as it is,' Linda said. 'Then Joss can come and visit whenever she wants. She chooses a time when Eric isn't there,' she added as Mark wrote. Again, I felt sorry that the integrated, happy family life Linda had hoped for had gone so disastrously wrong, with her daughter and husband unable to be in the house together at the same time and with little hope of that changing in the future.

Mark then asked Linda if she was satisfied with the improvements Joss was making at school, and Linda said she was pleased Joss was doing more school work but concerned that her behaviour wasn't improving.

'I've made a note of your concerns,' Mark said. 'And Miss Pryce will say more about Joss's behaviour and school work presently. Is there anything else you'd like to raise at this review?'

'Only that I wish Joss wasn't allowed out so much. That's when she gets into trouble. And with the summer holidays coming up I'm worried she will get into even more trouble if she's allowed out all day and evening.'

'Cathy would like to keep Joss in more too,' Jill added. 'But it's difficult with the contract of behaviour as it is. She's obliged to follow it.'

'Do I have a copy of this contract?' Mark asked Amelia, glancing at the folder he had on his lap.

'I don't think so,' Amelia said. 'It was drawn up after the last time I met with Joss. It isn't signed yet. I may have to make some changes.'

'Can you give me an outline of the issues we're talking about, then?' Mark said.

Amelia looked at Joss. 'You have to be in at nine-thirty during the week and ten-thirty at weekends, don't you?'

'Yes, but I'm not allowed out on Wednesdays,' Joss complained. 'And Cathy makes me stay in all day Sunday as well as in the evening. It's not fair.'

'I think I mentioned the issue of Sunday to you when we spoke,' Jill said to Amelia, and she nodded.

'I don't make Joss stay "in",' I clarified. 'We have been going out together as a family most Sundays, and Joss has enjoyed it.'

Mark looked at Linda. 'So you feel Joss should stay in more than one evening and all day Sunday?'

'Yes,' Linda said. 'And what about the summer holidays? What is she going to do for six weeks?'

'I have concerns too,' I said. 'I was hoping to go away for a week to the coast, but Joss said she doesn't want to come because she'd miss Kevin and her friends.'

'That's a pity,' Mark said. 'Are you sure you wouldn't like to go on holiday? You'd have a lovely time.'

Joss shook her head adamantly.

'Perhaps you'd prefer to go to a summer camp?' Mark suggested.

'No way!' Joss said, pulling a face.

'If we're not going away then I think it would be a good idea if Joss enrolled in some short leisure courses,' I said. 'For example, tennis, swimming, horse riding, orienteering or ice skating. There's a lot going on over the summer and my children will be doing some activities.'

'I'll go ice skating, then,' Joss agreed, as if it were a penance. 'But not for too long. I have to see my friends.'

'Perhaps you could find a suitable course?' Mark asked me.

'Yes.' I made a note.

'Thank you,' Mark said. 'That sounds positive.' He smiled at Joss, who looked away.

'That will help a bit,' Linda said. 'But what about all the other days Joss is allowed out? She won't be ice skating all the time.'

'What would you like to see happen?' Mark asked Linda.

'For Joss to just go out maybe twice a week, and not with that man she's been seen with.'

'He's my boyfriend!' Joss snapped. 'You can't stop me seeing him. We love each other.'

Everyone present was aware of the concerns surrounding Joss seeing Zach, but it wasn't really within the scope of the review to discuss that in depth.

'What are your feelings on Joss going out?' Mark now asked Amelia.

'I think if we put too many constraints on Joss she will not meet any of her targets,' Amelia said. This had been her view at the meeting when the contract of behaviour was drawn up. 'We have to be positive, and since coming to Cathy's, Joss hasn't gone missing all night, which is a step forward.'

Don't put the idea in her head, I thought.

Mark nodded. 'I take your point,' he said.

I could see nothing was going to change, so I said, 'If we're not going to alter the number of times Joss is allowed out, can we at least confirm that she is with me all day Sunday?'

'That seems reasonable,' Mark said. 'Do you agree, Linda?'

'Yes. At least I'll know where she is on Sundays.'

'Joss, can we confirm that you are happy to stay in with Cathy on Sundays as you have been doing?' Mark asked her.

'I guess,' she said.

I saw Mark look at the clock. Reviews usually last an hour, but forty-five minutes had already gone and there was still a lot to get through. Mark asked Linda if there was anything else she wanted to raise. There wasn't, so he turned to me. 'Cathy, would you like to go next, please?'

I glanced at the notes I held on my lap, but before I had a chance to speak, Joss – now having lost all her initial reserve

– remembered something she wanted to say. 'I still haven't got a front-door key,' she blurted. 'And it's been more than two weeks!'

Mark looked puzzled.

'Joss raised this at a meeting I had with Cathy,' Amelia explained. 'Cathy said she would give Joss a front-door key when she was acting more responsibly.'

'I have been,' Joss declared.

All eyes were now on me, although Linda threw me a knowing look. 'I'm still not comfortable with Joss having her own front-door key,' I said. 'And there really isn't any need. I am always home before her to let her in.'

'But you said after two weeks,' Joss said, glaring at me.

'I was at that meeting,' Jill said, coming to my rescue. Then, addressing Joss, she said, 'The agreement was that when you had been coming home on time for two weeks and your behaviour at school had improved then Cathy would consider giving you a front-door key. But I don't think we're there yet, and also there are other issues that would stop me from recommending Cathy gives you a key just yet.'

'What are the other issues?' Mark asked, looking up from writing.

'Joss has admitted to taking money from Cathy's purse and her daughters' money boxes,' Jill said. I was pleased Jill had raised this and I didn't have to.

'Joss!' Linda exclaimed, turning to her daughter. 'It was bad enough that you stole from me, but to steal from Cathy and her family is unforgivable!'

'I'm paying it back,' Joss grumbled.

I didn't mention that Joss had told me she was allowed to

help herself from her mother's purse. I could tell by Joss's expression that she knew she was in the wrong.

'Allowing Joss to have a key at this stage', Jill said, 'could also have implications for her house security and insurance if things were to go missing.'

'I think we'll make having a front-door key a goal that you're working towards,' Mark said sensibly to Joss. 'If this hasn't been achieved before your next review, we will discuss it again then, all right?'

Joss shrugged a begrudging acceptance.

'Please continue, Cathy,' Mark added.

I glanced at my notes. 'Joss has settled in well with my family. She generally has a good relationship with my children and she has met my parents. I include Joss in all family activities and, although she is reluctant to begin with, she always enjoys herself. We like Joss very much but understand she is hurting and this sometimes comes out in angry outbursts. I've talked to her about counselling, but as we've already heard she doesn't want that yet. Joss eats well and has a varied diet. Her bedtime is ten o'clock when she's in, and she does have nightmares. I always go to her room to settle her and she's fine in the morning.' I paused to allow Mark time to catch up as he took notes.

'I am especially pleased that Joss is doing some homework most evenings,' I continued. 'I hope this is improving her grades at school. I am very concerned, however, that when she is out of the house she is smoking – cigarettes and cannabis – and drinking alcohol. I've talked to her about the damage she is doing to her health and also that she is putting herself at risk of coming to harm. She promises to change, but once out with her friends – who are all older than her – she forgets.'

'Does she come home drunk?' Mark asked, glancing at me and then at Joss.

'Not always drunk, but she's obviously been drinking and she doesn't deny it.'

I heard Linda sigh.

'I am also concerned that Joss is regularly late for school in the mornings and also after the lunch break,' I said. 'Joss was also involved in an incident at a newsagents close to the school and Amelia is aware of this.' Mark nodded and I glanced at my notes. 'I think we've covered everything else I wanted to say already.'

'Thank you,' Mark said. 'And Joss can stay with you for as long as necessary?' This was a standard question.

'Yes,' I confirmed.

'I suppose I should have asked Joss this question, as she is old enough to answer,' Mark said, 'but health-wise, how is she?'

'Fine,' I said. 'I have no worries about Joss's health apart from the drinking and smoking and her unsafe lifestyle.'

'And she's up to date with her dentist and optician check-ups?'

'As far as I know. I understand she had check-ups before she came to me.'

'Joss still sees our dentist and optician,' Linda clarified.

Mark finished writing. 'Is there anything else you want to say, Cathy?'

'Only that we like having Joss live with us and I hope she will continue to build on the improvements she has already made.' I smiled at Joss and she managed a very small smile back.

'Thank you, Cathy,' Mark said. 'Jill, as Cathy's supervising social worker, would you like to add anything?'

'Cathy is one of our most experienced foster carers,' Jill said. 'I am satisfied that Joss is receiving a very high standard of care. I visit Cathy every month and also see her at training. Her record keeping is excellent, and she updates me regularly on Joss's progress and any issues that arise between my visits. I pass these updates on to Joss's social worker. I have no concerns about Cathy's care of Joss.'

'Thank you,' Mark said, throwing me an appreciative smile. 'We'll hear from Joss's social worker, Amelia, now.' He looked at her. 'I've read all the relevant information. Apart from Joss moving to Cathy's, has there been any other significant change since Joss's last review?'

'No,' Amelia said.

'Any changes to the care plan?'

'Not at present, although the department is still considering the option of a secure therapeutic placement should it become necessary.'

He nodded. 'Have all the decisions that were made at the last review happened?'

'Yes,' Amelia confirmed.

'And we know the contact arrangements are staying the same,' he said as he wrote.

'Yes.'

These were all standard questions that the IRO would probably know the answers to but needed to confirm for the sake of the review.

'My next question has to be: are there any complaints anyone wishes to raise?' This again was a standard question. He looked around the room and we all shook our heads. 'Good. And Joss is up to date with her medicals?'

'Yes,' Amelia confirmed.

'Exclusions from school?' Mark asked, working his way down a list.

Amelia briefly consulted her paperwork. 'Yes, but it was recorded at the last review. Joss is on report now.'

Mark wrote. 'Has there been any more involvement with the police since the last review?'

'Yes. I sent you the details,' she said.

'Thank you. Please continue.'

Amelia said she was reasonably happy with the way Joss was settling in, that she saw Joss regularly and was in contact with Linda and Joss's school. She said Joss knew she could telephone her any time and that counselling was available when Joss felt ready. She would have updated Mark prior to the review, so with nothing more to add, Mark asked Miss Pryce to speak.

Miss Pryce began positively by saying how pleased she was that Joss was now doing her homework, and she hoped she would continue to do some during the summer holidays. Joss pulled a face, but I nodded, confirming she would. Miss Pryce said Joss still had a lot of catching up to do, and although she'd begun her report positively it soon became clear that Joss did indeed have a long way to go. She read out some of Joss's grades in a range of subjects and they were very low – Es and Fs – mainly because Joss had failed to complete many of the assignments. Her test results were no better due to the large number of lessons Joss had missed and was still missing, Miss Pryce said, which was all very disappointing.

'But Joss is an intelligent girl,' Miss Pryce said, 'and if she applies herself in the new school year I am sure she can improve her grades dramatically. Next year is a very impor-tant one for Joss,' she continued. 'Her performance will largely determine which GCSE courses and exams she studies in the following year.'

'What is Joss on report for?' Mark now asked her.

'Swearing at a member of staff, after returning late from lunch break,' Miss Pryce said. 'It was the last in a number of incidents, and Joss was originally going to be excluded because of it. Joss knows this is her very last chance.'

Mark nodded gravely.

'The school is very supportive of its students,' Miss Pryce continued. 'We have a good mentoring service, which Joss can access any time. I'm pleased Joss is more settled here, and I am hoping that in September she will return to school ready to work and achieve what I, and other members of staff, believe she is capable of.'

'Thank you,' Mark said. He finished writing and then asked if anyone wanted to add anything to the review, but no one did. He set the date for the next review, thanked us all for coming and closed the meeting. It was now after six o'clock and understandably Jill, Amelia, Miss Pryce and Mark were eager to be away. I saw them to the front door while Linda stayed in the living room with Joss. When I returned I offered Linda a cup of coffee or tea, hoping she would stay and have a chat with Joss, but she said she had to go as Eric and Kevin would be wanting their dinner. The mention of Eric was enough to spark Joss to flare up at her mother. 'Sorry for taking up your time!' she snapped sarcastically. 'But this is my life we've been talking about. The one you and your precious Eric have fucked up!'

Joss jumped up from where she'd been sitting next to her mother, and with eyes blazing stormed out of the living room and upstairs. Linda sighed heavily. 'Sometimes I can see the advantage in doing what Steven did,' she said. 'End it all.'

'No, don't say that,' I said.

'Don't worry, I wouldn't. But I do wonder what I've done to deserve this. Perhaps I should do what Joss wants and leave Eric, but what a dreadful decision – my husband or my daughter. One thing's for certain, I can't take much more.'

She stood, and with a very heavy heart, I went with her to the front door.

CHAPTER FOURTEEN

TURNING POINT?

Later that evening, when Joss was in her bedroom, I went up and tried talking to her about how unhappy she was making her mother, but she wasn't moved by my words. 'She brought it on herself,' she said coldly. 'She didn't have to marry that creep, so don't blame me.'

'I'm not blaming you,' I said. 'But try not to be so hard on your mother, please. She has feelings too. She thought marrying Eric would give you all a family life again and make you happy, or she wouldn't have done it.'

Joss sneered.

'Joss, your mother is so miserable about what's happened that she is even considering leaving Eric, if it would help.'

'But she hasn't, has she?' Joss retorted sharply.

I could see I was getting nowhere, so I asked Joss to think about what I'd said and to try to be more considerate of her mother's feelings in future, then I left her to listen to her music before she got ready for bed.

That night Joss had a nightmare, and as usual when I went to her room she was half asleep, sitting up in bed with her eyes closed. She was mumbling something about 'mummy', which was hardly surprising given that I'd been talking to her about her mother in the late evening and she'd seen her at the review. It must have been playing on her mind. I sat on the bed and began talking to her gently before easing her onto the pillow, but instead of returning to sleep, she suddenly sat up in bed, making me start. Her eyes were open and she focused on me.

'Are you awake, Joss?' I whispered.

'Yes. I wish my mummy and daddy were still together,' she said sadly.

'I know you do, love.'

'If Daddy had stayed, we'd all be happy,' Joss said quietly. 'Why didn't he stay? Didn't he know we loved him?' In the half-light I could see tears glistening in her eyes. I felt so sorry for her.

'I'm sure your daddy knew you all loved him,' I said. 'His death had nothing to do with how much you loved him.'

'But if he was that unhappy, why didn't he tell Mummy or me?' Joss asked. 'I always told him when I was sad and he made me happy again. We could have made him happy so he didn't have to die.'

I swallowed the lump rising in my throat.

'Sometimes when an adult is very unhappy they become depressed,' I said gently. 'They can't find a way to ask for help or tell anyone how they are feeling. Sometimes a very depressed person can do something without thinking about the consequences. I'm sure that if your daddy had thought about the effect his death would have on you all, he wouldn't have done what he did.' Suicide must be unfathomable to a child; I wasn't even sure I understood it.

'Do you think Daddy thought about us when he tied that rope around his neck and hanged himself?' Joss asked. I went cold deep inside.

'We can't know that, love,' I replied honestly. 'But if he did think of you I'm sure they would have been nice thoughts, comforting thoughts. From what your mummy has told me, your father was a good, kind man and a caring husband and father. He loved you all very much and I think you must try to remember that and all the happy times. Many of the children I've fostered have never had a happy family life at all. They don't have happy memories, just painful ones. At least you have some happy memories.' My voice trailed off. I was choked up.

'I wish he was still here,' Joss said.

I took her hand in mine. She didn't resist. 'I know you do, love. You miss him, and that's natural. But I'm sure your daddy would want you to make the most of your life and be happy.'

'Do you think he's in heaven?' Joss now asked.

'If there is a heaven then I'm sure your dad is there.'

'Do you think he can see me from heaven?' she asked, as a much younger child might. I felt my eyes fill.

'I don't know, love, but if he can he will want to know you are doing all right, won't he?'

'Mum started taking us to church after he died,' Joss said. 'We never went before. She said it helped her feel closer to Dad. I think she still goes sometimes.'

'Having a faith does help some people when they lose a loved one. Would you like to go to church?' I asked.

'I don't think so,' Joss said. 'Daddy didn't go to church.'

'It's something you can think about. I'm sure your mother would be pleased if you went with her, or I could take you to our local church. We go sometimes, but not regularly.'

'Zach thinks religion is a load of nonsense,' Joss said.

I didn't comment, but I was pleased Joss was feeling able to talk to me. She was silent for a moment and I soothed her hand. When she spoke again her voice was flat. 'When I think of my dad the first picture that comes into my head is of him hanging in the garage. Sometimes I can force that picture out and force another one in, but the first one never completely goes. It's like a ghost picture you can see through. It's always there in the background. Even when I try to think of something really nice, like my birthdays and Christmas with him, I can still see his body hanging in the garage. It's like the memory is haunting me.'

'I understand,' I said gently. 'Counselling would help. Bad and sad memories can stay very vivid if they are not dealt with. You're not the only one to feel this way. When someone has suffered a dreadful trauma, as you have, the painful memory can remain vivid and blot out the good memories. It's not haunting you; it's just the way the brain works. Counsellors are specially trained to help people come to terms with bad things.'

'But I don't want to talk to a stranger about my daddy,' Joss said. 'It's personal and private.'

'They wouldn't tell anyone.'

'Sometimes I talk to my daddy in my sleep. Like a dream, only more real.'

'Does that help?' I asked.

'Sometimes, and just now I was talking to Mum.'

'I thought so,' I said with a small smile. 'When I came in you were saying "mummy".'

'Was I? I was telling her about my dad and how much I love and miss him,' Joss said. I thought this was positive.

'Joss, if you don't want to talk to a counsellor, what about talking to your mother?' I suggested. 'She would be a very good person to talk to because she was there with you. She knows the horror and tragedy of what you saw. She has suffered too. I know she would be very understanding and pleased to help you. She's just waiting for you to ask her.'

'But *he's* there,' Joss said, referring to her stepfather.

'So choose a time when he isn't there. If you tell your mother you need to talk to her, I know she will make time. She cares about you so much.'

'No, I mean he's there as in she's married to him. It's different now. They are a couple and she tells him everything. I don't want her talking to him about my daddy. It's nothing to do with him.'

I could understand why Joss was so protective of her father's memory, but I obviously couldn't tell Linda not to tell Eric.

'You feel very rejected by your mother remarrying, don't you?' I said gently.

Joss nodded.

'Joss, I can understand why you feel you can't live with your mum and stepfather at present, but don't let it ruin your life. You know how concerned your mother and I are about your unsafe behaviour, and it wouldn't please your father if he knew. You want him to be as proud of you now as he was when you were little and he was here on earth, don't you?'

'I do, Cathy,' Joss said. Then with a small sob she leant against me and began crying openly. I put my arm around her and held her close.

This was the first time Joss had shown her feelings or wanted me to comfort her, and I thought it was a very positive development. A big step towards releasing the pain and suffering she'd held deep inside for so long – since the day she'd arrived home from school at the age of nine and walked into the garage to discover her father's suicide.

I held Joss close while she cried silently for many minutes, and it's true to say I felt very close to her – the empathy that comes from sharing another person's pain. I also felt grateful that my own life had been so easy and pain-free. Yes, I'd had a few downers – my husband leaving, for one – but I had loving parents and a happy family life, so I hadn't suffered as Joss had, or as many of the children I'd fostered had, for many different reasons.

Joss's tears eventually subsided and she wiped her eyes and blew her nose. It was nearly 3 a.m. 'Do you think you can get some sleep now?' I asked her quietly.

She nodded. 'Thanks for being here.'

I smiled. 'Joss, you know you can talk to me any time – day or night. I'm always here to help you.'

'I know,' she said. 'Thanks.'

'So, starting from tomorrow, will you try to get your life back on course, for your father's sake? He really wouldn't want to see you angry and unhappy and behaving as you have been, would he?'

'No, I guess not,' Joss said. 'I'll try.' And I was sure she meant it.

'Good girl,' I said. I gave her another hug and then she lay back down in bed.

'Will you stay with me until I go to sleep?' she asked in a small, childlike voice.

'Yes, of course, love. Shall I stroke your forehead while you go off to sleep? It's very soothing.'

'Yes, please.'

She snuggled down and closed her eyes and I began lightly stroking her forehead. As she gradually relaxed, her face softened and her breathing regulated until at last she drifted into sleep. Once I was sure she was in a deep sleep, I stood and crept away from the bed and out of her room. My heart was light – lighter than it had been since Joss had first arrived – because I was certain we had turned the corner I'd been waiting for. Now that Joss was talking about her feelings and addressing her sorrow, her pain would surely start to ease and she'd become less angry and gradually get her life back. Healing the mind can take a long time, but once she came to terms with her father's death, I was sure she would slowly move forward towards a full recovery. I couldn't do anything about her mother's marriage, which seemed to cause Joss so much anguish, but I felt that now Joss was letting go of her pain, it wouldn't be long before she began to see that her mother had a right to happiness, which would hopefully pave the way for her accepting Eric and going home.

The following day I telephoned the leisure centre to find out about ice-skating courses and I booked Joss into one that took place three half-days a week: Monday, Wednesday and Friday, from 10 a.m. to 1 p.m. for four weeks in the summer holidays. It was expensive, but I was pleased Joss had shown an interest in something other than being with Zach and Chelsea. Adrian, Lucy and Paula were already booked to do some leisure courses. I thought Joss would be pleased, but when she came home from school that afternoon and I told her I'd booked the course she was more interested in how the time spent ice skating would impact on her seeing her mates.

'I suppose I'll have to tell Chelsea to meet me at the centre on those days so we can go out straight after,' she said, disgruntled. 'I'll come home for my dinner at five and then go out for the evening.'

'But you weren't thinking of going out all day and every evening during the summer holidays, were you?' I asked.

'Yes, of course,' she said, surprised I should think any differently.

'But you heard what Miss Pryce said about catching up with your school work over the summer.'

'OK,' Joss said testily. 'I'll do an hour when I come back for my dinner and then go out.'

Clearly Joss had it all planned out and the quiet, compliant child who'd wanted to turn over a new leaf the night before was fading fast. Two days later I had to admit that my midnight talk with her hadn't helped one little bit, and her behaviour was as bad as ever. The following week – the last week of term – there were three evenings when she didn't come home until 11.30 p.m., just as I was about to telephone the police and report her missing. Then more money disappeared from my purse on the day I became lax about leaving my bag unattended in the hall. I tried to talk to Joss about this, and her behaviour in general, but she was unresponsive and shrugged, saying, 'Yeah, whatever.' Meaning: I hear you but don't really care. I was so disappointed.

Joss went out of her way to avoid me in the house, and when she did have to see me her attitude was challenging and hostile – a clear warning for me to keep away. I thought she must regret letting me get close and confiding in me, and was now putting distance between us by making herself as objectionable and unlikeable as she could. She was also quite horrible to my children, making snide and derisive comments, so they kept away from her. I tried talking to Joss, hoping I'd catch a glimpse of the girl I'd seen that night, but she wouldn't engage with me at all and soon I had to admit that child was gone. She had more nightmares but didn't wake, so I settled her and came out.

One evening, when I was at my wits' end, I telephoned Joss's mother and asked her what Joss's behaviour had been like with her since the review. She said it was awful. The only person Joss was pleasant to was her younger brother, Kevin, and she blamed Joss's behaviour on the bad company she was keeping. Linda said, very tearfully, that she felt a secure therapeutic unit was probably the only place where Joss would be safe.

With the start of the summer holidays a new routine began, with all of us getting up later than usual and washing and showering at leisure, before doing whatever was planned for the day. On the days Joss had ice skating she left the house at 9.30 a.m. and returned at 5 p.m., made a drama out of the little school work she did and then went out straight after dinner without calling goodbye. I asked her if she was enjoying the ice skating and she said she was, but didn't offer any more. On the days she didn't have ice skating I suggested she might like to come out with me, shopping maybe, but I could see that held as much appeal as walking on hot coals. So Joss disappeared out straight after breakfast, at about 10 a.m., returned for dinner at 5 p.m. like a homing pigeon and then went out again. Then, on Friday morning in the first week, when she was supposed to be skating, one of the leisure centre's staff telephoned me and asked if Joss was ill, as she hadn't been attending the classes.

'Not at all?' I asked in disbelief.

'No.'

'And she's not there now?'

'No.'

'Are you sure?'

'Yes. I take it you thought she'd been attending?'

'Yes,' I said, feeling a complete fool and badly let down.

'Do you want to cancel the course? We can't give you a refund for this week, but we could for the other three weeks if you tell us now.'

'I don't know.' I sighed. 'No, leave it for now. Hopefully she'll be there next week.'

'All right. If not, let us know as soon as possible. Then we can refund for the two weeks left and also offer the place to someone else. There's a waiting list for these short courses.'

I apologized, said I'd phone as soon as I knew and then said goodbye.

I was fuming. Not only because Joss had wasted my money and stopped someone else from taking the place on the course, but because of her barefaced dishonesty. The trouble with anger is that it eats away at you like a canker, and so it gnawed at me for the rest of the day, although I tried not to let it. I knew I should be calm when I confronted Joss or there would be an argument, which would achieve nothing. Paula was in that afternoon and knew something was wrong, but I didn't tell her what. I never discuss one child's negative behaviour with another unless it has a direct bearing on them.

When Joss came home at five o'clock I told her to go into the front room, which was free, as I needed to talk to her.

'Why?' she asked, the picture of innocence. 'I need to do my school work so I can go out later.'

'You can do your work when we've spoken,' I said very firmly.

She could see I meant what I said, and without further protest she followed me into the front room where I closed the door so the others wouldn't hear.

I could have toyed with her. Having the upper hand meant I could have asked her if she'd enjoyed ice skating and then caught her out with her lies, but that wouldn't have helped our relationship, so I came straight to the point.

'Joss, one of the staff at the leisure centre telephoned me this morning and said you weren't there. Why weren't you there?'

She looked surprised. 'I didn't feel well, so I went to Chelsea's and had a rest,' she said, ready with another lie.

'And Monday and Wednesday? What happened then?'

'They told you about that too?'

'Yes, of course. Did you think they wouldn't?'

She shrugged and looked away.

'Joss, I'm very disappointed. Not only have you lied to me and wasted my money, you've stopped someone else going on the course. Someone who wanted to go. I don't understand.'

She shrugged again and kept her eyes down.

'Why didn't you go?' I persisted. 'You enjoyed ice skating when we all went. You agreed to go on the course and you knew I'd booked and paid for it.'

'I didn't fancy going alone,' she said.

'You wouldn't have been alone. There are others in the class.'

'But I don't know any of them,' she said, finally meeting my gaze with a frown.

Joss, usually so full of bravado, was telling me she hadn't gone ice skating because she didn't know anyone!

'You would have soon made friends,' I said. 'Everyone is in the same position on these short courses. You all get talking and make friends.'

Joss looked at me pathetically, and although I was annoyed I could appreciate that a teenager might feel self-conscious walking into a group where she didn't know anyone.

'It's a pity you didn't tell me how you felt sooner,' I said, softening my tone. 'You could have asked a friend to go – Chelsea, if she'd wanted to. But that's not an option now; the course is full.'

'Chelsea couldn't have afforded it anyway,' Joss said sullenly. 'Her dad's never got any money.'

'Joss,' I said seriously, 'if Chelsea had wanted to go and that's what it took to get you there, I would have happily paid for her too.'

Joss held my gaze and for a moment I thought she was going to apologize or say something nice, but the moment passed.

'I understand it can be difficult walking into a room full of people you don't know,' I continued evenly. 'I have to do it at some of the meetings I attend in connection with fostering. I can feel my heart racing and my stomach churning, but once I'm in the room and I start talking to others I relax. Most people feel the same. You coped well at your review, so I'm sure you can handle this. Will you go on Monday?'

'They'll all know each other now,' Joss bemoaned. 'They've had a week to make friends.' She had a point.

'But there's always room for one more friend,' I said. 'And most of the time you will be skating. You won't be standing alone, I'm sure. Will you try it on Monday, Joss? And if you really don't like it, I'll cancel the rest of the course.'

'OK,' she said.

'Good girl.' It was a small triumph.

CHAPTER FIFTEEN

DOING THE RIGHT THING

Joss attended the ice-skating class on Monday – I telephoned and checked – and when she returned home at dinnertime she said she wanted to continue going as there was another girl in the class she knew from school, and they'd teamed up. I praised her, and Joss agreed that she was glad she'd given the course a chance. However, the good feeling I had from this (small) achievement was to be short-lived. On Tuesday evening, while Joss was out, Linda telephoned with news I didn't want to hear.

'Has Joss told you?' she began anxiously.

'Told me what?'

'About the car they set fire to.'

'No!'

'Joss and some others were seen running away from a car they'd set fire to on the estate. Apparently it belonged to some chap they thought was a paedophile and they decided to teach him a lesson. Someone called the police and they arrested a couple of the gang, but Joss and the others ran off. The police have been here; they've just left. They want to talk to Joss. I told them she was in foster care and I've given them your address.'

'The silly, silly girl,' I sighed. 'Joss knows she has to stay out of trouble. When was this?'

'Friday evening.'

'Who else was involved? Do you know?'

'The police didn't say, but it was a large gang that is known to them. Joss seems to gravitate towards trouble. It draws her like a magnet. She never used to be like this.' Linda's voice fell away.

'I'll talk to her when she returns,' I said, aware that this would probably do little good.

'I thought I should warn you,' Linda said.

'Yes, thank you.'

There wasn't much else we could say – we'd said it all before – and I think we both knew that this time Joss had gone too far.

I was as fed up and worried as Linda was with Joss's negative, self-destructive behaviour, and when Joss came in that night – half an hour late and reeking of smoke – I told her straight away that her mother had telephoned and what she'd said. Joss actually had the cheek to smirk.

'I don't see anything funny, Joss. You're in trouble with the police again!'

'They can't prove I was there,' she said cockily. 'They haven't got any evidence. I outran one of the coppers,' she boasted. 'Charlie got caught, but she can't run as fast as me.'

'Who's Charlie?' I asked.

'Someone I know,' she said evasively.

'Joss, the police have been to your mother's and they will come here, to interview you about an arson attack. That's a very serious crime. They must have evidence you were at the scene or they wouldn't want to speak to you.'

'The coppers recognized me from the mall,' Joss said. 'But they can't prove anything. I'll say I wasn't there. Chelsea will give me an alibi. It's only the police's word against mine.' She looked pleased with herself.

'And you think the court is going to believe you and Chelsea over police officers?' I asked incredulously.

'Even if they don't, I'll only get another caution,' she said contemptuously.

'*Only* another caution!' My voice rose. 'You shouldn't have any cautions at all! You still don't get it, do you, Joss? After everything your mother and I have said to you, you still can't see that your behaviour is wrong. I really thought that after our chat the other week you were going to make a big effort to change – for the sake of your father.'

'Well, he's not here, is he?' Joss retorted sharply. 'So I can do what I fucking well want.'

'No, you can't,' I said.

She turned and stomped upstairs to her room.

When I checked on her later she was asleep, and then the following morning I woke her at 8.30 to go ice skating. I always start each day afresh, a new leaf, another beginning, and Joss was in a better mood. At breakfast she managed to ask Paula how her tennis course was going. Paula said she was enjoying it and they chatted for a while. Before Joss left the house that morning she asked me if she could have some extra money for a snack at break time and I gave her a couple of pounds. As I saw her off at the door, I wished her a nice day and said I'd see her later. Although I would have liked for Joss to return home straight after ice skating and spend the afternoon with us, I had to be realistic and manage my expectations, so I assumed she would be back around five o'clock for her dinner, as she had been doing.

When she hadn't returned by six o'clock I began to worry. She hardly ever missed dinner; she liked her food regardless of the mess the rest of her life was in. At 6.45 I telephoned Homefinders, the agency I fostered for, for some advice. Jill wasn't there, but a colleague, Trisha, was covering the out-of-hours service and I explained my concerns. She said that as it was only early evening I should wait until 9.30 had passed – the time Joss had to be home – before I reported her missing to the police, but to call her again if I had any more concerns or if she wasn't back by then. I thanked her and we said goodbye.

If a teenager who normally arrived home on time and didn't have a history of going missing failed to come home when expected, the parent or carer would call the police and report them missing much sooner. But with a young person like Joss, who was often very late back, there was some leeway before action needed to be taken and limited police resources were deployed. Yet, while part of me said that Joss wasn't in danger and would appear at some point as if nothing was wrong, I also acknowledged that this could be the one time when she was in danger and I was sitting here doing nothing.

When I answered the phone at 7.50 and heard Joss's voice I was very relieved. 'Oh, Joss. I'm so glad you've phoned,' I said. 'I'm not angry with you, but I am worried. Where are you?'

'At Chelsea's.' I could hear rap music and loud voices in the background. 'I thought I should phone you and let you know I'm not coming home tonight. I'm staying at Chelsea's.'

My spirits fell.

Children in care, like any other children, can occasionally stay overnight at a friend's house, providing the carer approves and is satisfied the child will be safe. The litmus test for the carer is: would I let my own child stay there overnight? And in this instance I certainly would not.

'Not tonight, love,' I said. 'You haven't got any of your things with you.'

'Chelsea's got night clothes I can borrow,' Joss said. I heard the two of them laugh and I could guess why: Chelsea was twice the size of Joss, so Joss would look ridiculous in Chelsea's clothes. 'I want to stay,' she said.

'Is Chelsea's father there?' I asked.

There was silence, some whispering and then Joss said, 'Yes.'

'Can I talk to him, please?'

More silence and whispering and then Joss said, 'He's sleeping, and we're not allowed to disturb him.'

'Are Zach and Carl there?'

'Not sure,' Joss said.

Then Chelsea's voice came on the line, 'Don't worry, Mrs Glass, I'll look after Joss for you.' There was more laughing and then the phone went dead.

I tried calling back a few times but no one answered, and then I telephoned Homefinders

'Joss isn't missing,' I told Trisha. 'She's at the flat of a friend, Chelsea. She wants to stay the night, but I'm not happy with that. I've been to the flat and there appears to be no parental control. I found her drinking and smoking cannabis with two much older lads. I'm going to collect her now.'

'All right, Cathy. Thank you for letting me know. I'll make a note and update Jill in the morning. If there's a problem call me. I'm on duty all night.'

'Thank you. I will.'

Lucy was out for the evening but Adrian and Paula were in. I told them that I was going to collect Joss and to let Lucy know where I was if she was back before me. I said I'd be about half an hour and called goodbye as I left.

As a foster carer I'd had to collect children before from places they weren't supposed to be, or where they'd stayed too late, or even from the police station, so I wasn't particularly fazed by the prospect of collecting Joss again from Chelsea's flat. I was more concerned that she was there at all. I assumed I'd find the two of them with Zach and Carl, smoking and drinking, as I had before. Joss would be angry with me, but so be it. She was my responsibility and I was doing what I thought was right to protect her.

Fifteen minutes later I was parking on the main road a little way from the parade of shops where Chelsea lived. It was 8.30 p.m. so still reasonably light in early August. The evening was mild and there were others walking along the streets. The off-licence was open and doing a good trade, but the rest of the shops in the parade were closed and shuttered. As I approached the building I could hear rap music coming from one of the flats above the shops, although none of the windows at the front were open. I went round to the rear and began up the metal stairs where it became immediately obvious the music was coming from Chelsea's flat. The upper windows were wide open. Pity the poor residents of the other flats, I thought, some of whom had their windows open. One door I passed had a child's tricycle outside on the landing, and

I wondered how the poor child slept if this music blasting out was a regular occurrence.

The chipped blue door to Chelsea's flat was shut, so I tapped on it loudly with the small rusty door knocker. No one answered; I doubted they could hear me over the music. I tried pushing the door and to my surprise it opened.

The small kitchen, previously littered with takeaway boxes, empty beer and drink bottles and unwashed pans and dishes, was now heaving with young people. There was evidently a party going on. The guys and girls draped over each other in the kitchen, drinking and smoking, were in their teens or early twenties. A couple of them looked at me disinterestedly as I entered, before returning to each other. I scanned the room for Joss but she wasn't there, so I continued towards the living room, edging around the cramped, sweating bodies and blinking from the smoke. The epicentre of the party was in the living room and, in contrast to the kitchen where everyone was standing or leaning against someone or something, they were all sitting in here: on the old sofa or the stained mattress, or just cross-legged on the floor. Cans of beer were everywhere and the unmistakable smell of cannabis hung thickly in the air. I couldn't see Joss but I could see Carl. He was sprawled on the sofa with a beer in one hand and a joint in the other. He had his top off, revealing a large serpent tattoo winding across his stomach and disappearing around his back. He saw me and, waving his beer can towards the stairs that led off from the far corner of the room, he shouted, 'She's upstairs.'

I stepped over and around the legs and bodies on the floor and headed towards the foot of the stairs. No one took much notice of me; they were too high or drunk. I wondered how long this had been going on. It was only 8.30. Thank goodness I'd come when I had. The need to get Joss out of there as soon as possible overrode my growing sense of unease for my own safety.

There was a door at the top of the stairs. I pushed it open and stepped into a small landing where three doors, all closed, led from it. A pile of dirty clothes was dumped at one end, presumably waiting to be washed. I opened the first door on my right. It was the bathroom, where a young man stripped to the waist was on his knees, throwing up into the toilet. In other circumstances I would have made sure he was OK, but right now I just wanted to find Joss and get out of there. I closed the door and went to the next one. It opened into a bedroom, which was littered with piles of rubbish. My eyes immediately went to the double bed against the wall where a middle-aged man sat propped up, with Chelsea on one side and Joss on the other. He had his arm around Joss and all three of them had an open can of beer; Chelsea was smoking a joint.

'Oh, shit!' Chelsea said, seeing me, while Joss stared at me, horrified.

'Hello, lovely lady,' the man said, grinning inanely and making no attempt to move. 'Who might you be?'

I took a step into the room.

'This is Joss's foster carer,' Chelsea said quietly, stubbing out the joint into an already overflowing ashtray.

'Nice to meet you,' he said, stupefied. 'Would you like a beer?'

'No. I've come to take Joss home. Who are you?' With long hair, a stubbly chin, tattoos and his shirt open to the waist, revealing a large medallion against a hairy chest, he looked like an old rocker.

'Dave,' he said, still grinning. 'They call me Dave the Rave.'

'He's my father,' Chelsea said, moving slightly away.

'Really.' I was shocked. 'Do you know how old Joss is?' I asked him.

'Old enough, I guess.' He grinned.

'Thirteen! Your daughter is only fifteen. Neither of them should be drinking or smoking. You want to be ashamed of yourself.'

He took a swig of his beer, but had the decency to remove his arm from around Joss.

'We're going home now,' I told Joss.

'But I don't want to,' she protested.

'Now,' I said. 'Or I'll call the social services and the police and ask for their help. I'm sure they'd be interested to know what is going on here.'

'Do as your foster carer says,' Dave said, suddenly alert. 'I don't want any trouble.'

Joss glared at me but got off the bed.

'Leave that here,' I said to her, referring to the can of beer she still held.

She set the can down angrily on what had once been a dressing table but now, like everything else in the room, was covered with rubbish, filth and grime.

I turned, and Joss followed me out.

'Bye!' Chelsea called.

Joss didn't reply.

'Why did you do that?' she hissed as I opened the door at the top of the stairs. The noise and smoke coming from below hit me.

'Because this isn't a suitable place for young girls,' I said, and began downstairs.

'You've shown me up in front of everyone. I'll never live this down,' Joss said.

'Better that than leave you here,' I said.

As we picked our way across the living room, Carl shouted above the music, 'Is it your bedtime?'

'Ignore him,' I said to Joss.

She followed me out of the living room and through to the kitchen. I breathed a sigh of relief once we were outside. 'Whatever do you see in that lot?' I asked, walking quickly, my heart still racing.

'They're my friends,' she said defensively.

As we neared the bottom of the metal staircase, Zach appeared from around the corner with an armful of beers, presumably having been to the off-licence. He looked surprised to see us. 'Are you off?' he asked Joss, ignoring me.

'She's making me,' Joss complained.

I think Joss was expecting Zach to commiserate, possibly protest and take her side against me, because she looked rather taken aback when he said, 'See you around, then,' and continued up the stairs.

We walked in silence to my car, but I could feel Joss's hostility radiating towards me. Once we were in the car, I said, 'Why were you upstairs with Chelsea's father?'

'We were talking.'

'Joss, it's completely inappropriate. A man of his age, lying on the bed half dressed with his arm around you and encouraging you and Chelsea to drink and smoke.'

'He wasn't encouraging us,' Joss said, trying to defend him.

'He didn't stop you,' I said. 'And as a parent he should be setting an example.'

'Don't have a go at Dave!' Joss snapped. 'I like him – he listens to me.'

'Joss, I always listen to you whenever you want to talk, but I won't always tell you what you want to hear. Responsible parents guide their children. They show them the best path and help them make the right decisions. It's a wonder the social services haven't taken Chelsea into care.'

'They tried,' Joss said, 'but she wouldn't go. Chelsea's got more sense.'

I put the key into the ignition, started the engine and pulled away. Joss was angry with me for removing her from the flat, but I had no doubt I'd acted correctly. 'I don't want you going to Chelsea's again,' I said as I drove. 'If you want to see her, you invite her to our house.'

Joss didn't reply.

'How often do they have those parties?' I asked after a few moments.

'Dunno,' Joss said. 'When Dave's around, I guess. About once a week.'

'And they start in the afternoon?'

'They aren't planned. People just drift in with beer and then someone puts the music on and it all takes off.' I could hear the excitement in her voice, the lure of the prohibited and risqué. Of course the scene at Dave's was attractive to an impressionable thirteen-year-old who had lost her way in life. It was enticing, but she was vulnerable – easy pickings for the likes of Dave, Zach and Carl.

'Who supplies the drugs?' I asked.

Joss didn't reply. I glanced at her. 'Dave?'

'Dunno,' she said with a shrug. So I thought it might be.

* * *

Once home, I asked Joss if she wanted anything to eat, but she didn't. She poured herself a glass of water and went up to her room. I took the opportunity to telephone Trisha at Home-finders. I was still thinking that perhaps I should call the police and hopefully they would raid the flat. It concerned me that, while I'd taken Joss out, Chelsea was still there, and who knew how many of the other teenagers there were underage? But when I told Trisha what I'd found at the flat she said to leave it to her – she'd speak to the social services and they'd take any necessary action. She also said she'd update Jill the following morning.

I went upstairs and checked on Joss. She was still angry with me. 'I'm just doing what I believe is right to keep you safe,' I said.

She turned her back on me, so I came out. A while later I heard her go to the bathroom and when I checked on her again she was asleep.

I knew Joss would go to Chelsea's again – the attraction of what was going on there would make any family outing or home entertainment I could offer pale into insignificance. I also knew she wouldn't tell me if she went there, and I couldn't trail her twenty-four seven. But Chelsea's flat would be the first place I'd look if Joss went missing, and it was the address I'd give to the police. I couldn't stop her going, which was a huge concern, but then, ironically, two days later Dave helped me out.

Joss came home that evening in a foul mood. 'You've ruined my life!' she said as soon as I opened the front door. 'I hate you. You've taken Chelsea away from me. She's not my friend any more.'

'How is that?' I asked, perplexed.

'You coming to Dave's like that and making a fuss. He's worried now that you'll cause him trouble and call the police. He's told Chelsea I'm not to go there any more. He's banned me from his flat!'

I didn't say I was pleased, because I could see how unhappy Joss was by this exclusion. 'Joss, if Chelsea is a good friend, this won't end your friendship,' I said. 'You will find other things to do and other places to go. And you know you can bring her here any time.'

'It's not the same, I've told you!' Joss thundered. 'You've ruined everything. I hate you.'

Sometimes as a parent or carer you have to be very thick-skinned and stand your ground when you know you are doing the right thing.

CHAPTER SIXTEEN

FAILED TO PROTECT HER

On the days in the summer holidays when Paula, Lucy, Adrian and Joss didn't have an activity planned, I arranged some days out – to the coast, the zoo, a museum, a wildlife centre and the Tree Top Adventure Park again. Although Joss initially moaned about going – preferring to 'hang out' with her 'mates' – she always enjoyed herself once we were on our way. And to her credit she also continued attending ice skating, so earned back her lost pocket money. When she came home on the Monday of the final week of the ice-skating course she said they were putting on a little show on the last day, Friday, and asked me if I would like to go. I was touched that she wanted me there. She'd asked her mother, but she couldn't get the time off work, and Kevin was attending a full-time play scheme. I said I'd be delighted to go and that I'd take plenty of photographs and have a set printed for her mother and brother.

Paula was free that Friday morning, so we both went to see the show. All the summer ice-skating classes had combined to put on the show and it was very impressive. When the organizer introduced the event he pointed out that some of the participants had only been skating for four weeks and the youngest participant was only three years old. Joss proved to be a competent skater and had developed her skills since the time we'd all gone skating. She could now skate backwards, turn with ease and make a small jump. After the show Paula and I congratulated her and said how much we'd enjoyed the display. I suggested to Joss that she might like to continue going to classes when school returned – in the evenings or at weekends, but she didn't immediately jump at the opportunity.

'I'll think about it,' she said. 'I wouldn't want you wasting your money if I changed my mind and didn't go.'

'I'm sure you would go,' I said. 'You've enjoyed it. But it's your decision.'

It was now the end of August, and the start of the new school term was a week away. I'd bought everyone their new uniforms and shoes, and to be honest I was quite relieved that Joss would soon be back at school. I'd know where she was, and with most of her days occupied there should be less opportunity for her to find trouble. We were still waiting for the police to visit in connection with the car she'd set on fire, and while Joss was blasé about it – 'They know they can't prove anything,' she said – it weighed heavily on my mind.

Although Joss had been, and still was, going out far more than I would have liked, I felt that, overall, the summer holidays hadn't been too bad. She'd been late back a number of times and had clearly been drinking and smoking, but as far as I knew she hadn't got into more trouble with the police, and neither had she gone missing overnight as she had done many times at her previous carers. Where and when she met up with Chelsea I didn't know, and Joss didn't say – she never mentioned her now. Occasionally she volunteered that Zach and Carl had brought her home in the car, so I assumed Chelsea had been with them.

Amelia came to visit at the very end of the summer holidays for one of her statutory visits. Jill had been updating her, so I filled her in on the last few days, emphasizing all the positives. As usual Amelia wanted to speak to Joss alone, so I left them in the living room to talk in private. When they'd finished Joss came to find me. 'You can go in now – she's done with me,' Joss said, and went up to her room.

'Thank you for all you're doing for Joss,' Amelia said as I sat down, 'but try not to be so critical of Joss's friends. I know they're not your choice, but criticizing them is upsetting for Joss.'

'What have I said?' I asked, realizing they must have been discussing a comment I'd made.

'When you collected Joss from Chelsea's flat you made it clear you didn't approve of her friends.'

'I didn't approve of what was going on in the flat and the people Joss is associating with,' I said. 'I can't stand by and say nothing. I'm also worried that Chelsea is living in that environment. I think my fostering agency passed on my concerns?'

'Yes,' Amelia said. 'But I can't discuss Chelsea's case with you.' Which I knew.

'I'm sorry my comments upset Joss,' I said. 'That wasn't my intention, but I believe Joss is in real danger from going to that flat and hanging out with those people. Foster carers are expected to look after the children they foster as they would their own children, and I certainly wouldn't let my children go there or associate with the likes of Zach, Carl or Dave. What's a middle-aged man doing with all those young people?'

'But part of growing up is choosing your own friends and being allowed to make your own mistakes,' Amelia said, missing the point. As I'd observed before, Amelia was pleasant but naïve, and clearly didn't have children of her own. Obviously we had different views on parenting, and it crossed my mind that had Amelia actually looked after teenagers she might have felt differently. She asked me if Joss had everything she needed for school and I confirmed she had, so with nothing else to discuss she went upstairs to say goodbye to Joss, and then left.

What happened next showed I'd been right to be very worried about the company Joss was keeping, although I gained no satisfaction from being right, none at all.

It was the last Saturday in August and my family were making the most of their 'last weekend of freedom', as Lucy called it, before school began again the following Tuesday. Adrian had spent the afternoon bowling and the evening at the cinema with friends, and was now relaxing on his bed. Lucy and Paula were at friends' houses for sleepovers and Joss was out. It was Saturday, so I wasn't expecting her home until 10.30 p.m. – far too late for a thirteen-year-old in my opinion, but it wasn't my decision. The nights had started to draw in now, and there was a chill to the evening air suggesting autumn wasn't far away. I was snug in the living room with the curtains closed, the television on and Toscha curled up on the sofa beside me. At around 10.15 Adrian came downstairs and said he was turning in now, as he was tired, so we said goodnight. He and Paula were seeing their father – my ex-husband, John – the following day. They saw him about once a month when he took them out for the day. At 10.45 I was still waiting for Joss, but I wasn't unduly worried. She was often fifteen minutes late. When she still hadn't returned by 11.15 I was worried and also annoyed that she was acting so irresponsibly again. When the doorbell rang five minutes later I headed down the hall relieved, but also ready to give her a big lecture.

'Where on earth have you been –' I began, as I opened the door. I stopped. Joss was in tears and obviously distraught. 'What's the matter?' I asked, stepping forward, very concerned. 'What's happened?'

She shook her head, unable to speak. I gently took her arm and drew her into the hall. 'Joss, what is it? Tell me.' It wasn't like Joss to cry.

'I can't,' she said, between sobs.

I closed the front door. 'Come into the living room.'

I led her down the hall and into the living room, where I sat her on the sofa and passed her the tissues. I sat beside her. Her cheeks were red from crying, but there were also some other marks on her face, which I thought could be bruises. My concerns grew.

'Joss, you need to tell me what has happened,' I said. 'Have you been in a fight?'

'No.' She pressed the tissue to her eyes.

'What is it then, love? Please tell me. Is it about Chelsea? Have you fallen out?'

She shook her head and fresh tears fell.

'Have you broken up with Zach?' I tried. I knew how distressing it was when a first love ended.

Her breath caught. 'It's not like that. It's bad. If I tell you, you mustn't tell anyone.'

I looked at her and gently rubbed her arm. 'I'm afraid

I can't promise,' I said. 'If it's something serious that affects you, I have to tell your social worker, and she may tell your mother, if it's appropriate.' This was something I had to make all children I fostered aware of: I wasn't allowed to keep their secrets if it affected their well-being. 'Amelia will be very sympathetic,' I added. 'And she will be able to help us. Are you in trouble with the police?' I thought this was likely, although it had never upset Joss before.

'No, it's Zach,' she sobbed.

'So you have split up?' I said. I had my words of comfort and reassurance ready.

Joss turned to me in anguish. 'Cathy, it's a lot worse than that,' she said through her tears. 'He attacked me. I know it's my fault. You were right. He's no good. He raped me. I'm sorry.' She fell against me sobbing and I went deathly cold.

I knew I had to stay calm. I'd fostered children before who'd disclosed shocking abuse, and it was important for the child that I didn't go to pieces.

'He raped you,' I repeated mechanically. 'When?'

'Just now, in the car,' she sobbed on my shoulder. 'He and Carl gave me a lift home, but they didn't bring me here. Carl parked up on the wasteland at the back of the allotments and Zach raped me while Carl watched.' Her sobbing rose and I held her very close.

'All right, love. You're safe now,' I said. My words sounding far off and inadequate. 'You're safe with me.'

'Carl was going to do it too,' Joss sobbed. 'But I fought him off and managed to get out of the car. They were laughing. I ran to the bus stop in town where there were people, and then came here. You tried to warn me, Cathy, so did my mum. I know you did. But I thought Zach loved me. I really did.'

I held her close and waited for her sobbing to ease. My heart was pounding and I felt sick to my core, but I knew what we needed to do. 'We have to tell the police,' I said. 'Was Chelsea in the car?'

'No. She's not well. She didn't come out with us. But you can't tell the police. They'll say it was my fault. We went to some bars first. I'd been drinking and having a laugh with them. Zach was my boyfriend. They won't believe me.' She was crying uncontrollably now.

I turned slightly so I could look at her. 'They will believe you,' I said. 'It's not your fault. You've been horrifically attacked. We need to report this as soon as possible, but I'm going to phone my agency first for some advice. You've done right in telling me, Joss.'

I gave her a hug and then reached for the phone on the corner table. Trembling, I keyed in the number for Home-finders. Joss was sobbing quietly and I held her hand. The phone connected and then went through to the agency's out-of-hours number. To my relief, Jill answered – she was on duty that night. 'It's Cathy,' I said. 'Joss has just come home. She's been raped.' I heard Jill gasp. 'Do I dial 999 or take her to the police station?'

'Does she need emergency medical attention?' Jill asked.

'Are you badly hurt?' I asked Joss. 'Do you need a doctor?'

She shook her head.

'She says no.'

'Take her to the police station, then,' Jill said. 'They have a rape suite there. I'll phone the station and tell them to expect you. The poor child.'

'What's a rape suite?' I asked. 'So I can tell Joss.'

'It's a private room at the police station that is used for interviewing victims of rape and sexual assault. Reassure Joss that she'll be well looked after. The police are specially trained and will treat her sensitively. She'll also be examined by a doctor if necessary. Cathy, it's important to preserve as much evidence as possible, so make sure she doesn't wash, brush her teeth, eat or drink or change her clothes, otherwise vital DNA evidence could be lost. It's best if she doesn't go to the toilet either before the doctor examines her and takes swabs, but obviously if she's desperate she'll have to go. And, Cathy, take a change of clothes for her. The police might want to keep the ones she's wearing for evidence.'

I was grateful Jill knew exactly what to do.

'Should I telephone Linda before we go?' I thought to ask.

'I want my mum,' Joss said, her voice small and vulnerable.

'I'll phone her mother,' Jill said. 'And also the council's duty social worker, who will tell Amelia. Will you be all right taking Joss to the police station? What about your kids?'

'There's just Adrian in. I can leave him here.'

'OK. Go straight away. Phone me if there's anything else you need.'

'I will. Thank you.'

I replaced the handset and turned to Joss. 'Is Mummy coming?' she asked, childlike.

'Jill is phoning her now,' I said. 'We have to go to the police station. Jill said it's important you go as you are, and we need to take a change of clothes for you, as the police might want to keep your clothes for evidence. Shall I go and fetch some clothes from your bedroom, or do you want to?'

'You go,' Joss said, her eyes brimming again.

'Oh, love,' I said.

I gave her hand a reassuring squeeze and left her sitting on the sofa while I went upstairs. Before going to Joss's room I went to Adrian's as I needed to tell him I was going out. His light was off and he was asleep in bed. As I approached the bed his eyes flickered. 'Mum?' he asked groggily.

'I have to go out for a while,' I whispered. 'I need to take Joss to the police station.'

'Why? What's the matter?' he asked, his eyes opening.

'She's been attacked. She's all right, but we need to see the police as soon as possible.'

'Do you want me to come with you?' he asked. Bless him.

'No. I'll be OK. Thanks, love.'

I came out, drawing the door to behind me. In Joss's room the clean laundry I'd left for her to put away was still in a pile on her bed, so I quickly selected fresh underwear, leggings and a top. I returned downstairs and put the clothes into a carrier bag, and then went into the living room. Joss was as I'd left her, sitting on the sofa with a tissue pressed to her face. Toscha had taken up the space I'd left and was now curled close beside her as though sensing she needed to be looked after.

'All right, love, let's go.' I threw her a reassuring smile.

She stood, and Toscha raised her head to look at her.

In the hall I slipped on my shoes, unhooked our jackets from the stand and passed Joss hers. Leaving the hall light on, we went out. The night was clear but chilly. As we got in the car Joss said quietly, 'Thanks for not going on at me.'

I looked at her, a pale and frightened child. 'There's no need to thank me,' I said. 'You're not to blame. You're a victim.'

'But if I'd done what you'd said and stayed in more and found some other friends, none of this would have happened.'

I couldn't disagree. In my heart of hearts I'd known that something like this might happen, but what else could I have done to prevent it? It was a question that not only I, but also the social services and all those involved in Joss's care would be asking ourselves in the future. Joss was a vulnerable thirteen-year-old, and together we'd failed to protect her.

CHAPTER SEVENTEEN

REMORSE, GUILT AND REGRET

J oss was silent as I drove to the police station, and other than offering a few impotent words of reassurance I was quiet too. It was nearly midnight and there was little traffic on the roads, although some late-night revellers were hanging around on street corners in the town. An ambulance sped by with its light flashing and siren blaring. Ten minutes later I was parking in the side road adjacent to the police station, anxious and desperately worried for Joss.

'I hope Mum comes,' Joss said as I cut the engine.

'I am sure she will if she can,' I said. I could appreciate that despite everything that had happened between Joss and her mother, she would want her with her in a crisis.

'You'll stay with me if she doesn't come, won't you?' Joss said, her eyes filling again.

'Yes, of course. Try not to worry. I'll be with you.'

We got out and Joss linked arms with me for support as we walked round to the front of the police station and then up the steps to the main entrance. Arriving at the security-locked glass door I pressed the button for the bell. Through the glass I could see into the brightly lit reception area where a young male police officer stood behind the counter, working on some papers. He looked at us and then released the security lock. I pushed open the door and we went in. The second door opened automatically into the reception area. There was only one other person in reception – a young man with long hair, sitting on one of the chairs. I approached the counter while Joss waited to one side.

'How can I help you?' the officer asked, still holding his pen and his elbow resting on the counter.

'My name is Cathy Glass,' I began quietly, so the man waiting couldn't hear. 'My fostering agency, Homefinders, telephoned this station a short while ago to say we were coming. Joss, the girl I'm fostering, has been sexually assaulted.' I felt my pulse rise.

'Is this the young lady?' he asked, straightening and looking past me to Joss.

'Yes.'

'What's her full name?'

I told him.

'Take a seat, please, and I'll find out who is dealing with this.'

'Thank you,' I said.

We went over to the steel-framed chairs as the officer disappeared through a door behind the counter. Joss sat beside me. The young man opposite kept his gaze down and away from us. Distant voices could be heard coming from elsewhere in the building and a police officer's radio sounded. A couple of minutes passed and then the bell on the main door rang, making Joss start. The three of us looked out to see a middle-aged man, poorly dressed and who could have been sleeping rough, gesticulating through the glass that he wanted to be let in. Clearly we couldn't do that. The man opposite us shrugged and looked away, while I pointed to the empty reception desk. The man outside banged on the glass and then went away as two uniformed officers let themselves in.

As the officers passed through reception the first one said a polite 'Good evening', then paused as he recognized Joss and added a playful, 'Not you again!'

It wasn't appropriate, but he wasn't to know why we were here, and I caught a glimpse of the Joss who was well known to many of the officers from all the times she'd been in trouble.

Joss forced a smile. 'Yeah. It's me,' she said.

They disappeared through a door at the rear of the station and we were left to our thoughts again. Joss concentrated on the floor and chewed her bottom lip as the man opposite sat with his arms folded and legs outstretched, staring straight ahead.

'Hopefully it won't be too long,' I said to Joss after a while, touching her arm reassuringly – although in truth I had no idea how long it would take, as this was new ground for me.

A couple of minutes later the officer who had been on reception reappeared. 'Come through,' he said, releasing a lock on the small gate in the counter. We went through and he locked it again behind us.

'You can wait in the suite,' he said. 'It's more comfortable in there. The interviewing officer is on her way.'

I thanked him and we followed him down the corridor, past closed and open doors on either side; some were signed as interviewing rooms while others led to offices. At the end of the corridor he opened a door on the right and stood aside to let us in.

'Make yourselves comfortable. Would you like a drink?'

'No, thank you,' I said. Joss shook her head.

'Give me a shout if you need anything,' he said. 'Ann, the interviewing officer, should be with you in about half an hour.'

'Thank you,' I said again.

He went out and closed the door behind him.

It was a pleasant room – if a room designated for victims of sexual assault could be described as such – and I could see why the officer had said we'd be more comfortable in here. As well as being private, it was designed to try to put those waiting at ease. Furnished like a living room, it had a fitted carpet, a sofa and an easy chair with scatter cushions, and a coffee table with some reading material on it. The walls had been painted a light beige. Yes, it was like a small living room, except for the examination couch – which, although partially shielded from the room by a movable screen, was a chilling reminder of why we were here and what was to come. Jill had said that the interviewing police officer would be specially trained and sensitive to the victim's ordeal, but it didn't stop me from worrying about what lay ahead. Joss would be interviewed and then examined by a doctor. She sat beside me, a frightened child. I put my arm around her and we leant back on the sofa.

She snuggled into my side and we were silent for some time. There was one small window in the room, very high up, suggesting the room could previously have been a standard interview room. The air felt stuffy, although not exactly warm, and the room was quiet save for the occasional voices and footsteps that drifted in from the corridor outside.

Ten minutes or so went by and Joss yawned. 'How long do you think they're going to be?' she asked. 'I'm so tired.'

'Hopefully not much longer,' I said. 'Joss, when the police officer interviews you, you know you must tell the truth. All of it.'

'Yes,' she said quietly.

'Even the things you don't tell me, like how much you've had to drink tonight, and if you've been smoking dope. They won't blame you, but they will need to know all the details.'

'OK,' she said quietly, and began sucking her thumb.

Another five minutes passed and I thought Joss might be asleep on my shoulder, but then I heard her breath catch and she began to cry again. 'I want to go home,' she said. 'I don't want to stay here any more. I'm tired. Can we go now, please, Cathy?'

'Oh, love,' I said, holding her close. 'It's important we stay and tell the officer what happened while it's fresh in your memory. And the doctor needs to see you.'

'We can come back tomorrow. I want to go to bed now.'

I could appreciate that, exhausted and traumatized, Joss just wanted her bed, but from what Jill had said, if we left now and came back tomorrow valuable DNA evidence could be lost.

'Why don't you stretch out on the sofa and try to have a little sleep,' I suggested. 'I'll sit on the easy chair.'

'No. I want you to stay next to me,' she said, clutching my arm.

'All right, love.'

I stayed where I was and held her close. How dearly I wished I could turn back the clock and undo all that had happened to her that evening – indeed, undo all the bad that had happened to her in the last four years, starting with her father's death. Joss had already suffered so much, and now this. Would she ever get over it? I doubted it.

Another five minutes passed and more footsteps sounded along the corridor. They stopped outside the door and we heard the duty officer say, 'They're in here.'

The door opened and Linda came in. Joss immediately stood and rushed into her mother's arms and wept.

'Is everything all right?' the officer asked me, looking concerned.

I nodded. 'She's very upset.'

'Ann shouldn't be too long now,' he said. 'Do you need anything?'

'No, thank you.'

He nodded stoically and left the room, closing the door behind him.

Linda and Joss stood in the middle of the room, clutching each other and crying openly. 'Oh, Joss,' Linda said. 'Whatever happened?'

'I'm sorry, Mum. I'm so sorry,' Joss wept.

'I knew something like this would happen,' Linda said through her tears. 'As if we haven't had enough upset in our lives, and now this.'

It was pitiful to see and I felt my own eyes fill. I stood and went over to them. 'Come and sit down,' I said, touching Linda's arm.

'Thanks, Cathy. I'm sorry.' Then to Joss, 'Come on, love. Let's go and sit down.' She put her arm around her daughter and led her to the sofa, where they sat side by side. I took the easy chair, while Joss rested her head on her mother's shoulder and snuggled into her as she had done previously with me.

'It's going to be all right,' Linda said, trying to comfort and soothe her daughter. 'We'll get through this. You'll see.' She reached down into her handbag and took out a packet of tissues. Taking one out, she turned to face Joss and began wiping the tears from her eyes as the mother of a young child would. 'We need to be strong and face this together,' Linda said. 'We can do it, just as we've faced other bad times.' It was heartbreaking to watch.

As Linda continued to wipe away Joss's tears and comfort her, I could see the mother and daughter bond that had been there before Linda had remarried and their relationship had gone so horribly wrong. It crossed my mind that perhaps this catastrophe, this appalling attack on Joss, might lead the way to them building the bridges they desperately needed to regain what they'd had. Sometimes it takes a tragedy to steer families back on course.

Linda wiped her own eyes, and now Joss was calmer they sat back together on the sofa. Linda put her arm around her daughter and Joss relaxed against her.

'They said the interviewing officer has been delayed,' Linda said to me. 'Apparently she'll be about another twenty minutes.'

Joss groaned. 'I want to go, Mum.'

'Not until you've given your statement,' Linda said. 'I want that bastard prosecuted.'

I was pleased Linda recognized how important it was Joss stayed and that she was being firm with her. We sat quietly for a while and then Linda began making light conversation, probably as a displacement for her own anxiety. She said how nice Jill had been when she'd telephoned and that she must be very supportive and a great help with fostering. I said she was and we talked a bit about fostering. Then Linda looked at her watch and said, 'It's nearly quarter to one, Cathy. Why don't you go home? I can stay with Joss.'

Because Joss was in care under a Section 20, I could leave her with her mother. Had she been the subject of a Care Order from the court, I would have had to stay with her.

'I don't mind waiting,' I said.

'It's OK. You go,' Joss said. 'Mum can stay with me.'

'Go and get some sleep,' Linda said. 'I'm grateful for all you've done.' So with that, I thought they would prefer it if I left.

'All right, if you're sure,' I said, moving to the edge of my seat. 'Phone me when you've finished and I'll come and collect Joss.'

'There's no need. I have my car,' Linda said. 'I'll bring her back afterwards.'

'Thank you,' I said. 'Take care.' I didn't know what else to say. I smiled weakly and left the room.

I walked down the corridor and to the rear of the reception.

'You going?' the duty officer asked.

'Yes. Joss has her mother with her now.'

He unlocked the small gate and I went out. The middle-aged man we'd seen earlier through the glass door was now inside and sitting on one of the chairs. His clothes were badly stained and he smelt unwashed, but as I walked past him he tipped his hat and said a polite 'Good evening'.

'Good evening,' I said, and continued to the door, which opened automatically.

I stepped out into the cool night air and made my way to my car.

* * *

Remorse, guilt and regret can befall anyone at any time, but never more so than in fostering, with the sensitive and emotionally charged situations we often have to deal with. As a carer looking after children with challenging behaviour, I'd often found myself regretting something I'd said or done, a decision made or not made, and then beating myself up about the outcome until I eventually took the lesson from the mistake and moved on. I was grateful Linda wasn't blaming me for what had happened to Joss, as I certainly felt responsible. Linda had placed her faith in me, given me responsibility for her daughter, and I'd failed her and Joss miserably. If there was anything to be learned from what had happened I couldn't see it as I drove through the now deserted streets, sinking deeper into a gloom of guilt and regret. I had two daughters of my own and certainly wouldn't have allowed them out as Joss had been allowed out. True, they didn't want to go out and challenge the boundaries as Joss had, but if they did I would pin them to the floor rather than allow them to place themselves in danger.

As I parked on the drive and cut the engine I was at an all-time low. What had happened to Joss would blight her life for many, many years to come. She would never forget it and I felt responsible. I let myself in and saw the light flashing on the answerphone. I pressed play and heard Jill's voice, flat and emotionless: 'Cathy, can you phone me when you return, please.' The message was timed at 12.55, ten minutes previously.

I mechanically slipped off my shoes, hung my jacket on the coat stand and went through to the kitchen where I poured myself a glass of water and drank it straight down. It was quiet upstairs, so I assumed Adrian was still asleep, and the girls wouldn't return from their sleepovers until the following day. At least they hadn't had to go through this with Joss and me. I went into the living room. Toscha was still curled up on the sofa. As I sat beside her she looked at me as though expecting to be taken through to her bed in the kitchen, where she spent the night. I picked up the telephone from the corner table and dialled Homefinders' number. It rang and then there was the usual few seconds' delay as the call was transferred to the agency's out-of-hours service, then Jill answered.

'You're back sooner than I thought,' she said.

'Linda wanted to stay with Joss, so I left them. I hope that was all right. The interviewing officer hadn't arrived by the time I left.'

'That's fine, but you sound very low. How are you?'

'I'll get by,' I said.

'I don't think you could have done any more for Joss,' Jill said, which didn't help and seemed to emphasize my failings.

'Do you know the details of what happened to Joss?' she asked.

I told Jill what I knew. I heard Jill give a heartfelt sigh.

'The poor kid. When you have a moment can you write it up? For now, though, try to get some rest,' Jill said kindly. 'You must be exhausted. They'll be a couple of hours at the station at least. I've informed the duty social worker at the social services, and I'll speak to Amelia tomorrow. How was Joss when you left her?'

'Quiet, upset and coping as best she can,' I said. 'I would have stayed but she wanted her mother, so I thought it best to leave them.'

'Yes. Linda is sensible. How is Joss getting back?'

'Linda is going to bring her.'

'OK. I'm on duty until seven o'clock tomorrow morning, so phone me if you need anything, even if it's just to talk. Otherwise I'll speak to you tomorrow – or rather, today.'

'Thank you, Jill.'

'And Cathy. Try to get some rest.'

'I will.'

I slowly replaced the handset and then spent some moments staring unseeing across the living room. Toscha had gone back to sleep beside me and I absent-mindedly stroked her fur. Jill was right when she said I was exhausted, but I knew I couldn't sleep. I didn't know when Joss would be back, and my head was throbbing and my thoughts were racing with the horror of what had happened that evening. Joss had gone out, a young teenager with attitude, and had arrived back a broken woman, a victim of a dreadful sexual attack. How had all this been allowed to happen? I played through the sequence of events in my mind over and over again. Then I forced my eyes to close and rested my head on the sofa back, trying to ease the tension. But the thoughts persisted, torturing me like red-hot needles. If it was bad for me, how much worse was it for Joss – the victim? And her poor mother. They would probably be with the interviewing officer now, Joss going into the details of what had happened to her, and her mother having to listen. It was every mother's worst nightmare to have to hear the details of her daughter's rape.

Despite the torment of my thoughts I must have eventually dozed off, for when my eyes opened again the clock on the mantelpiece showed 2.45 a.m. I sat forward and then stood to go and make myself a coffee. Toscha looked at me. As I left the room, she followed me into the kitchen, where she put herself to bed. I made a mug of coffee and took it into the living room where I sat on the sofa and switched the television on low as a background distraction. I hadn't had the television on in the early hours since my husband, John, had left me many years before, when the children were little. Then I'd been up all night worrying and fretting, and had regularly passed the long nights with the television for company.

I slowly sipped my coffee, placed the empty mug on the corner table and closed my eyes again. Some time later I came to with a start as the front doorbell rang. And for a moment, before I was fully awake, I thought I'd been dreaming and that everything that had happened that evening had been a dreadful nightmare, until reality set in and I remembered.

CHAPTER EIGHTEEN

LYING?

The clock on the mantelpiece showed it was 4 a.m. I quickly switched off the television and went down the hall to open the front door. Joss and her mother stood side by side, pale and drawn.

'Come in,' I said, opening the door wider.

'I'm going to bed,' Joss said as they stepped in. She was wearing the change of clothes we'd taken with us.

'Do you need anything?' Linda asked her.

'No,' Joss returned. I closed the front door.

'I'll see you, then,' Linda called as Joss began upstairs.

'Yes. Goodnight.'

'Night, love,' I said.

Linda and I watched Joss go upstairs until she'd turned the corner on the landing to go to her bedroom.

'Do you want to come and sit for a while?' I asked Linda.

'I wouldn't mind,' she sighed. 'I'm tired, but I'm not ready to go home yet and explain all of this to Eric.'

We went through to the living room. 'Can I get you a drink?' I asked.

'No, thanks. I had one at the police station. They were very kind.'

We sat down. Linda took the sofa, and I one of the chairs. She looked shattered, and I too felt the weight of all that had happened that evening.

'I don't know, Cathy,' she sighed, shaking her head in despair. 'Joss made a statement, but I'm not sure if it's strong enough to have them convicted. She was very confused and kept changing her mind. Ann and her colleague were very patient, but they had to keep stopping Joss to clarify points. I hope I'm wrong, but I felt it didn't look good on Joss.'

'Did she tell them all they needed to know?' I asked.

'In the end, but she was reluctant to say how she first met Zach and Carl, which they wanted to know. Apparently it was at Chelsea's flat. I think Joss was trying to protect them all. As if they've done her any favours! I gather that flat is a right mess and has been raided by the police for drink and drug offences. The police seemed to know it.'

'I wasn't aware of that, but when I first went there I reported my concerns to the social services. I'm sorry I didn't do more to stop Joss from going there.' I felt even guiltier now.

'It's not your fault,' Linda said quietly. 'Joss can be very strong-willed when she wants to be. I wish she hadn't changed her story, though. First she told the police she'd been at the flat all evening and that Zach and Carl had offered her a lift home, but then she admitted she'd been out with them all evening.'

'That's what Joss told me,' I said. 'I think she thought it might reflect badly on her if she admitted she'd been out drinking with them.'

Linda nodded sadly. 'I hope the police realized Joss was still in shock and couldn't think straight.'

'I'm sure they did,' I said, trying to reassure her.

'When Ann asked Joss which bars they'd been to, how much they'd had to drink and who had bought the drinks, she kept saying she didn't know. Ann asked if she was frightened of what Zach and Carl might do to her if she told the truth and she admitted she was. It took a lot of reassurance before she was able to give them the details of the rape – or rather, attempted rape. It seems from Joss's description that – to use the term the police used – "full penetration" didn't take place.' Linda's eyes immediately filled and she pulled a tissue from her pocket.

I went over and sat beside her on the sofa; I lightly rubbed her arm as she wiped her eyes.

'I'm sorry,' she said. 'But the things I've had to listen to tonight. It was dreadful.'

'I can appreciate that. But the more details the police have, the more likely they are to be able to prosecute.'

'That's what they said. They asked Joss to describe Zach's underwear, and if he'd been circumcised and if he had an erection. I mean, Cathy,' Linda said, turning to me, her brow creasing again, 'Joss is thirteen. She may have seen her little brother in the bath, but she's never seen an adult male naked. And we've never really talked about that sort of thing. I was going to leave it until she was older.'

Linda began to cry openly so I put my arm around her and comforted her as best I could. My thoughts turned to Lucy and Paula, of similar ages to Joss, and how absolutely horrendous it would be for them if they had found themselves in Joss's situation. It didn't bear thinking about.

After a while Linda wiped her eyes and continued. 'From what Joss told the police, it seems Zach had had so much to drink that he couldn't "enter her", as the police put it. That's when Carl said he wanted to have a go. Those were his words, Cathy: "Let me have a go and see if I can do it." They were laughing. But when Carl began climbing over from the front seat to get in the back of the car, Zach loosened his grip on Joss and she managed to knee him in the crotch and get out. She ran into town and then caught the bus here.'

Tears streamed down Linda's face again and she sobbed uncontrollably. I held her and soothed her until eventually her tears were spent and she couldn't cry any more.

'I'm sorry,' she said, straightening. 'I've had to be strong for Joss and it just built up inside me. I've always tried to be strong for her. I feel a bit better now, thank you.' She leant forward and threw her tissue in the wastepaper basket.

'Would you like a drink now? I can make a tea or coffee?'

'No, thanks. You've been so kind. I'd better get back. Eric will be wondering where I am. Is it all right if I come round later this afternoon to see how Joss is?'

'Yes, of course. Whenever you like. I'll be here.'

'Thank you. I'll phone before I set off.'

'Did the doctor examine Joss?' I asked.

'Yes. She also bagged up all of Joss's clothes to take away for examination. Thanks for sending a change of clothes. I wouldn't have thought of that.'

'Jill told me, or I wouldn't have known.'

'She's good, your Jill,' Linda said, and then she stood, ready to leave.

It was nearly 5 a.m. I saw Linda out and closed and locked the front door. I switched off all the downstairs lights and went upstairs to bed for what was left of the night. Despite the turmoil of my thoughts, I was so tired I fell asleep quickly.

When I woke my bedside clock showed 9 a.m. I didn't feel refreshed, but at least I'd had some sleep, which would hopefully see me through the day. I could hear water running in the bathroom as Adrian showered, getting ready to go out with his father. Paula was being brought home by her friend's parents at ten to join them, and Lucy would be returning a little later.

I hauled myself out of bed, put on my dressing gown and went round the landing to Joss's room. I quietly opened the door and looked in. She was on her side and fast asleep, so I came out again. I went downstairs, fed Toscha and made a cup of coffee, which I drank while leaning against the work surface in the kitchen and gazing out of the window. The sky was grey and overcast, suggesting rain wasn't far away, but the birds were busy at the bird feeder, which was always nice to watch. The bright golden marigolds and red geraniums were still flowering well, but I noticed the grass needed cutting – a job Adrian and I shared. Presently, I heard him cross the landing and go into his bedroom, having finished in the bathroom. I drained the last of my coffee, put the mug in the sink and went upstairs to bathe and dress.

At breakfast Adrian naturally asked after Joss and if she was hurt. I said she'd been badly assaulted and was obviously shaken, but I didn't go into details. If Joss wanted to tell him, Lucy, Paula or anyone else more about it then that would be her decision.

Paula returned promptly at ten o'clock, tired from the sleepover but having had fun. She and Adrian were ready when John arrived shortly after 10.30, and I greeted him as I usually did with a polite good morning. Whenever Paula went out with her father she always wanted an extra hug and kiss goodbye from me. When she'd been very young and hadn't understood the implications of divorce, she'd asked if I could go out with them, which had broken my heart and made me hate John even more for leaving us. Now time had passed and we'd all adjusted to the arrangements, so I gave her that extra hug and kiss and wished them a nice day out.

Once I'd seen them off, and while Joss slept, I set about some household chores. Just before midday Lucy telephoned and asked if she could stay a bit longer at her friend's house, as her parents had invited her for lunch. They'd told her to check with me that it was all right and said they'd bring her home between three and four that afternoon. I said it was fine with me as long as it was all right with them, and reminded Lucy to thank them.

A few minutes later I heard Joss's bedroom door open and I immediately went upstairs.

'Are you all right, love?' I asked, meeting her on the landing.

'I'm going to have a long bath,' she said.

'That sounds good. Do you need anything?'

'Could you bring me up a glass of water?'

'Of course. Anything else? Are you hungry?'

'Yes, but I'll have my bath first.'

I thought it was a good sign that Joss was up and having a bath. I fetched the glass of water and then left her in the bathroom. She was in the bath for nearly an hour; I heard the water drain and then the bath refill. I understood she was probably trying to wash away the 'dirt' from yesterday and cleanse herself of the dreadful experience. It was a pity she couldn't wash away the horrendous memory as well. While

Joss was in the bath, Jill telephoned to see how she was. I told her she hadn't got back until 4 a.m., had gone straight to bed and was now in the bath. I said that Linda had been very upset and was concerned about Joss's statement.

'Hopefully the police have enough to prosecute,' Jill said. 'Joss is going to need a lot of support.'

'I know. Linda's coming back later to see her.'

'Good. I'll speak to Amelia tomorrow, but if you have any concerns or need to speak to one of us today, call the usual number. I'm not on duty, but one of the team will help you.'

'Thank you.' I thought it was kind of Jill and a sign of her dedication as a support social worker that she'd telephoned on Sunday, her day off.

When Joss came down after her bath, having also washed her hair, she did look a bit fresher. I told her that her mother was planning on coming over later and I asked her what she'd like to eat. She said her stomach was rumbling, as she hadn't eaten since yesterday afternoon, so I set about making her a cooked breakfast – brunch, really – and then sat at the table with her to keep her company while she ate. But as I sipped my coffee and made light conversation, I could feel the horror of what had happened the day before sitting between us like an unacknowledged wall, until I couldn't ignore it any longer.

'Joss, I won't keep mentioning what happened, but if you want to talk, any time, day or night, you know I'm here to listen, and I'll do what I can to help.'

'Yes, I know,' she said. 'There is one thing.'

'Yes?' I asked, and set down my coffee.

'Will I get my clothes back from the police?'

'I don't know, but you've got plenty and we can always buy some more.'

'But those were my best jeans,' she said.

'We'll replace them,' I said without hesitation. And I thought it was another good sign that the old Joss who loved her clothes was still in there somewhere.

Shortly after we'd finished at the table, when Joss was in her room, Linda telephoned and said she was planning to visit in about half an hour, if that was all right with me. I said it was, and told her that Joss was up and dressed and had had a bath and something to eat.

Linda said, 'So it sounds like Joss is recovering quickly. See you soon.'

I went upstairs and told Joss her mother was on her way, but she pulled a face, the old hostility towards her mother returning.

'What's she coming here for?' she grumbled. 'There's no need.'

'Your mother is very worried about you,' I said. 'You were pleased to see her last night.'

'That was different,' Joss said.

I was disappointed. I had hoped that the bond I'd seen between Joss and her mother last night would continue, although I could see why it hadn't. Last night, after that brutal attack, Joss was a scared and frightened child again, in need of her mother's love and comfort. Now she was feeling a bit better, her guard was back up.

'Be nice to your mother,' I said. 'She was very upset last night – we all were.'

'Whatever,' Joss said dismissively, and turned away.

I didn't feel able to tell her off, given what she'd been through, so I said, 'I'll call you when she arrives,' and came out.

Five minutes later the grey, overcast skies that had threatened rain finally delivered as promised, and it began to pour down. Toscha shot in through the cat flap, hating the feel of water on her fur, then sat in the living room staring out through the patio doors with her tail lashing, annoyed that she couldn't go outside and catch more crane flies, which were abundant at this time of year. I wondered where John, Adrian and Paula would go in the rain; to the cinema or the leisure centre possibly – that's where they often went when the weather was bad. By the time Linda arrived the storm was peaking; thunder crashed overhead and lightning flashed on the horizon.

'What a day!' she exclaimed, closing her umbrella and leaving it in the porch. 'I could hardly see out of the windscreen.'

I thought Linda seemed much brighter now and far more composed.

'Did you manage to get some sleep?' I asked as she took off her coat and I hung it on the coat stand.

'A little, and Eric and I have had a good chat, which helped a lot.'

'That's good. I'll tell Joss you're here. She's in her bedroom.'

'Cathy,' Linda said, lowering her voice and placing her hand on my arm to stop me. 'Could I speak with you first, please, alone? There's something I need to tell you before I see Joss.'

'Yes, of course,' I said, wondering what it was. 'Let's go into the living room.'

I switched on the light, as the storm had made the room dark. Rain was sheeting against the window and Toscha was trying to dab the rivulets of water through the glass. Linda sat on the sofa and I took the chair, just as we had in the early hours, and I waited to hear what she wanted to tell me. After a moment she leaned forward slightly and looked at me carefully.

'Eric and I have been talking, going over everything Joss claimed happened last night, and I'm sorry to say we've come to the conclusion that she's made it all up.'

I stared at her, shocked. 'No, that's not possible. Not the attack?'

Linda nodded solemnly. 'Yes, all of it.'

'But why?' I asked, amazed.

'For attention,' Linda said.

'No. I'm sure you're wrong. Joss wouldn't do that.'

'It wouldn't have occurred to me either if Eric hadn't said it, but then it made perfect sense. Think about it, Cathy. There are no witnesses. It's only Joss's word against theirs. Chelsea was conveniently ill. Joss has been doing all she can to get attention, but we're not shocked any more by her bad behaviour, and you've been coping with it. So she needed to stage something really dramatic to get attention, and it doesn't get more dramatic than crying rape.'

I stared at her, my mouth dry, my heart racing from shock. 'But you saw how distraught Joss was last night after the attack. She couldn't have made it up. And there were bruises on her face.'

'They could have come from anywhere. Perhaps she fell over or got in a fight. Don't kid yourself; Joss is very good at theatricals. She says she'd like to be an actress when she's older. Look at all the lies she's told us in the past. You, me, her social worker and teachers have all been taken in.'

'But the police believe her,' I said, my thoughts reeling. 'They are taking it seriously. And Joss was examined by a doctor. That should help prove she's telling the truth.'

'The doctor couldn't or wouldn't tell me anything yesterday other than she'd taken some swabs and they'd be sent to the lab for testing. Eric and I are sure the results will come back negative or inconclusive, so there won't be any evidence. The guys involved will deny it and back each other up, so there won't be a prosecution. You wait and see. I bet we're right.'

I was stunned. What Linda was saying was to some extent plausible, but I still couldn't believe that Joss would make it all up. 'So you really think Joss is lying?' I asked incredulously.

'Yes, we do,' Linda said.

Joss must have been outside the door and heard what her mother had said, for she now burst into the room.

'He would say that, wouldn't he!' she shouted, eyes blazing, advancing towards her mother. 'You believe everything that fucking idiot tells you!'

For a moment I thought she was going to hit her mother, and I was on my feet. 'Joss!' I said firmly, taking her arm. 'Calm down and sit down. We can talk.'

'I'm done with talking to her,' Joss yelled, jabbing a finger towards her mother. 'She always takes his side. It's *his* fucking fault it happened. I wouldn't be here if it wasn't for him!'

With her fists clenched and her face white with rage, Joss turned and stormed out of the room.

'Joss!' I called, going after her.

'I'm going to my room,' she yelled. 'Tell me when she's gone. They can both go to hell!' She began upstairs.

At that moment the front door opened as Lucy let herself in, having returned from her friend's sleepover. 'Hi,' she said, smiling. And then, seeing Joss, 'Oh no. Not again,' she sighed, her face clouding.

'I'm sorry, love,' I said. 'Joss is upset and her mother is in the living room.' Joss's bedroom door slammed shut overhead.

'We'll catch up later,' Lucy said. I would normally have spent time with her hearing about the sleepover. 'I'll unpack. Do you want me to look in on Joss?'

'Yes, please. Thank you, love,' I said gratefully.

As Lucy went upstairs I returned to the living room, thankful I had such an understanding family.

'See what I mean?' Linda said. 'Joss loves a good scene.'

'But I can understand why she's upset,' I said, sitting on the sofa. 'The last time she saw you, you were sympathetic and supportive, and now you and Eric are accusing her of lying.'

'Well, she is,' Linda persisted. 'And she's angry with me because I've seen through her lies.'

I still wasn't convinced. 'You may be right,' I said despondently. 'But until the police prove differently I think we need to believe Joss. Can you imagine what it would do to her if she is telling the truth, and she's had the courage to report the attack, and we didn't believe her?'

This wasn't what Linda wanted to hear. 'Well, that's up to you,' she said tartly. 'But I agree with Eric, and tomorrow we're going to phone the social worker and the police and tell them the truth.'

'But we don't know what the truth is,' I said. 'There's no real evidence to say Joss has made it all up.'

'There's no evidence to say she hasn't,' Linda said. 'But when the police start investigating, Joss's story won't stack up.'

I didn't want to antagonize her by disagreeing further, so I chose my words carefully. 'I've been fostering for a long time and in my experience children usually tell the truth. I know some do make up allegations, but the majority do not. So until there is firm evidence to the contrary, I have to believe Joss and support her as best I can.'

'That's up to you,' she said, and stood ready to leave.

'If you stay a while longer, I could try to persuade Joss to come down and we could all talk about it,' I said.

'I don't think that will help,' Linda replied tersely, and she took a step towards the living-room door. 'And to be honest, Cathy, I've had enough of all this. Joss and her lies. I'm exhausted and sick of it all.'

She went down the hall and pulled her coat from the stand. 'Tell Joss I said goodbye,' she said. 'And for all our sakes, try to persuade her to tell the truth.'

I opened the front door and we said an awkward goodbye. The rain had stopped now, but the sky was inky black, suggesting that another downpour wasn't far away. I closed the door. My heart was heavy and my thoughts were in chaos. While I could appreciate what Linda had said about Joss lying in the past and her theatrical outbursts, I couldn't make the huge leap that she and Eric had to decide Joss was lying about this.

CHAPTER NINETEEN

ALONE

I went up to Joss's room, where Lucy and Joss were sitting side by side on the bed.

'Her mother called her a liar!' Lucy exclaimed indignantly, taking up the fight for Joss. 'Can you believe it? How mean is that? Your own mother calling you a liar!'

I looked at Joss. 'How are you?'

'OK,' she said quietly, her anger largely gone.

'If I told you something like that,' Lucy continued, 'you'd believe me, wouldn't you?'

I nodded but didn't say anything. Lucy meant well, but I didn't think criticizing Joss's mother was going to help. She was, after all, her mother, and Lucy seemed to have forgotten how loyal she was to her own birth mother despite all her failings.

'Your mum is very upset right now,' I said to Joss. 'She's also exhausted. When she's had time to think clearly I'm sure she'll feel differently.'

'Not if *he* has anything to do with it,' Joss said, her anger flashing again.

'Her stepfather sounds horrible,' Lucy commiserated. 'Pity your mother ever married him.'

'It was,' Joss agreed.

'Perhaps they'll get divorced,' Lucy suggested.

'I doubt it,' Joss said.

I could see that the girls were comfortable talking together and Joss didn't really need my input right now. Sometimes a similar-aged young person can offer the empathy and words of understanding that an older adult cannot.

'If you two are all right, I'll go downstairs.'

'Sure,' Joss said easily.

'We'll be fine,' Lucy said.

'And you had a good time at your friend's?' I asked Lucy.

'Yeah, great.'

I left them and went down to the kitchen. As I worked it crossed my mind that perhaps I should telephone Homefinders' out-of-hours service to report and discuss what Linda had said, but Jill wouldn't be on duty. Although I could have talked to another member of the Homefinders team, it wasn't an emergency so I decided to wait until the following day, Monday, when Jill would be at work again. Jill knew Joss and I greatly valued her opinion. It was at times like these that I very much missed the support and views of a partner. Couples who foster can support each other and discuss their worries and concerns, but as a single carer I bore it all. I was deeply troubled by Linda's abrupt turnaround and that she had withdrawn her support for her daughter. It had only been a matter of hours since she'd sat on my sofa and, believing Joss to have been viciously attacked, had broken down. Then, as a result of listening to Eric, she'd completely changed her mind and now thought her daughter was lying. But then again, I supposed Eric wouldn't have suggested Joss was lying unless he had genuinely believed it. What a mess.

* * *

About half an hour later I heard the girls' voices on the land-ing and I went up to make sure they were all right. They'd changed rooms, and Joss was now sitting on Lucy's bed while Lucy unpacked her overnight bag. She could have stayed for a week for all the clothes she'd taken to her friend's, most of which were now being consigned for the laundry, despite just needing an iron.

'Are you OK?' I asked Joss. She seemed to be.

She nodded and managed a small smile. So, reminding them again that I was downstairs if they needed me, I left them to it.

John brought Adrian and Paula home shortly after five o'clock and they said goodbye at the door. They'd been to the cinema. Everyone did their own thing until dinner was ready, and then I called them to the table. Although Joss had confided to Lucy what had happened, she hadn't told Adrian or Paula, so the conversation over dinner was reasonably light-hearted and general, which wasn't a bad thing. Joss would obviously be suffering inside, but she was coping with it in her own way, and I didn't think she needed glum faces and endless sympa-thy. When we'd finished eating Paula suggested a game of Monopoly, as we were all home, and everyone liked the idea. We hastily cleared away the dishes and dumped them in the sink, and then set up the Monopoly board on the table.

The competition is always fierce when we play Monopoly – we play to win; even Paula and me, who aren't normally competitive. There's just something about that game! It wasn't long before our voices had risen in excitement and good-humoured arguments had broken out over ownership deals and land development. I seemed to spend a lot of time in jail while Adrian was busy acquiring older sites. Paula's pile of money grew from developing Park Lane and Mayfair; Lucy reaped a steady return from the utilities, and Joss from owning Regent Street to Bond Street. We had a break at nine o'clock and I made some snacks and poured us some lemonade. The game resumed and the excitement grew as fortunes were made and lost. Although I was tired from lack of sleep the night before, it was put on hold until we finally finished the game at 10.30, with Adrian the outright winner.

'Good game,' I said, as Lucy gave him an affectionate slap on the arm.

'He always wins,' Paula told Joss.

'It's luck,' Joss joked.

'In your dreams. It's skill,' Adrian quipped back.

The atmosphere was good.

'Can we start taking turns in the bathroom,' I said. 'And I need a volunteer to help me pack away the game.'

'I'll help you,' Joss said. She remained at the table while Adrian, Paula and Lucy made their way upstairs. 'That was fun,' she said, as we began sorting the money and cards into piles. 'We used to play Monopoly at home with Dad.'

'That's a lovely memory,' I said, smiling.

She nodded. 'I just wish they weren't memories and he was still alive.'

I paused and looked at her. 'I know you do, love. You've had a lot to cope with.'

We continued sorting the money and then Joss suddenly said, 'I'm not lying, Cathy. About what happened with Zach. I wouldn't lie about that.'

'I'm sure you wouldn't,' I said, meeting her gaze. 'Not something as serious as that.'

'So you believe me?'

'Yes.'

'Mum doesn't. She always takes his side.'

'I suppose it must be difficult for your mother,' I said. 'She's trying to make her marriage work and probably feels caught in the middle. Did you and your stepfather argue a lot?'

'Yes, but Mum never believed what I said and always took his side.'

'What caused all the problems?' I asked, feeling that Joss wanted to talk.

'Oh, you know what he's like – the usual.' She shrugged and continued sorting the money.

'I don't know him, really,' I said. 'I've only met him once. Is he very difficult to live with?'

'Mum says I never gave him a chance, but that's not true. I thought he was all right to begin with. He was kind to Kevin and me. He used to buy us presents, but that was just so he could win us over.'

'To gain your affection?'

'Sort of.'

We placed the money, cards and playing pieces into the Monopoly box and secured the lid with a large elastic band. The box was a bit ragged from years of use, but it had protected the game. I was about to stand to put the game away before going to bed when Joss said, 'I know why it was easy for him to persuade Mum I was lying.'

I remained in my chair and looked at her. Her gaze was down and she concentrated on the table.

'Why?'

'Because she never believed me about all the other stuff either.'

'What other stuff?' I asked, expecting Joss to start telling me about all the other arguments they'd had.

'The other stuff he did,' she said with a shrug.

'Like what?' I asked, naïve and hoping I could go to bed soon.

'You know. Things he shouldn't have done.'

Perhaps it was because I was very tired that I didn't understand straight away what Joss was trying to tell me, or maybe I didn't want to understand.

'Joss, love, you'll have to explain to me. I'm sorry, I don't understand. Your mum doesn't believe you about Zach because she didn't believe you in the past about Eric?'

'Yes. He persuaded her that I was lying when I told her he used to walk around naked and stuff. So now she doesn't believe me about anything.'

I turned in my chair so I was facing her. She continued staring at the table. 'Some people do walk around naked at home,' I said. 'They see it as natural. But it made you feel uncomfortable and I can understand why. We don't do that here.'

There was a small pause before Joss said, 'It wasn't just that.'

'No? What else?'

She took a breath and kept her eyes down. 'He used to come into my bedroom when I was dressing or when I was in the bath. We didn't have locks on the doors, but you are supposed to knock and wait, like you do here. But *he* didn't. He used to come straight in and stand and stare at me. I told Mum, but she didn't believe me. They both said I was lying.'

I was now starting to feel very uneasy, not just about the implications of what Joss was telling me, but about whether she was telling the truth. The problem when someone has a history of lying is that it's very difficult to know when they are telling the truth. I believed Joss when she'd said Zach had attacked her – I'd seen her distress just after it had happened, and I'd met Zach and Carl and those they associated with and could believe they were capable of what Joss had claimed. Eric was another matter entirely, though. He was a middle-aged, respectable man, with a responsible job – although that didn't mean he couldn't be an abuser. He'd seemed pleasant enough the one time I'd met him, and from what Linda had said he appeared to be doing all he could to be a successful stepfather. Was it possible Joss so greatly resented him trying to replace her father that she was making this up? I didn't know, but as I'd told Linda, in my experience children rarely lied about sexual abuse. I needed more details.

'Joss, what you are accusing Eric of is very serious indeed.'

She nodded. 'I know,' she said quietly.

I looked at her. 'When did it start? Can you remember?'

'A few weeks after they got married and he moved in. The first time it happened I thought it was an accident and he'd come into my room by mistake. I liked him then. He seemed nice and he made Mum happy. Kevin was already calling him Dad. Then one evening Mum went out to a fundraising event. She does charity work to help families where someone has committed suicide. Kevin was in bed and I was in my room. I didn't have my top on and I was standing in front of the mirror. I know it sounds silly, but I'd just started developing and I used to stand in front of my mirror every evening to see if my breasts had grown. Without knocking, Eric suddenly came in. I grabbed my top and held it against me. I thought he'd apologize and quickly go out, but he stood there leering and going red in the face. He was sweating and breathing heavily – it was disgusting. And then he said, "You naughty girl. Look what you've done to me." He undid his trousers and his pants were wet at the front. I thought he'd peed himself, but later I realized what it was. I felt sick, and I was frightened too. I told him to go. He grinned, a horrible smile, and said, "I'll be seeing you again, young lady," and he left.' Joss shivered, and I felt icy cold too.

'He went to the bathroom,' Joss continued, nervously rubbing her finger along the edge of the table. 'I heard the shower turn on. I was shaking. I stayed in my room until Mum came home. She came up to say goodnight. She always did. She knew something was wrong, but I couldn't tell her what, so she just thought I was ill. I didn't sleep. I lay there all night thinking about what had happened. Then the next day I sort of convinced myself it had been an accident, him coming into my room, but deep down I knew it wasn't. I kept thinking about what he'd said and the way he'd undone his trousers.'

Joss took a breath before continuing and I sat very still and quiet. 'He tried it again the next time Mum went out. I was in my bedroom with all my clothes on. I wasn't going to change for bed until Mum came home. He came in without knocking and asked me to show him my breasts so he could see how much they'd grown. I don't know how he knew that's what I'd been doing. I told him to go and leave me alone and that I'd tell Mum. He grinned, all pervy, and said I could tell her because she wouldn't believe me. He'd make sure of it. I didn't tell her straight away – I didn't know how to tell her. That's when the arguments started. I ignored him, or if he tried to talk to me I was rude to him. So Mum would tell me off and try to make me apologize, but I wouldn't. Then, when other stuff started to happen, I finally found the courage to tell Mum. She didn't believe me, but she must have said something to him because later, when she wasn't around, he told me to keep my mouth shut if I knew what was good for me.

'After that, it was just arguments and more arguments. I hated him, and I began hating Mum for believing him and not me. Even little Kevin was getting upset by all the shouting. We never used to shout and argue before *he* came along. I started getting into trouble at school. I was angry the whole time, even with my teachers. I felt like everyone was against me. And I stayed away from the house as much as possible. It wasn't my home any more. I began hanging around the streets. It felt safer on the streets in the dark with strangers than it did at home.' She stopped. 'Oh, Cathy,' she suddenly cried. 'If only my dad hadn't died, none of this would have happened. I feel so alone.'

I put my arm around her and comforted her as best I could while she cried. Did I believe her? Yes, I did. The childlike details and the logic in what she'd said convinced me she was telling the truth. My thoughts went to all the times Joss had referred to Eric as a creep, and I knew now it wasn't just name-calling. Why hadn't I picked up on this sooner? I should have done. But there had been so many issues with Joss it had slipped through the net. Her hatred of Eric should have been another indicator – a clue I'd missed. She didn't hate him because he was trying to replace her father; she hated him because he'd been abusing her. With a sinking heart I remembered I'd actually defended Eric and had told Joss he was probably being nice to her because he was trying to build a relationship. How insensitive and inappropriate that sounded now! I also remembered that when I'd met him he'd told me he wanted to foster, and my stomach heaved. That would have given him a steady supply of children to abuse. Then another horrendous thought struck me.

'Joss,' I said, holding her close, 'has Eric abused Kevin?'

'I don't think so,' she said, raising her head slightly and sniffing. 'I think it was just me.'

But, of course, she couldn't be sure.

She straightened and looked at me, her eyes red and her cheeks stained with tears. 'Do you believe me?' she asked, her voice shaking. 'Do you see why Mum changed her mind about Zach?'

'Yes, I do, love. I can see why, and I believe you.'

'Oh, thank you, Cathy!' she cried, and threw her arms around me.

I held her for some time. She'd said 'other stuff' had happened too, but it wasn't for me to question her now. I needed to leave that for the police.

'I'm sorry I couldn't tell you sooner,' she said through her tears. 'I should have told you – I nearly did a few times, but I was worried you'd think I was lying, like Mum did.'

'It's all right,' I said. I stroked her hair. 'I understand why you couldn't tell me. You've been very brave to tell me now.'

'Will I have to talk to the police again?' she asked. 'I'm so tired. I just want to go to bed.'

'You will have to talk to them at some point, but I don't think it has to be tonight.'

'Can I go to bed?'

I nodded and helped her stand – she was exhausted and drained from the emotion of crying and reliving the abuse. She leant heavily against me and we went upstairs. I saw her to her bedroom and left her to change while I went to my bedroom. I wanted to telephone Homefinders for confirmation that Joss wouldn't have to talk to the police straight away. I explained what had happened to the member of staff on duty, and she said she'd speak to the duty social worker at the social services and then call me back. I went to Joss's room to tell her, but she was already in bed asleep, her clothes in a tumbled pile by her bed, left where they'd fallen as she'd taken them off. I tucked her in, came out and went downstairs to wait for the telephone call from Homefinders. It was nearly 1 a.m. by the time they phoned and said the social worker had confirmed that, as Joss wasn't in any immediate danger, the social services would initiate action the following morning, so there was no need to go to the police station tonight. I thanked her and went to bed.

The next day would be Monday, and it was the last day of the summer holidays before school returned for the autumn term. Normally, I would do something a little special with the family for the last day – lunch out, swimming or a similar activity – but I knew that was out of the question now. Tomorrow would be given over to supporting Joss as the social services and police began their investigations into her new claim of abuse. As I lay in the dark, tired but unable to sleep, I wondered how Linda would react now that it was out in the open. Would she still refuse to believe Joss? Or would doubt start to creep in to her previously unshakeable belief in her husband? Or – the worst-case scenario – had she known all along? Certainly she had failed to protect Joss, and questions would be asked.

CHAPTER TWENTY

MONDAY

Having had little sleep, I was up but not dressed at 7.30 the following morning when the doorbell rang. Surprised and apprehensive at an early morning visitor, I checked the security spyhole first. To my horror, two uniformed police officers stood at my door. Oh, hell! I thought. I was in my dressing gown and Joss wasn't even awake yet. I unlocked and opened the door.

'I'm sorry,' I said, embarrassed. 'I wasn't expecting you so early. Joss isn't up. Come in.'

'Early morning is usually a good time to catch young people, before they head off out,' one of the officers said with a smile as they came in. 'We made this our first call of the shift. Looks like we've been lucky again.'

I thought his smile and casual approach was inappropriate considering they were here to take a statement from a victim of sexual abuse. Linda had said that Ann had been lovely at the station. It was a pity she hadn't come.

'This is PC Mike Salmon and I'm Joe Davies,' he said.

'Come and have a seat in the living room,' I said, leading the way down the hall. 'I'll wake Joss now.' I thought that, while I was upstairs, I'd also quickly put on some clothes.

'Has she been behaving herself, then?' Joe Davies asked. Both officers stood with their feet apart in the centre of the living room, looking around. I nodded. 'You're Joss's foster carer, aren't you?' he said. 'Linda told us we'd find her here.'

'That's right. But I don't understand. You've been there? We gave this address at the station.'

'It's possible they have it, but Mike and I were given it by her mother a while back. We weren't busy this morning, so we thought we'd follow it up. Do you want to fetch Joss now and get it over and done with?'

I took a step towards the living-room door and then stopped. 'Sorry. Why have you come to see Joss?' I asked.

It was their turn to look confused. 'Apologies, I thought you knew. She was in the vicinity of a car that was set on fire a few weeks back. I've got the exact date here.' He took out his notepad.

'It's OK,' I said. I understood now. I returned to the centre of the room. 'You obviously aren't aware that Joss reported a serious sexual assault at the weekend. I thought you were here to interview her about that.'

Their expressions immediately changed and grew serious.

'We didn't know,' Mike said. 'That's a separate unit. This weekend?'

'Yes.'

He exchanged a glance with his colleague. 'We'll confirm it with the station, but I think we should probably leave this enquiry for now.' Joe nodded. 'We'll call them from the car and let you know what's decided.'

'Thank you,' I said. I followed them down the hall and saw them out.

As soon as I'd closed the front door I quickly ran upstairs and put on some clothes. My bedroom is at the front of the house and, once dressed, I discreetly looked out through my bedroom window. The police car was parked on the opposite side of the road and I could see the officers in the front talking on their radio, presumably to someone at the police station. The children hadn't woken, so I returned downstairs where I made a quick coffee, which I took into the front room. I could see the police car from behind the net curtains, and a few minutes later I saw Mike get out, leaving Joe in the car. I left my coffee mug in the front room and went to answer the doorbell.

'We've decided to leave this enquiry for now,' Mike said. 'Joss has enough to cope with.' Which I thought was a kind and sensible decision. 'Hope she's OK.'

I thanked him, we said goodbye and I closed the front door. I didn't know if their decision was based solely on the allegation Joss had made against Zach or if they were aware of the new one too, and it didn't matter. It was the right decision. Joss didn't need any more stress right now, and neither did I.

Joss woke just after 8.30 and came downstairs in her dressing gown. I asked her how she was and she said she felt a bit better and had slept well. I told her of the police visit and she too was relieved that she didn't have to answer questions about setting the car on fire now. 'I was very angry then,' she said pensively. 'I wouldn't do that now.'

'I'm pleased to hear it, Joss, and when the police come back you must tell them that.'

'I will.'

In my experience, once a child starts to disclose the abuse they've suffered their anger begins to leave them almost immediately, as a huge burden has been lifted. I could already see a lighter, more open and responsive side to Joss, and she wasn't always on the defensive now. She poured herself a juice and then went upstairs to shower and dress. Adrian was up and dressed next, and appeared in the kitchen, hungry as usual, just before nine o'clock. I scrambled his eggs while he toasted bread and I explained that I was expecting to spend most of the day dealing with something Joss had told me late last night. From being in a family that had fostered for many years, he understood the implications and didn't press me for details. He said that once he had his school things sorted and ready for tomorrow, he'd probably see a friend in the afternoon. We ate breakfast together and then he went up to his room.

Jill telephoned about twenty minutes later, having been updated about Joss's disclosure in respect of her stepfather by the team member on duty the night before. She began with a heartfelt sigh. 'Dear me, it never rains but it pours. Do you believe her?'

'Yes.'

'And Joss said she'd told her mother but wasn't believed?' This was significant, as Linda could be accused of covering up the abuse and failing to protect her daughter.

'That's what Joss said,' I confirmed.

'You know what her mother will say, don't you?' Jill said. 'That Joss has never liked Eric, resented him for trying to be her father, and has made this up to get rid of him.'

'I know, but I'm sure Joss is telling the truth.'

'And Joss is prepared to make a statement to the police?' Jill asked. This could be another indicator of the sincerity of a young person; if they were lying, they were likely to back down and withdraw the allegations at the mention of making a statement to the police.

'Yes, she is,' I said.

'OK. I'll telephone Amelia when she's had a chance to speak to the duty social worker. She'll want to talk to Joss as soon as possible. There will be concerns about her brother too, although Joss is saying she doesn't think he touched Kevin. Is Joss with you now?'

'She's upstairs.'

'How is she?'

'Relieved that it's finally out in the open, I think. She looks less anxious. She did say she should have told me sooner.'

'And the reason she didn't is because she thought you wouldn't believe her?' Jill asked.

'Yes. That's what she said.'

'I guess it makes sense.'

I then told Jill about the visit we'd had that morning from the police officers about the burning car.

'I'm glad common sense prevailed,' Jill said. 'I'll let Amelia know when I phone her. And when you have a moment, Cathy, can you write up your notes while it's still fresh in your mind? Then we'll have a copy ready on file if it's needed.'

'I will,' I said.

'And keep Joss with you today. I can't imagine she wants to go out, but Amelia will want to talk to her at some point.'

'All right.'

We said goodbye and I replaced the receiver. Lucy and Paula were up now, and I could hear their voices and Joss's as the three of them talked on the landing. When Lucy and Paula came down in their dressing gowns a short while later, they both looked very shocked.

'Joss told you?' I asked.

'Yes. It's awful. What a pervert Eric is,' Lucy said.

'He was supposed to be her new dad!' Paula said, disgusted.

And for a moment an uncomfortable thought flashed across my mind that Joss might have told them for dramatic effect, which would have given credence to her mother's assertion that she made things up for attention. But then we all handle trauma in different ways, and sharing it with her peers was probably Joss's way of coping – now that it was out in the open, she felt comfortable telling others she trusted. Not for the first time, though, I worried about the effect all of this was having on my children. Paula had gone very pale.

'Try not to worry,' I said to them both. 'Now Joss has been able to tell us, she'll receive the help she needs.'

'First her boyfriend and now her stepfather. It's dreadful,' Lucy said.

'Yes, it is,' I agreed.

I then told them, as I had Adrian, that my day would largely be taken up with Joss, which they understood, and I suggested that they might like to go out after lunch for a while, once they'd got everything ready for school in the morning. They decided to go into town together window shopping. Lucy had a birthday coming up and I asked her to look out for some present ideas.

They had some cereal and toast and then went upstairs to shower and dress. I sat in the living room and wrote up my log notes. There was a lot to write, and I used Joss's words as much as possible – a verbatim account – when she'd described the abuse. Although the telephone was silent, I knew there would be a lot going on at the social services, and as I wrote, I was on tenterhooks, half expecting it to ring at any moment.

Joss was also waiting for news and she came down a couple of times just to ask if I'd heard anything from her social worker or the police. I reassured her that I'd tell her as soon as I did. It would have helped her if she'd been able to go out with Lucy and Paula and take her mind off it, but that wasn't an option.

Although I was expecting the telephone to ring, I was completely unprepared for the next call. I was making lunch for us all before Adrian, Lucy and Paula went out. I answered the phone in the kitchen, expecting to hear Jill, Amelia or even the police, but it was Linda, distraught, angry and in tears.

'How could you?' she began. 'I can't believe what you've done. Why did you have to pass on all those lies to the social services? You know what Joss is like!'

I spoke calmly. 'Linda, I have to tell the social services what a child says if they make an allegation. I am sure it will be properly investigated.'

'Yes! They are investigating us!' she cried. 'They already think we're guilty. They're coming here this afternoon, and they want to see Kevin. My little boy. How could you, Cathy? Supposing they take him!' She broke down, sobbing.

'Linda,' I said gently, 'the social services won't just take Kevin. They can't remove him without a court order, and they wouldn't be able to get that unless there was a very good reason.'

'Well, there isn't!' she snapped. 'But how am I going to convince them after all the lies Joss has told? You've believed her, and they will too. You should have just ignored her.'

Which, of course, was what Linda had done.

'I can't believe you'd do this!' Linda cried. 'You've ruined my life, the two of you, with these lies. You can tell Joss she's never to set foot in my house again. I'm finished with her. That's it.' And with a sob, she put down the phone.

I took a deep breath. I could appreciate why Linda was so upset – she'd had a big shock, and now she felt threatened at the possibility that Kevin could be removed. She obviously loved her children, I didn't doubt that, but she'd failed to protect Joss, and she'd have to convince the social services that Kevin wasn't in any danger. Contrary to what I'd previously thought might happen, far from having any doubts about Eric, Linda now seemed even more convinced that her daughter was lying. I'm not sure I would have been so certain in her position, but then you never know how you would react in the face of trauma.

A few minutes later the phone rang again. 'Cathy, it's Jill. Are you free to talk?'

'Yes. Linda has just telephoned. She's very upset and angry and is blaming me.'

'What did she say?'

I told her.

'I'll mention it to Amelia when I next speak to her. It's not appropriate for Linda to be phoning you while she and Eric are being investigated. Although she's right that the social services have concerns around Kevin. Amelia wants to see Joss first – she'll phone you later with a time – and then she'll visit Linda and talk to Kevin.' Jill paused, and I knew she was choosing her words carefully. 'Cathy, I know you believe what Joss told you about her stepfather, and the social services are taking it seriously, but can you make sure Joss under-stands the gravity of her allegations? That Kevin could be taken into care? Don't frighten her, just make sure she knows the implications.'

'I will,' I said. 'Does Amelia have doubts that Joss is telling the truth, then?'

'She raised the question, as I did, of whether it was possible that Joss was doing this to get back at Eric because she resented him. But the department is taking Joss's allegations seriously and acting on them.'

'I'll speak to Joss and make sure she understands,' I confirmed.

'Thank you, Cathy. And if Linda telephones you again, tell her to call Amelia if she needs to speak to someone.'

'Thanks. I will.'

I replaced the handset and went upstairs to speak to Joss. I knew I had to be careful how I phrased what I'd been asked to say. It had taken a lot of courage for Joss to speak out and I didn't want to undermine the trust she'd placed in me and the social-care system by suggesting we didn't believe her. Her bedroom door was partly open, but nevertheless I knocked as usual. 'Come in,' her little voice called from the other side. 'Be careful where you step. I'm tidying up.'

I took one step into her room but couldn't go any further as the floor was covered with the contents of her drawers and wardrobe.

'I thought I'd sort out my stuff while I had the time,' she said.

'Excellent,' I said, impressed.

'I heard the phone ring – is there any news?' she now asked, looking at me anxiously.

'Jill just telephoned,' I said. 'Amelia will be coming to see us later. Then she'll visit your mother and Kevin. Joss, you need to prepare yourself for the fact that if the social services believe Kevin is at risk of being abused, they may take him into foster care.'

'But I told you, that perv didn't touch him. It was just me,' she blurted.

'I know. I've passed that on, and you can tell Amelia yourself when she visits. But the social services have to be certain Kevin is safe, and while Eric is in the house he could be at risk.'

'But Kev is only a little kid, and he's a boy,' Joss said naïvely. 'Perv wouldn't be interested in him.'

Despite all the news stories we see and hear in the media, many people struggle to believe in the existence of paedophile activity. 'Joss, love,' I said gently. 'If Eric is a paedophile, the fact that Kevin is a young boy won't stop him. I'm afraid paedophiles find young children sexually attractive, boys and girls.'

'That's horrible,' Joss said, visibly shaken.

'I know, so you understand why the social services need to make sure Kevin is safe.'

'Yes, but it's unfair if Kev has to leave home. It's perv who should have to leave.'

'I know, but that might not happen.' I didn't tell Joss that her mother was standing by Eric and her faith in him appeared to be unshakeable.

'If Kev has to go into foster care,' Joss said thoughtfully, 'can he come and live here? He could have my bed and I'll sleep on the floor. I don't mind.'

I smiled. 'Children in care have to have their own bedrooms,' I said. 'And anyway, it may not come to that. I just thought you should know in case.'

'I understand,' Joss said. 'As long as Kev is safe.'

So I had the confirmation Jill had requested, that Joss understood the impact her allegations could have on Kevin, and with it the added proof that she was telling the truth, not that I needed it.

'I'll leave you to your sorting out, then,' I said. 'I'll let you know when I hear more, and lunch won't be long.'

'Thanks, Cathy,' she said with a small smile, and returned to her clothes.

As I returned downstairs I thought again how Joss seemed like a different person now she'd spoken about the abuse she'd suffered at home and her allegations were being acted on. Here she was, in her room contentedly sorting out her clothes, which would have been unheard of a few days ago. I felt my talk with her had gone well and she appreciated that in order to protect Kevin he might have to go into care. I hadn't told her that her mother had telephoned, because there was nothing positive to say about the call and it would only have upset her.

I put the finishing touches to lunch and was about to call everyone to eat when the phone rang again. It was Jill, telling me that Amelia was aiming to be with us by three o'clock.

'The poor woman is so busy,' Jill said. 'I told her I'd phone you to save her time.'

'Thank you. I've spoken to Joss and she understands that Kevin might have to go into care.'

'And she was all right about that?'

'Well, she thought Eric should be the one to leave the house, but she appreciates that might not happen.'

'OK. You can tell Joss that Zach and Carl have been taken in for questioning by the police. Amelia will talk to her about that too when she sees her this afternoon.'

We said goodbye and I went straight upstairs to Joss's room. She'd heard the phone and then my footsteps approaching. 'Come in, Cathy,' she called before I'd knocked on her door. She looked at me expectantly.

'That was Jill again,' I said. 'Amelia will be coming to see us at about three o'clock this afternoon. And Zach and Carl have been taken in for questioning by the police.'

'Really? So soon?' Joss said, surprised.

'Oh, yes. Serious allegations have to be acted on straight away.'

'I'm glad I told you,' she said reflectively. 'I just wish I'd told you sooner about Eric, but I really felt like it was my fault and everyone would blame me.'

'Joss,' I said firmly, 'abuse is never the fault of the victim. Never, ever. Although the abuser might try to make them feel it is. Hear me and believe me, please.'

'I'll try,' she said quietly.

CHAPTER TWENTY-ONE

WAITING FOR NEWS

At three o'clock I was sitting with Joss in the living room, waiting for Amelia to arrive. We were the only ones in the house apart from Toscha, who'd just strolled into the room and was taking up residence on Joss's lap, circling to find herself the most comfortable position. Outside the day was overcast but not cold or wet; indeed, the air was quite humid for early September, and I'd left the patio door slightly open. Joss and I were making small talk, mainly about pets, as a distraction from the anxiety we were both feeling. Joss said she and Kevin had always wanted a cat or a dog, but Kevin was slightly asthmatic and had an allergy to animal fur, so they'd had to settle for a goldfish instead. Joss mused that when she was older and had a job and flat of her own, she was going to buy two dogs so they would be company for each other while she went out to work. I smiled and said that was nice, although dogs needed regular exercise, unlike cats, who could take themselves for a walk.

Amelia didn't arrive until 3.30 p.m. She came in flustered and apologized for being late. 'Don't worry,' I said. 'Would you like a drink?'

'Oh, yes. Coffee, please,' she said gratefully. 'Milk, but no sugar. Thank you.'

I showed her into the living room and left her talking to Joss while I made coffee. Little wonder she was stressed, I thought. She'd arrived at her desk on Monday morning to face a caseload that included two new serious allegations of abuse, in addition to her usual work. As with most local authorities, the funding wasn't available for more much-needed social workers. I returned to the living room with her cup of coffee and set it on the table within her reach. 'Thank you so much,' she said.

I sat on the sofa beside Joss as Amelia drank half of her coffee straight down and then set the cup in the saucer before looking up and addressing us.

'I'll talk to you both first, to update you,' Amelia said. 'Then I would like to talk to Joss alone.' I nodded. 'Joss tells me she's feeling a bit happier in herself now she's been able to tell us what has been going on at home.'

'Yes, she certainly seems more at ease,' I said.

'Good.' Then, looking at Joss, Amelia said, 'I'll be able to arrange some counselling for you, but not until after any court cases. If you begin therapy now it could weaken your evidence.' This was normal practice and it made some sense, as counselling helped a person overcome abuse so that harmful memories faded. 'But you know you can talk to me or Cathy at any time,' Amelia added.

'Yes,' Joss said, keeping her gaze down and stroking Toscha.

'I want to talk about what happened with Zach first,' Amelia said, glancing at the papers she held. 'Joss, you did very well going to the police station on Saturday straight after the attack. You were able to give a statement to the police, and you were examined by a doctor. I can appreciate what an ordeal that must have been and you did very well.' Joss nodded but didn't look up. 'When the results of the tests are known,' Amelia continued, 'the doctor will write her report. That will form part of the evidence, together with the statement you made and any other evidence the police gather. They will then make a decision on whether to prosecute, and we will be told.'

'Is there a chance the police might not prosecute?' I asked, feeling this was something Joss would want to know.

'It will depend on the strength of the evidence against them,' Amelia said. I glanced at Joss, but she didn't look up. I sincerely hoped there was enough evidence to prosecute Zach. Joss had been through so much, and for it not to go to court would be a big blow to her.

'Zach and Carl are being interviewed at the police station,' Amelia continued. 'When they've finished they will be released. Joss, it's important you don't have any contact with either of them. That means not going to Chelsea's flat or places where Zach and Carl hang out. If they approach you in the street, ignore them and tell me, Cathy or the police. Do you understand?'

'Yes,' Joss said, still not looking up.

'Good. I'll tell you as soon as I have any news, but don't expect to hear anything for some time. It takes many months for the police to fully investigate, so we have to be patient.'

'Will they talk to Chelsea?' Joss asked, finally glancing at Amelia.

'Possibly. I don't know. Why? Are you worried about something?'

'No, I just wondered.'

'OK. Do you have any other questions?'

'Will I have to go to the police station again?' Joss asked.

'Yes, very likely, to make a statement about your stepfather, but it may not be for a while, and it will be different to Saturday. You may be interviewed by Ann again, but you won't need another physical examination, and it will probably be a taped interview. I'll know more when I've spoken to the police.'

Joss nodded.

'You're being very brave,' Amelia said.

'She is,' I agreed.

Amelia paused, drained the rest of her coffee and then looked at Joss. 'When I leave here I shall be going to see your mother and Kevin. I believe Cathy has explained this to you?' We both nodded. 'Then the police are likely to want to question your stepfather.'

'He'll lie,' Joss said. 'Like he always does.'

'The police will be aware of that. They are highly trained and know which questions to ask to get to the truth. Is there anything else worrying you? Or anything you want to tell me that you haven't told Cathy?'

'Not really,' Joss said.

'I spoke to your mother on the phone this morning,' Amelia continued. Joss immediately looked up. 'One of the things she said was that for the time being she thinks it's better for everyone if you don't go home.'

'Why?' Joss blurted. 'Better for who? *Him?* It's my home and I want to see Kevin.'

'I know, but we can't be sure Eric won't be there, and at present your mother is very upset. If Kevin is brought into care then I will arrange for you to have contact with him, but for now it's best if you don't go home until we know what is happening.'

'That's not fair,' Joss protested.

'We need to do what Amelia tells us,' I said, lightly touching Joss's arm.

In the past I'd felt that Amelia had been naïve in the way she'd dealt with some of the issues relating to Joss, but now I felt she was handling this exactly right – sensitively but firmly, and telling Joss what she needed to know. Possibly she'd had a shock by what had happened, but she had a much stronger presence now, and I was seeing her in a new light.

'And the same restrictions apply to seeing Eric as they do to Zach and Carl,' Amelia said to Joss. 'These are serious allegations and while Eric is being investigated you mustn't have anything to do with him.'

'I wouldn't want to,' Joss said.

Then to me Amelia said, 'Eric will be told not to contact Joss, but if he does try to see her, refuse and refer him to me, please. Don't let him speak to her in person or on the telephone.'

'I understand,' I said. 'What about Linda, if she telephones?'

'She won't,' Joss said, scowling.

'There's no reason why Linda shouldn't talk to Joss if they both want to speak to each other,' Amelia said. 'But obviously not if it upsets Joss. Perhaps you could monitor it?'

I nodded.

'School starts tomorrow,' Amelia now said to Joss. 'Do you feel up to going?'

'Yes,' Joss said without hesitation.

'OK. But we'd all understand if you didn't want to go this week. You're under a lot of stress right now, and either Cathy or I would explain to the school.'

'I want to go,' Joss said.

'All right, but remember you have to come straight home after school,' Amelia said. 'No going to Chelsea's flat, or the shopping centre, or any of the other places you've been going.'

'I won't,' Joss said. 'I'm not daft.'

'I know you're not, love,' I said, 'but I'd feel happier if I took you and collected you in the car.'

Amelia and I both looked at Joss for her reaction. There was a moment's hesitation before she said, 'OK.'

'Good,' Amelia said, with a smile, and she made a few notes. Then, checking her watch, she looked at me. 'Cathy, if there's nothing else, I'd like to speak to Joss alone now, please.'

'Of course,' I said, and immediately stood. I left the room, closing the door behind me.

While they talked in private I took the opportunity to do a few jobs around the house that I'd put on hold with everything else that had been going on that day. I took the clean laundry upstairs and was distributing it around the bedrooms for the kids to put away when I heard the front door open and close as Lucy and Paula returned from shopping. I went to the top of the stairs and motioned to the living room. 'Joss and her social worker are in there,' I said quietly.

They understood that they weren't to be disturbed and came upstairs. We went into Paula's room where they showed me their purchases – some teen novels, nail varnish and body spray, bought from their allowances. Lucy had also seen a leather jacket she wanted for her birthday, so I said I'd go into town with her as soon as we had the opportunity, probably next Saturday, and if it was suitable I'd buy it for her.

'It really does suit her,' Paula said.

Presently we heard Joss call from downstairs, 'Amelia is going now!'

I went down as Joss came up to join Lucy and Paula. Amelia was standing by the front door. 'I really must go now to see Linda and Kevin,' she said. 'I'm late already. Joss is doing very well, and I'll phone you or Jill as soon as I have any news.'

We said goodbye and she left as she'd arrived – rushed off her feet and without enough hours in the day.

It was now five o'clock. I went into the living room, closed the patio door, collected up Amelia's empty cup and then went through to the kitchen to start making dinner. Adrian arrived home half an hour later and we all ate together at six, chatting and laughing, outwardly a normal, happy family enjoying their evening meal, if you didn't know what had happened to Joss. I glanced at her every so often and thought she was probably putting on a brave face, although she did seem far more relaxed and amicable now the abuse she'd been suffering was out in the open.

After dinner the children cleared away and then did their own thing, sometimes upstairs and sometimes downstairs, where I was. During the evening my thoughts often returned to what was unfolding away from my house. Amelia had been going to see Linda and Kevin. What had she learned from them? Perhaps nothing. Zach and Carl had been at the police station. Were they still there? What had they said? And Eric? Had he come home from work and found Amelia there? Or perhaps he was already being questioned by the police. I didn't know. Foster carers often have to wait on the sidelines for news while important and life-changing decisions are being made, and the wait can be agonizing. I guessed Joss must have been thinking about what was going on too, although she didn't say so until bedtime, when I went up to say goodnight.

'I hope Kevin is all right. Do you think he's still at home with Mum?'

'I would think so,' I said. Joss was sitting up in bed with her lamp on. I perched on the edge of the bed. 'It's a bit soon for any decision to have been made,' I said, although I knew that if a child was in immediate danger, they could be removed quickly with an Emergency Protection Order.

'I really want to see Kevin,' Joss said.

'I know, love, and Amelia said she'd arrange contact if he was brought into care.'

'I hope he's not,' Joss said. 'That's his home and he'll miss Mum. He'll be with strangers ... but I understand he has to be safe.'

I appreciated how difficult and worrying it was for children when they or their siblings were brought into foster care, especially when siblings couldn't be together.

Joss looked tired and soon gave a small yawn.

'I think you should try to get some sleep now – you've got school in the morning.'

'It seems ages since I was last at school with everything that has happened,' she said.

'It does,' I agreed. 'Are you sure you feel up to going tomorrow?'

'Yes, I want to,' Joss said. 'It'll help take my mind off what's going on. Miss Pryce won't be my form teacher any more – we have a new one – but she said at the end of last term that I could still talk to her any time, if I wanted to.'

'That was nice of her. She's very caring. Do you think you will tell her what's happened?'

'I don't know.' She stifled another yawn.

'Come on, love, snuggle down. You must be exhausted. I know I am.'

Joss hesitated and looked at me, so childlike and unpretentious now she was shedding the layers of hostility and anger that had been her armour for so long. 'Cathy?' she asked.

'Yes, love?'

'I know you've asked me loads of times before and I've always said no, but can I have a kiss and hug goodnight, please?'

My eyes immediately filled. 'Of course you can, love. Come here.' She moved closer and I encircled her in my arms, a child in need of protection and reassurance.

We held each other for some time and when she eventually drew back she was smiling. 'That was a nice hug,' she said. 'Just like Mum used to give me when I was little.'

I smiled too. 'Good, now snuggle down and try to get some sleep.'

She lay down, resting her head comfortably on the pillow, and I drew the duvet up to her chin. She looked up at me, her hair trailing out around her on the pillow. I gently stroked away a strand from her face and then kissed her forehead. 'Goodnight, love. Sleep well, and I'll see you in the morning.'

'Goodnight, Cathy, and thanks for being here for me.'

I kissed her again. 'You're welcome, love.'

I came out and then went round the landing, going in and out of the bedrooms, saying goodnight and dispensing hugs and kisses to my other children, including Adrian. As big as he was, he still liked his goodnight hug and kiss, unless he had a friend sleeping over and then I knew not to embarrass him. I went downstairs, locked up, settled Toscha for the night and then had an early night myself. I was in bed by ten o'clock and was asleep as soon as my head touched the pillow.

I slept soundly, waking at 6.15 a.m. with the alarm clock. As usual on a school day I showered and dressed before I woke the children, and did they take some waking! It's always a wrench for them to get up at the start of a new term, and they needed a lot of cajoling to fall into the school routine. Although I woke them in plenty of time, there wasn't a minute to spare. Joss and I had to leave the house before they did and my departing shot was: 'Will you all get a move on, please, or you'll be late for your first day, and that won't look good!' But I trusted them not to be late.

Most young people don't want to chat first thing in the morning and Joss was no exception. She switched on the radio as soon as we were in the car, although I'm not sure she was really listening to it. Five minutes from school she turned it off and looked at me thoughtfully. 'Do you think Kevin is going to school today?' she asked.

'Yes, I would think so,' I said.

'Even if he's in foster care?'

'Yes, the carer will take him, like I'm taking you.'

'He won't like that. Mum always takes him on her way to work,' Joss said.

'I know it will be a bit different, but he'll be fine. Try not to worry.'

How Joss was going to concentrate on her school work I had no idea, although I agreed it was probably better for her to be in school than at home with little to occupy her thoughts and only me for company. I parked the car as close as I could to the main entrance of the school and we said goodbye. As

Joss got out someone called her name, and with a smile and a wave she went over to join them. I waited until she'd gone into the building before I drove away. On the way back I stopped off for essential groceries and then went home to await any news. The house was uncannily quiet with everyone at school. Toscha must have felt it too, for she kept wandering aimlessly from room to room as though looking for everyone.

'They're at school – they'll be back later,' I reassured her, and she answered with a meow.

Although I was busy, with housekeeping, fostering training and paperwork, I was continually listening out for the phone and wondering how Joss was faring at school. The telephone didn't ring until the middle of the afternoon, and I rushed to answer it.

'Cathy, it's Jill.'

'Yes?' I asked expectantly.

'No news yet. I'm phoning to check you've remembered I'm due to visit you tomorrow morning at ten o'clock.'

'Yes, it's in my diary. I haven't forgotten.' This was one of Jill's scheduled four-weekly visits.

'I'll phone you as soon as I hear anything, otherwise I'll see you tomorrow.'

'Yes, OK.' With a feeling of anticlimax, I returned the phone to its cradle.

When I collected Joss from school later that afternoon her first question was naturally, 'Have you heard anything about Kev?'

'Not yet. It could take some time for the social services to complete their investigation and decide what to do for the best.'

'Miss Pryce came to find me at lunch break,' Joss said. 'She asked me if I'd had a nice summer.'

I looked at Joss. 'What did you say?'

'That it was all right, but I'd had to talk to the police about some stuff that happened. I didn't tell her what. I didn't want to go into it all again. I've told you and Amelia, and the police, and I know I'll have to see the police again, but I don't want to keep going over it all. I'm not telling my friends either. I'm trying to forget it.'

'I completely understand,' I said. 'But it was nice of Miss Pryce to ask after you.'

Joss nodded and looked thoughtful. 'I had to tell her about something else,' she said after a moment as I drove. 'She's going to sort it out.'

I glanced at her. 'Oh, yes?'

'Someone Chelsea knows has been spreading rumours about me, saying I got Zach and Carl into trouble and I've been telling lies about them. I told Miss Pryce and she said she'd look into it straight away.'

'Good. That was the right thing to do.'

Joss then changed the subject and chatted about her day at school, and the rest of it seemed quite positive.

Paula, Lucy and Adrian were already in when Joss and I arrived home, and I asked each of them how their first day had gone. Adrian said fine, Paula said she was tired from having to wake up early and Lucy said her brain hurt from all the learning she'd had to do and that it shouldn't be allowed. They relaxed while I made dinner, and after we'd eaten they read for a while and then watched some television. Around 8.30 p.m. we all began taking turns in the bathroom, ready for a reasonably early night. I find it always takes a few days to adjust to a new term and I too longed for the more relaxed routine of the holidays. When I said goodnight to Joss she said she wanted a kiss and a hug, as she had done the night before, and was sitting up in bed ready. Since the weekend I'd noticed Joss was making a bigger effort to integrate with my family, reaching out to us at every opportunity and wanting to be part of it. It was just a pity it had taken such a horrendous event to bring this about. I didn't know how long Joss would be with us, but I thought it could be long term, as there was no chance of her returning home now. As she hugged me she asked again if I thought Kevin was still at home. I had to say I didn't know, but that I was hoping to hear more when I saw Jill the following day.

As it turned out I did hear more, although it wasn't what I'd imagined it would be – events in fostering rarely are.

CHAPTER TWENTY-TWO

MISSING

On Wednesday morning, having taken Joss to school, I went straight home to prepare for Jill's visit at ten o'clock. Jill was always very punctual, and part of her visit would be quite formal as she checked and signed my log notes, assessed my training requirements and made sure my fostering was meeting Joss's needs. By 10 a.m. I had all the paperwork ready beside me on the sofa in the living room and was waiting for the doorbell to ring. Instead, the phone rang, and it was Jill.

'Sorry, Cathy, I'm running late. I'm leaving the office now. I'll update you when I see you, but I've just finished speaking to Amelia and I'm afraid it's not good news.'

Jill said a hurried goodbye and I was left to imagine the worst for the next agonizing half-hour – the time it took Jill to drive from her office to my house. When I answered the door she looked very serious and came in with a no-nonsense, business-like efficiency.

'Would you like a coffee?' I offered as she strode down the hall towards the living room.

'Not now, thank you, Cathy. Maybe later.'

In the living room I returned to the sofa as Jill took one of the chairs. Placing her bag on the floor beside her, she then sat upright, hands in her lap, and looked at me.

'Monday,' she began, coming straight to the point. 'After Amelia left you she went to see Linda and Kevin.' I nodded. 'This is what happened. Linda was, and still is, convinced Joss is lying – about Eric and Zach. Linda told Amelia that Joss has never liked Eric, bitterly resented his intrusion into the family and has often threatened to leave if he didn't. She also said she thought Joss should have psychiatric care in a hospital, as she's so delusional.' I went to speak but Jill held up her hand. 'I know, of course she's not. Joss could do with some counselling, but she certainly doesn't need hospitalizing.'

'Amelia spoke to Linda first,' Jill continued. 'Then she asked to see Kevin alone. Linda was reluctant to let her see him to begin with. She said she didn't want him involved, as it was about Joss. But Amelia explained that when one child in a family discloses abuse then any other children are assessed as a matter of practice. Linda wasn't happy and wanted to phone Eric for advice – she appears to rely on him heavily – but he wasn't available, so eventually she agreed to let Amelia speak to Kevin alone. Kevin told Amelia there had been a lot of arguments in the family, between Joss, Mum and Dad – he calls Eric "Dad" – and it had upset him. He said he missed Joss very much and wished she'd come home so they could all live together again. He was unaware of Joss's allegations of abuse. Amelia steered the conversation to Kevin's relationship with Eric and much of it seemed positive. Kevin said he liked Eric; that he played with him a lot, helped him with his school work and bought him presents. But when Amelia asked him if there was anything he didn't like about Eric, Kevin admitted that he didn't like the way Eric put him to bed when his mother was out, and also didn't like it when he had his bath. Amelia asked him what exactly he didn't like, and Kevin said that he was old enough to wash himself and didn't like having his private parts washed for him. He wouldn't say anything further about Eric after that.'

'He didn't have to,' I said. I had that dreadful sinking feeling that comes from knowing a child has been abused.

'No,' Jill agreed, 'but obviously the social services have to be certain. Amelia then spoke to Linda again and put to her what Kevin had said. She was very upset, but defended Eric. She said of course he bathed Kevin and put him to bed, it was what fathers did, and he was trying his best to be a good dad. She then suggested that perhaps Amelia had misunderstood what Kevin had said, which she hadn't. Amelia asked her if Kevin had ever told her he didn't want her to go out and leave him with Eric. She admitted he had, but that this was because – like many young children – he didn't like his mummy going out, and it had nothing to do with Eric.

'Then Eric came home,' Jill continued. 'Amelia thinks Linda had managed to speak to him on the phone while she'd been talking to Kevin, because he seemed prepared. He was unnaturally calm, considering the serious nature of the allegations being made against him – by Joss and now Kevin. He said Joss must have put Kevin up to it because she hated him so much, and Linda agreed. Although Eric was calm, Linda was distraught and kept telling Amelia that Eric did his best for the children. Eric asked Amelia what would happen now, and Amelia explained that she'd report back to her manager and she'd advise them of the outcome of that meeting. Yesterday afternoon the social services held a child-protection strategy meeting and it was decided that there were sufficient concerns to bring Kevin into care.' Jill sighed. 'There have already been too many missed opportunities to help Joss; they couldn't afford to make another mistake with Kevin.'

'What do you mean by "missed opportunities"?' I asked. 'Joss only disclosed that Eric had been abusing her at the weekend.'

'Yes, but it seems Linda had told Amelia last year that Joss was making up lies about Eric – without giving any details. With hindsight, Amelia feels she should have delved further and asked questions about what Joss was saying, but because Linda was being cooperative and working with the department, and there was so much going on with Joss, it got missed.'

'I can understand that,' I said. 'When I think of all the times Joss referred to Eric as a creep and how much she hated him, I wonder why I didn't spot the warning signs sooner.'

'Because you were so busy dealing with Joss's challenging behaviour,' Jill said. 'Don't blame yourself. Joss was a very angry young person, although of course we now know why. Her behaviour wasn't only the result of her father's death and her mother remarrying, but also because she was being abused by her stepfather and her mother didn't believe her.'

'Exactly,' I said. 'I feel I could have been more aware and should have better protected her, but that contract of behaviour didn't help. I said all along that it was wrong to allow a thirteen-year-old out until late nearly every night of the week.'

'Amelia sees that too now,' Jill said. 'She admits that with hindsight she would have done many things differently. She's taken a lot away from this case and has been on a sharp learning curve.'

'Her and me too,' I said, ruefully.

'Joss is going to need a lot of support, and it won't be coming from her mother while she's refusing to believe Joss and defending Eric.'

'I know. I'll do all I can. So when will Kevin come into care?' I asked. 'Pity I haven't got a spare bedroom.'

'Tomorrow, I think. We're trying to find a carer in the area so Kevin can go to the same school.'

'Joss keeps asking about him. She's worried. Shall I tell her he's going into care tomorrow?'

'I don't see why not, but let me ask Amelia first. I'll be speaking to her again later today. I'll phone you and let you know. Also, Joss will need to make a statement to the police about Eric. Amelia hopes she'll be able to go with her, but if not she's asked if you could go. I said I was sure you would. She'll let us know the date as soon as she knows.'

I nodded. 'What's happening with the Zach and Carl investigation?'

'They've been released from police custody, but we're not expecting to hear anything further for some time, while the police investigate. I know Amelia has spoken to Joss about not having any contact with them, and she'll let us know when she has the police report.' Jill now dipped her hand into her bag and took out a pen and folder. 'Before you give me an update on how Joss has been doing and we go through any other business, could I have that coffee, please?'

'Yes, of course.' I stood.

'And a biscuit, please, if you have one,' she added.

I paused and looked at her with a smile. 'Jill, when have you ever known me not to have a biscuit in the house?'

'Chocolate digestive?'

'Absolutely.'

While Jill drank her coffee and ate the chocolate biscuits, which were not only her favourite but my family's too, I updated her on Joss. She made notes and then went through her checklist of questions, which formed part of every supervisory visit and covered Joss's education, her physical and mental health, contact arrangements, compliance with the care plan, times I'd had to use out-of-hours emergency cover and any changes in my household. Jill finished by reading and signing my log notes and arranging a date for her next visit. Reassuring me that I was doing a good job she left, saying she'd phone when she'd spoken to Amelia.

It was now after midday. I made a sandwich lunch, which I ate while reading through the printouts Jill had left on forthcoming training events. My thoughts kept returning to Linda and the anxiety and pain she must have been going through. Amelia would have notified her after the strategy meeting of the decision to remove Kevin and had probably asked her to pack some clothes and toys for him to take with him. How ever was she coping? I couldn't begin to imagine. Her sorrow must be immeasurable and my heart went out to her. Yes, I appreciated that she'd failed to protect her children, didn't believe them and was still siding with Eric, but she was their mother and was about to lose her second child, which was inconceivably heartbreaking.

Jill telephoned shortly before I was due to leave to collect Joss from school and said that Amelia didn't want Joss told at present that Kevin was going into care; I should wait until after the move, when I could reassure Joss that Kevin was settling in. 'To be honest, Cathy,' Jill said, 'we're struggling to find a carer for Kevin. All our local carers are full. We may have to place him out of the county, which will mean either a change of school for him or a very long car journey to and from his present school.' This was a familiar problem. There were never enough foster carers for the number of children coming into care, and sometimes children had to be placed many miles from their home and in an entirely different part of the country.

When I collected Joss from school she asked about Kevin almost immediately. I said Jill didn't know any more, but she'd phone us as soon as she did.

Joss sighed. 'So when can I see him?'

'Amelia will arrange contact –' and I nearly said 'once Kevin is settled in care', but stopped myself and said instead, 'if Kevin is brought into care.'

'But what if he isn't?' Joss asked. 'What if he stays at home? How will I see him? I'm not allowed to go home because of the creep being there, and Mum doesn't want me there anyway.'

'I'll ask Amelia,' I said evasively, knowing that before long I'd be able to tell Joss the arrangements that had been made for Kevin. As it turned out I didn't have to tell her – she found out, and in very distressing circumstances.

It was seven o'clock that evening. We'd had dinner and the children were now in various locations around the house, finishing homework, reading, listening to music or generally chilling out. The phone rang and Lucy, who was passing the phone table in the hall, answered. She then shouted through to Joss, who was in the living room, 'Joss! It's for you.'

I immediately left what I was doing in the front room and went to Lucy in the hall. She was just replacing the handset as Joss picked up the extension in the living room.

'Who is it?' I asked Lucy.

'Joss's mother,' Lucy said. She saw my face drop. 'Sorry, I thought she was allowed to speak to her.'

'She was. It's OK, you weren't to know.'

Although Amelia had previously said there was no reason why Linda couldn't talk to Joss, that was before Kevin had disclosed abuse and the decision had been made to bring him into care. I hurried down the hall and into the living room. I would monitor the call and do what I could, but I knew straight away from Joss's expression that Linda was already telling her the devastating news. I hovered indecisively for a moment and then sat on the sofa beside Joss as Linda continued talking and Joss listened, staring straight ahead, her face pale and her body tense. I couldn't hear what Linda was saying, just the rise and fall of her distressed voice.

Joss looked at me, horror etched on her face. 'They think Kev has been abused too,' she said as her mother continued. 'They're taking him into care, but Mum is going to run away with him.'

'She mustn't do that,' I said, even more concerned. 'Tell her.'

'Mum, listen,' Joss tried, but Linda was sobbing. 'Here, you talk to her,' Joss said, thrusting the phone into my hand.

'Linda,' I said. 'It's Cathy.'

'What?' she blurted between sobs. 'Haven't you caused enough trouble?'

'Linda, I'm trying to help. Don't think about running away with Kevin; it will make things a whole lot worse.'

'It can't get any worse. I'm going to lose my other child.'

'Linda, listen. Please. If you disappear with Kevin the social services will notify the police and they'll have every police officer in the country looking for you both. They'll alert the ports and airports, and when you're found it will make your case a great deal worse.'

'Case! You sound like one of them. Leave me alone. I wish I'd never been born.'

'Think of Kevin and how distressing it would be for him if you ran away,' I tried. 'Nothing has been proven yet, and it may be that Kevin is allowed to return to you once the social services are satisfied he will be safe.'

'I'm not taking that risk,' Linda said, and the line went dead.

I immediately dialled Linda's number, but she didn't answer. Joss stared at me in horror, her eyes filling. 'What shall we do?' she asked.

'Keep trying to phone her back,' I said. 'I'll see if I can talk some sense into her.'

I tried again, but the phone rang and rang.

'I'm going to have to report it,' I said at last. 'Did she say where she was going?'

'No, only that she was going tonight.'

I now pressed the number for Homefinders. Michael, on out-of-hours duty that night, answered. I quickly told him what Linda had said and the circumstances leading up to it. Joss sat beside me, anxious and wide-eyed with fear.

'I'll phone the duty social worker straight away,' Michael said. 'They'll contact the police. I suppose Linda and the child could still be at home. If not, they can't have got far. And Joss doesn't have any idea where they could be heading?'

'No.'

'All right. I'll get back to you.'

I replaced the handset and looked at Joss. 'That's all we can do,' I said.

Nearly an hour passed and then the duty social worker telephoned. 'Amelia has given the police a description of the missing persons,' he said. 'Ideally they'd like a photograph. Do you have one?'

I thought for a moment. 'I don't, but Joss has a family portrait in her bedroom. It's of her, her mother and brother. Will that do?'

'Is it recent?'

'Reasonably. Last year.'

'It should do. Does she have one of her stepfather too? It seems he might be with them.'

'No, she doesn't. I'm sure.'

'OK. Can you take the photo to the police station?'

'Now?'

'Yes, as soon as possible, please. And obviously if any of them contact you, phone us or the police straight away.'

'I will.'

I replaced the handset and turned to Joss who, having heard the phone ring, had come into the living room. 'The police have asked for a photograph. It's usual with a missing person,' I explained. 'The framed photograph on the shelf in your bedroom – is that the only one you have with you?'

'Yes. I've got a small one of my dad in my purse, but they're not having that.'

'They won't need it,' I said. 'Just the one showing your mum and Kevin. We'll have to remove it from the frame first.' I knew this from having to supply a photograph previously when a teenager I was fostering went missing.

I went upstairs with Joss and we carefully removed the photograph from the frame.

'I didn't know you had a photograph of your father,' I said gently as I put the frame to one side.

'It's just of me and him,' Joss said quietly. 'It's one of the last ones taken. I keep it with me at all times. It's like it makes me feel closer to him, as if he's by my side.'

'That's lovely,' I said, and I saw her eyes fill.

Downstairs I found a large, strong envelope to put the photograph in for protection. Joss wanted to come with me to the station, which was understandable. We quickly told the others where we were going and then slipped on our shoes and jackets and called goodbye. There was a chorus of 'Bye', 'See you later' and 'Take care'. Outside, the night air was damp but not cold, typical of early autumn, and a slight wind blew.

As we climbed into the car Joss asked, 'Is *he* with Mum and Kevin?'

'The police think he could be,' I said.

Her silence and look of anguish said it all.

CHAPTER TWENTY-THREE

THE ENDLESS WAIT

It was 9.15 p.m. when we entered the police station – our second visit within a week. I recognized the duty officer at the desk from Saturday. He recognized us too and looked mildly surprised.

'Good evening,' he said. 'How can I help you?'

We crossed to the counter and I explained that Joss's mother and brother had been reported missing and we'd been asked to bring in a photograph. Joss slid the envelope across the counter.

'I'm afraid I don't know anything about this,' he said. 'Please take a seat and I'll check with my colleagues.'

He took the envelope and disappeared through the door at the rear. Joss and I sat in the waiting area beside a couple of very talkative teenage girls who, we quickly learned, had reported their dog missing and were now checking to see if it was in the police compound.

Five minutes later the duty officer reappeared and called us to the desk. He said the officer who was dealing with the missing persons was on the telephone right now, but we should write our contact details on the envelope and he'd make sure he got it.

'What will happen to my photo?' Joss asked.

'We'll take a copy and circulate it. Then we'll return it to you.'

He passed me a pen and I wrote Joss's name and our address and telephone number on the envelope and handed it back. 'Thanks,' he said. 'Someone will be in touch.' And that was it. There was nothing more we could do but wait.

Joss was quiet as I drove home, but as we turned the corner from the high road I saw her attention go to a group standing on the street. 'Do you know them?' I asked.

'They're some of the crowd from Dave and Chelsea's. I wonder why they're out here and not at the flat. There's always a party there on Thursdays. It's when they get their benefits.' Which presumably meant they would all know Zach and Carl.

'Joss, you know you have to keep away from them and that flat,' I reminded her.

'Yes, I know. It used to seem like fun there, but it doesn't any more.'

At home, Adrian, Paula and Lucy had taken turns in the bathroom, so Joss was able to go straight in. Lucy was in Paula's room, both of them waiting to hear how we'd got on at the police station. Matters affecting a foster child, positive and negative, impact on the whole family – we share and celebrate their good news and worry over the bad and distressing. While Joss was in the bathroom, I went to Lucy and Paula and reassured them that the police would find Joss's mother and brother soon.

'What will happen to them when they're caught?' Lucy asked.

'Will Joss's mum be put in prison?' Paula wanted to know.

'Hopefully not,' I said. 'Although she will be in trouble for taking Kevin away.'

'So you can't ever take us away?' Paula asked, puzzled.

'That's different,' I said. 'We're not being investigated by the social services. Kevin was considered at risk, and Linda has done the wrong thing and put him at more risk by running away.'

'But she's not a bad person, is she?' Paula asked. 'She's not hurting Kevin?'

'No, but she failed to protect him, which is why he was being taken into care.'

'Protect him from that perv?' Lucy asked.

Joss had clearly told Paula and Lucy what had happened, so there was no reason why I shouldn't answer their questions.

Once the girls were as reassured as they could be – although none of us would be happy until Linda and Kevin were found safe and well – I said goodnight to Paula, while Lucy went to her room. I then said goodnight Lucy and finally to Adrian. He was in bed, reading by the light of his lamp.

'Everything all right?' he asked. Adrian had a different disposition to the girls and I knew he wouldn't want all the details, just to know that Joss was OK.

'Yes,' I said. 'Joss is getting ready for bed now. Are you all right? How's the new term going at school?'

'Good,' he said, setting down his book. 'I'll be late back tomorrow. I've got rugby practice after school. I'm in the team.'

'Great!' I said. 'Well done.'

'And I'm in the swimming team,' he added modestly.

'That's fantastic. You should have told me sooner.'

He shrugged. 'There was a lot going on.'

'But never so much that I haven't time to listen to your good news,' I said. Adrian wasn't one to boast about his achievements. 'I'm very proud of you, son,' I said, and kissed his head.

'I'm proud of you too, Mum, but don't ruffle my hair.'

I did anyway, and having said goodnight I came out.

Joss was in her room now, waiting for me to say goodnight. She looked very worried, unsurprisingly, and I sat on the edge of the bed. 'I'm sure the police will find them soon,' I said. 'There aren't many places you can hide with a child.'

'I hope Mum doesn't leave Kev alone with *him* like she used to,' Joss said. She'd never been able to use Eric's name.

'I'm sure she won't,' I said. 'Try not to worry.'

'I'll kill him if he hurts Kev.' Her eyes filled and I took her hand between mine. 'I can't think of anywhere they could be,' she said. 'That creep didn't have any friends. There's my nana and grandpa, but they never liked him, so they wouldn't have gone there. And anyway, we haven't see them in a long while.'

I sat with Joss for some time, stroking her hand and reassuring her as best I could that her mother would look after Kevin and they would be found soon. Eventually she said she'd try to get some sleep and snuggled down. I gave her a kiss and hug goodnight and came out.

I was half expecting someone from the police station to telephone, but when no one had called by eleven o'clock I went to bed. Exhausted but too worried to sleep, I lay for over an hour in the dark, agonizing over where Linda and Kevin could be and if they were safe. I appreciated that Linda's act had been a 'fight or flight' response and she hadn't meant Kevin any harm, but to flee with the person who'd been accused of abusing her children was totally irresponsible and would make her situation with the social services much, much worse.

The following morning we fell into the school routine again, but of course, as I woke Joss, Lucy and then Paula, their first response was to ask if I'd heard anything. I had to tell them I hadn't. When I woke Adrian he groaned and turned over, which is his usual response to being woken for school. However, when he came downstairs for breakfast he said to Joss, 'How are you doing? You must be worried. I hope your mum and brother are found soon.'

I could see she appreciated it. 'Thanks, Adrian; that's kind,' she said with a small smile.

Joss and I left the house first, and once in the car Joss switched on the radio, clearly not wanting to talk. When I dropped her at school I said, 'Take care, love. See you later.' She nodded and went in. I didn't go straight home but drove to the supermarket on the edge of town, as I needed to do a big grocery shop. Once I was home and I'd unpacked, I telephoned Jill and told her I'd taken the photograph into the police station the evening before. She thanked me and said the social services had taken out a court order in respect of Kevin, which would give them greater powers. It wasn't necessary to do so for Joss, as she was already in care and therefore not at risk of harm. Jill asked how Joss was and I told her that she was obviously very worried but had gone to school as usual. 'And she has no idea where her mother and brother could be?'

'No. She mentioned her mother's parents, but they've never liked Eric so they're not close.'

'The police will have covered that. Family and friends are the first place they look for a missing person,' Jill said.

I heard nothing further on Thursday and our anxious wait for news of Joss's mother and brother continued. On a positive note, Adrian had a good rugby practice after school, Lucy said she was going to try for the school netball team and Paula had been praised by a teacher for a piece of written work she'd done in history, so I congratulated them all. Tired from their first week back at school, they were in bed at 9.30 p.m., and having said goodnight to them I sat with Joss until she fell asleep. When I still hadn't heard from the police or social services by Friday lunchtime, I was frustrated and also a little angry. I was hoping that someone would telephone, even if it was only to say that there hadn't been any developments, so when the phone rang at 12.45 I answered it immediately with trepidation and relief. But it wasn't the social services or the police; it was Miss Pryce.

'Is this a good time to call?' she asked. 'I wanted a word with you about Joss.'

'Yes,' I said. I thought Joss had probably vented her anger and frustration at school, or had broken down crying, unable to cope.

But Miss Pryce's voice was upbeat as she said, 'I thought you'd like to know that Joss has had a really good first week back at school. I've had feedback from most of her teachers and she's attended all her lessons, hasn't been disruptive in class and has sat quietly, listening. Neither has she been leaving the school at lunchtime. This is a huge improvement since last term and we're all very pleased.'

'Excellent,' I said, mustering as much enthusiasm as I could. While I was obviously pleased Joss had turned over a new leaf, I knew there were other reasons why she was quiet and staying in at lunchtime, which Miss Pryce clearly wasn't aware of – and it wasn't for me to tell her.

'So I wanted to say well done,' Miss Pryce continued chirpily. 'Joss has obviously had a very good summer with you. She's come back to school a different child.'

'That is good,' I said. 'Thank you for telling me. I'll pass it on to Joss.'

'There's no need,' she said. 'I saw Joss at morning break. I always like to give the students positive feedback as soon as possible, especially if there have been behavioural issues in the past.'

'Thank you,' I said again. It was all I could say.

When I collected Joss from school that afternoon the first thing I told her was that there hadn't been any news about her mother and brother. She sighed heavily and slammed the car door shut. The next thing I told her was about Miss Pryce's telephone call. 'So well done, I'm very pleased with you,' I said. 'I know this has been a difficult week, but you've coped well.'

She shrugged despondently and turned on the radio, signalling that she didn't want to talk.

I could understand why Joss was running out of patience. The worry of her mother and brother being in hiding with Eric must have been excruciating, and my words of reassurance and kindly meant platitudes sounded jaded and hollow. She didn't say anything during the drive home, and when we got in the others knew from her obvious dejection that there was no news and she wanted to be left alone. We all ate together at six o'clock, but without our usual Friday-evening light-heartedness at the start of the weekend. Once we'd finished our meal and cleared away, Adrian, Lucy and Paula went to do their homework so it wasn't hanging over them all weekend, and Joss ambled into the living room.

'Would you like me to help you with your homework?' I offered. I thought it might help take her mind off the worry for a while.

She sat on the sofa, looking very downhearted, and gave a small nod. I sat next to her. 'Cathy,' she said, 'before we start, I was thinking I might phone my nana and grandpa.'

'Oh yes?' I said, surprised.

'I know I haven't spoken to them in a long while, but we used to be close. And with Mum and Kev gone, they're the only real family I have.'

I felt so sorry for her. 'I understand,' I said. 'When was the last time you saw them?'

'About a year ago. Before I left home. I'm sure they wouldn't mind if I phoned them now.'

'Do you have their telephone number?' I asked. 'I haven't got it.'

'I know it off by heart,' Joss said. 'I used to phone them every Friday evening to tell them what sort of week I'd had. It started after Dad died and stopped when I left home.'

A lump rose in my throat. 'Joss, I wish you'd told me that before. You could have phoned them from here every Friday.'

'I didn't really think about it until now,' she said. 'And I was always out on a Friday evening.' Which was true.

Yet while it seemed a good idea for Joss to be in touch with her grandparents again, I had some reservations. Given the lapse in time since they'd last had contact, and that they would

273

have been told their daughter and grandson were missing and must be worried sick, it was difficult to know what their reaction would be. People deal with grief and stress in different ways and it was possible they might blame Joss for causing trouble and lying, as her mother had done. However, Joss wanted to phone them and I could stay close and intervene if the call became distressing for her.

'I'm sure they won't mind if I phone,' Joss said again. 'They're really nice people. I should have kept in touch.'

'OK, but remember they're likely to be very worried and upset.'

'I know,' Joss said.

I passed her the handset. She keyed in the number and then, when it started ringing, she tilted the handset a little away from her ear towards me so I could hear too. As it rang I could see Joss growing increasingly nervous, and she began fidgeting with the cuff on her jersey. Then a woman's voice answered and stated the phone number.

'Nana?' Joss said very quietly. 'It's Joss.'

There was a second's pause and then, 'Joss! Oh my! It's so good to hear from you. We've been talking about you. How are you, love?' I was relieved.

'Not too bad, Nana,' Joss said sweetly.

'Are you well?' her nana asked.

'Yes. Are you?'

'Yes, thank you, love. But we've missed you so much.'

'I've missed you too,' Joss said. I could see tears welling in her eyes. I placed my hand on her arm to reassure her.

'I'm so pleased you've got in touch,' her nana said. 'I thought you would eventually. We used to be a close family before all of this. Are you still living with the foster carer?'

'Yes. Cathy.'

'Oh, love. It'll be so nice when you can all live together again as a family. I hope it won't be too long.'

'Yes,' Joss said quietly, clearly very emotional.

'Fancy you phoning on a Friday,' her nana said, brightening up. 'Do you remember all those chats we used to have every Friday evening? You used to tell me all about your week at school, what you'd been doing in lessons, who your best friend was and even what you'd eaten for your school dinner. I loved those chats.' I heard her voice tremble.

'I did too,' Joss said.

'Anyway, love, enough of me. I know you'll want to talk to the others.'

Joss looked at me, puzzled. 'Grandpa?' she asked her nana.

'Yes, he'll want to speak to you, but talk to your mum first. She will be pleased you've phoned.'

'Mum!' Joss exclaimed. 'Is Mum there?'

'Yes, of course, pet. I'll call her now.'

'What?' Joss said, turning to me, the colour draining from her face.

We heard her nana call 'Linda!' Then she said to Joss, 'She's coming.'

'Is Kev there too?' Joss asked, shocked.

'Yes, of course. He's with Grandpa. Speak to them when you've spoken to your mother.'

'Nana, is my stepfather there?' Joss asked tightly.

'Good heavens, no, love. Of course not. Not after what he's done. Your mother's told us what happened and it's shocking. I just wish we'd known sooner.'

There are times in life when you don't have the information you need to make an informed decision, but a decision is

275

required. With no idea what was going on or what part Joss's grandparents had played in their daughter and grandson's disappearance, I was tempted to take the handset from Joss and find out. I was sure Joss wouldn't mind, for she was looking as shocked and confused as I felt. But Linda was already on the phone. 'Hello, Joss?' her mother said in a small voice.

'Mum, what's going on? You're supposed to be missing. The police are looking for you.'

'I can't talk now,' Linda said under her breath, presumably so her parents couldn't hear. 'I'll try to phone you later.'

'No. I want to talk to you now!' Joss demanded.

'I can't, not now.' There was desperation in Linda's voice. 'Please, love. I'm sorry. I'll phone as soon as I can, I promise. Kevin is fine, so there is no need for you to worry.'

'Mum!' Joss said. But the line went dead. Joss and I stared at each other.

CHAPTER TWENTY-FOUR

UNBELIEVABLE

'Let me phone her back,' I said, taking the handset from Joss. I cleared the line and pressed redial.

The phone rang about half a dozen times and then Joss's nana answered. 'Hello?' she said tentatively.

'It's Cathy, Joss's foster carer.'

'Oh, I see. I don't understand what's going on here. My daughter was supposed to be talking to my granddaughter, but she's fled upstairs, crying. She's saying she has to leave straight away.'

'She mustn't do that,' I said. I didn't know what Joss's nana had been told, but I guessed it probably wasn't the truth. 'I'm sorry, I don't know your name.'

'Joan.'

'Joan, I'm not sure what's going on either, but we need to ask you – did you know that Linda, Kevin and Eric are registered as missing?'

'Missing? No. What do you mean?'

'They left home on Wednesday evening and haven't been heard of since. No one knew where they'd gone, because Linda didn't leave a forwarding address. The police have been looking for them.'

'What?' Joan exclaimed. 'But Linda and Kevin have been here with us all the time. I don't know where Eric is and I don't care. Linda didn't tell anyone where she was going because she's left her husband and doesn't want him to find her.'

'So Eric hasn't been there at all?'

'No. I wouldn't have him in my house again after what he's done.'

'And the police and social services haven't been in touch with you?'

'No. Why should they? It's Eric they're looking for.'

I realized Joan knew some of what had happened but not all.

'Joan, the police are looking for Eric, but they thought the three of them were together. I don't understand why no one has contacted you, they should have done. Do you know why Linda and Kevin are staying with you?'

'I told you,' Joan said a little sharply and clearly stressed. 'Because Linda has left her husband. She had nowhere else to go. She confided in me. I now know what a wicked man he is and the bad things he's done to Joss and Kevin. She needs time to adjust and the support of her family.' Her voice trembled.

'Joan, I'm afraid there's more to it than that, and Linda mustn't run away again. She has to contact the police or social services.'

'Why? She hasn't done anything wrong.'

This was so difficult. What I needed to say was going to shock and upset Joan. 'I'm afraid she has,' I said. 'I appreciate why Linda ran away, because she couldn't bear to lose Kevin as well as Joss, but the social services have a court order to bring Kevin into foster care.'

'Why?' Joan cried, distraught.

'Because Eric has been abusing Kevin, and Linda failed to protect him. She's been standing by Eric, defending him, and he has been living at the house. The social services had no alternative but to apply to the court for a Care Order to remove Kevin for his own safety. That's why Linda ran away, and I'm afraid it's a police matter now.' Harsh though it was, Joan needed to understand the seriousness of what had happened, and she did.

'I can't believe this is happening to us,' she cried.

'I'm so sorry, but you had to know. Linda mustn't run away again with Kevin. It will make her case even worse.'

Joan was crying, and Joss, who had heard some of the conversation, was looking at me, concerned and close to tears herself. Then I heard a male voice in the background say, 'Joan, whatever is the matter?'

'Oh, Andrew,' I heard her sob. 'The police are looking for Linda. They want to take Kevin into foster care, like Joss.'

There was a pause and then the man came on the line: 'Hello, I'm Andrew, Linda's father and the children's grandfather. Please tell me what is going on. My wife is very upset.'

'I'm Joss's foster carer, Cathy,' I began. 'I appreciate how upsetting this is for you both.' I then told him the sequence of events that had led to Linda fleeing with Kevin and arriving at their house, finishing with the present position – that there was a court order to take Kevin into care and the police were looking for Linda, Kevin and Eric, as no one knew where they were.

Andrew gave a long, heartfelt sigh. 'What a mess,' he said. 'My wife and I had no idea. Linda told us she'd left Eric because he'd been abusing the children. We didn't know the police were looking for her, or that Kevin was going to be taken into care. But once we tell the social services that Kevin is with us then everything will be all right. Linda, Kevin and Joss can stay here until they can return home.'

I knew it wasn't going to be that simple. 'It may take a while to sort out,' I said gently. 'There's a court order in place for Kevin, and the child protection services will need to be satisfied he's safe.'

'Of course he's safe with us,' Andrew said brusquely.

'I know, but the social services will need to see for themselves, so what I'm saying is, it may take time to sort out.'

'I can't see why,' he said bluntly. 'We're the children's grandparents.'

'I know,' I said, and left it at that. Andrew clearly didn't know the workings of the social services as I did and that grandparents had very few rights when it came to children in care.

He cleared his throat. 'So what is the next step? How do we progress?' he asked a little more amicably. 'Linda can't return home while Eric is there.'

'No,' I agreed. 'One of us will need to contact the police or social services to tell them they've been found and where they are.'

'Then what will happen?'

'I'm not sure of the exact procedure,' I said honestly, 'but someone, probably a social worker, will visit you.'

'And when they see that Kevin is fine they'll get rid of that ridiculous court order and concentrate on finding the person responsible for all of this – and hopefully lock him up for a long time. I know what I'll do if I find him first.'

'The police *are* looking for Eric,' I said, 'but they thought he was with Linda and Kevin.'

'He's not, and never has been. He won't come here if he knows what's good for him. So we need to phone the social services or the police and tell them they're here?'

'Yes. As soon as possible.'

'Perhaps you should do that as you're used to dealing with them. Linda told me you have a lot of experience and know how to talk to the social worker. I might make things worse if I get angry with them.'

'I can phone them,' I said. 'I'll need your contact details.'

'I'll give them to you now.'

I reached for the pen and paper by the phone. 'Go ahead,' I said, and I wrote down the address Andrew gave me. 'I should phone them straight away.'

'I understand, but before you do I'd like to speak to my granddaughter, if that is all right?' he asked in a more conciliatory tone. 'And I'm sure she'll want to talk to her brother. Her mother is too upset to talk now.'

'I'll put Joss on,' I said, and passed the handset to her.

'Hello, Grandpa,' she said in small voice. 'I've missed you all very much. I'm sorry I've caused you so much trouble.' And the tears that had been building in her eyes now escaped and ran down her cheeks.

I passed her a tissue and she wiped her face as her grandpa spoke. I couldn't hear all of what he said, but I caught the gist of it. He sensibly reassured her that it wasn't her fault and that they all loved and missed her very much. He said Kevin and her mother were safe and well, and that she mustn't worry about them, as everything would be sorted out soon and they would all be reunited.

Joss nodded and managed a small smile. I just hoped he was right.

When they'd finished Kevin came on the line and Joss's tears fell again. She told him she missed him, loved him loads and blew kisses down the phone. 'I forgive you for all the horrible things you've done to me,' she said, smiling through her tears. 'I even forgive you for putting those slugs in my shoes and salt in my orange juice.'

Kevin must have said he was worried he would never see her again, for Joss said, 'Don't worry, Kev, you'll see me soon. Grandpa is going to sort everything out. You be a brave boy and give teddy a kiss from me. We'll all be together soon.'

Blowing a final farewell kiss down the line, Joss passed the phone back to me. 'Grandpa wants to speak to you,' she said, wiping her eyes again.

I put the phone to my ear. 'Hello?'

'Cathy, you can make that call now,' Andrew said sombrely. 'But please make sure they understand that Linda was only doing what she thought was best. She didn't mean any harm. She loves her children more than anything. Tell them, Cathy.'

'I will,' I said.

I felt as though I was betraying them as I pressed the number for Homefinders, but as bad as I felt, I had no choice other than to notify the authorities. For an agency carer it's usual practice to contact the agency first, unless it's an emergency, when the carer would obviously call the emergency services. The phone rang, and Joss stood. 'I'm going upstairs to tell the others Mum and Kev have been found,' she said.

I nodded as the phone connected. Jill answered, on out-of-hours duty, which I was grateful for as it saved me from going over all the background with a colleague. 'Linda and Kevin have been found,' I said with utter relief. Then I told her what had happened – from Joss wanting to phone her grand-parents, to the conversation I'd just had with her grandfather.

Jill had been a social worker for a long time and not much surprised her any more. She listened in silence until I'd finished, when she said stoically, 'Well, at least they've been found. I'm glad you explained to the grandpa that the social services will need to make sure Kevin is safe. It won't happen overnight. They'll run background checks first and assess them. I'll phone the duty social worker now and they'll notify the police. They may leave Kevin where he is for the night if he's not in danger. Give me the grandparents' contact details, please, and I'll get things moving.'

I read out their details.

'I can't imagine why they weren't contacted by the police,' Jill said as I finished. 'Family is the first place they look for a missing person.'

'I know, and I'm sure they were telling the truth when they said no one had contacted them. They both seemed genuinely shocked when I told them.'

'I guess we'll find out what went wrong in time,' Jill said with a certain resignation. 'I wonder what made Linda change her mind and believe Kevin and Joss rather than Eric.'

'I don't know. I didn't speak to Linda. She was too upset.'

'And Joss is OK?' Jill asked.

'Very relieved. She's upstairs now telling Paula, Lucy and Adrian that her mum and brother have been found.'

'I wonder where Eric is, if he's not with them,' Jill said.

'No idea, but Andrew was adamant he wouldn't go there.'

'OK. I'll pass all this on. The police will find him. Thankfully, he's nowhere near Kevin or Joss. I'll phone you this evening if there's anything you need to know, and then a colleague will be on duty over the weekend. Call us if you need to, otherwise I'll speak to you first thing on Monday. You should sleep easier now they've been found. I know I will.'

'Most definitely,' I agreed.

There is a common expression that foster carers often have cause to use in their work when a situation is even stranger than fiction: 'You couldn't make this lot up.' What happened next is a perfect example of that: it was so incredible that I struggled to believe what I was seeing.

Having said goodbye to Jill, I went upstairs and headed to Lucy's room, where Joss was still excitedly telling the girls about her mum and brother being at her grandparents' house all along. Joss hadn't told Adrian the good news yet, but given the level of her voice and the girls' squeals of delight I thought he probably already knew. I'd just stepped into Lucy's room when the doorbell rang. I went out again and downstairs to answer the door. I thought it was probably a charity collector, or a salesperson, or possibly my good neighbour Sue, who occasionally popped in on a Friday. It was just before seven o'clock, and although it was beginning to get dark outside it was still reasonably early and there was no reason for me to be extra-vigilant (as I'd had to be with some children I fostered), so I didn't check the security spyhole first before opening the door.

I immediately regretted my decision.

Standing in the porch, unshaven and in a crumpled suit, was Eric.

'Please don't be alarmed,' he said, seeing my shocked expression. 'I know what you've been told, but it's not true. I've come to explain.'

'You don't need to explain to me,' I said sharply. 'It's the police and court you'll be telling.'

'But I don't want you to think badly of me,' he said pathetically. 'If I could just take a moment of your time and explain.'

'No,' I said, and began to close the door.

'Please,' he said, putting his hand lightly on the door. 'Just for a moment. You owe me that.'

'I don't owe you anything,' I said bluntly. 'I'm going to call the police.'

He glanced at the telephone on the hall table, which could be seen from the door. 'But you don't understand, Cathy,' he said imploringly. 'If I could come in for a few minutes and explain, you'd understand then.' It was said so rationally and reasonably you could almost believe him, if you hadn't heard his stepdaughter describe what he'd done to her.

'No. You can go to the police station and tell them,' I said. 'The police are looking for you.'

'I know, they came to the house. I had to hide until they'd gone.'

I began to close the door again.

'No, listen, please,' he said. 'Just for a moment. I love those children – I would never harm them. I just didn't know how to treat them. I've never had children of my own. I can see now that they may have misinterpreted some of my actions, but I never meant them any harm, honestly.'

'Tell the judge,' I said, and closed the door.

My heart was pounding, my legs were trembling and I felt physically sick. I sat heavily on the chair by the phone table, picked up the handset and dialled 999. The operator asked which emergency service I wanted and I replied, 'The police.' I was put through immediately and the woman officer asked for my name and address, and then what the emergency was. I said that a man called Eric – who was registered missing and was being sought in connection with a child-abuse enquiry – had just come to my house. I was asked to hold as she logged the details into her computer.

'Are you the foster carer?' she asked a moment later.

'Yes.'

'Is Eric still outside?'

'I don't know. Do you want me to look?'

'Only if you can see without going out.'

'I'll use the security spyhole,' I said, standing.

With the phone in my hand I took the step to the front door and looked through the spyhole. The porch was empty.

'He appears to have gone, unless he's hiding out of sight,' I said.

'OK. Don't go outside. Lock your doors and I'll send the nearest available police car.'

'Thank you.'

The doors were already locked. I replaced the handset and looked again through the spyhole, but the porch was still empty. I felt cold and scared; not because of the harm he could do me – he was physically quite small and pathetic, rather than aggressive – but because of his sickening lies and the way he'd tried to justify what he'd done by blaming the children and saying they had misinterpreted his actions. So plausible and sincere it was chilling. But then abusers are good liars, having had plenty of practice covering up their evil ways. Did I believe him? Not for one moment.

The girls were still upstairs talking in Lucy's room, and I hoped they hadn't heard. I wanted to keep Joss out of this, if possible. It would be upsetting for her if she knew he'd come to the door. I went into the front room and, leaving the light off so I couldn't be seen, I stood behind the window and looked out for the arrival of the police. The night was clear and still. Fifteen minutes later a police car pulled up outside the house. I could make out two officers in the front, and someone sitting in the rear. The officer in the passenger seat opened his door and got out. I reached the front door before he'd rung the bell.

'Mrs Glass?' he asked.

'Yes.'

'Just to let you know we have Eric – in the car. We picked him up at the end of your road, so there's no need for you to worry further.'

'Thank you,' I said.

'You're welcome. Thank you for your prompt action. We've been looking for him for a while.'

I hesitated – I didn't want to get anyone into trouble, but then I thought it would probably come out anyway. 'He told me he'd been hiding at his house all along.'

'I'll pass it on,' the officer said. 'Thanks again, and goodnight.'

'Goodnight.'

I went upstairs and into Lucy's room, where I told Joss that Eric had been found and was in police custody.

CHAPTER TWENTY-FIVE

AND SHE WEPT

Once I'd recovered from the shock of finding Eric on my doorstep, I telephoned Jill.

'Incredible. The gall of the man, turning up like that!' she said, as astounded as I was. 'Had he been at home the whole time?'

'I think so. Should I phone the grandparents and tell them he's been found?' I asked.

'No. Leave it to the social services. I'll phone the duty social worker now,' Jill said. 'Once Eric has been questioned, he's likely to be released, pending further enquiries and the court case. In law he's innocent until proven guilty, but obviously if he comes to your house again, call the police straight away. Just seeing him could be very intimidating for Joss.'

'I understand,' I said. 'I think we might have a day out tomorrow and give everyone a change of scenery after everything that's happened this week.'

'Good idea. It could be some time before the cases against Eric and Zach go to court, so it's best for Joss if she continues her life as normally as possible.'

'Yes,' I said. Although easier said than done, I thought.

* * *

I returned upstairs and told the girls that if everyone had completed most of their homework by the end of the evening, I was thinking we could go out for the day on Saturday. They were delighted and I asked them to think about where they'd like to go. I then went into Adrian's room and asked him what he thought, and he agreed it was a good idea. Ten minutes later they came down and said they'd made a unanimous decision that they'd like to go to the seaside for the day. I was slightly surprised, as it was out of the holiday season.

'OK, but I doubt it will be warm enough to swim in the sea.'

'I'll take my shorts anyway,' Adrian said.

'We can paddle if it's too cold,' Paula suggested.

'And make sandcastles,' Lucy said.

'And have fish and chips like we did when we went in the summer holidays, and just chill out right away from everything,' Joss added.

'Sounds good to me,' I said.

So, with most of their homework done, the following morning we were up earlier than usual for a Saturday. We packed the buckets and spades I kept for when I fostered younger children in the boot of the car, together with our quilted jackets (it can be windy on the coast in September), and set off. It was a bright, clear day and the traffic was light, so we were on the motorway by 8 a.m. Everyone was in good spirits as we left the enormity of all that had happened during the week behind us. The radio was on and the girls began singing along to pop songs while Adrian listened to his music on his earphones. We made one stop for the toilet and a drink just over halfway and were walking barefoot on the beach by 11.30 a.m.

As I breathed in the fresh, blustery air, which really did blow the cobwebs away, I gazed out to the horizon, tantalizingly close yet unattainably far away. I find that looking into the distance, like gazing up at the stars, helps put problems and anxieties into perspective, and yet I was still worried. While I didn't for one moment doubt Joss's claim that Eric had been abusing her, I'd become unsettled by the plausibility of his excuse: that not having had any previous experience of children, he had mismanaged his care of Joss and Kevin and had never intended them any harm. Added to this was his previous assertion that Joss, having resented him from the start, was lying and had persuaded Kevin to lie too. If there was no DNA evidence – unlikely after the amount of time that had elapsed – it would just be his word against theirs. I knew that many cases of child abuse never reached court simply because there wasn't enough evidence to stand a reasonable chance of securing a prosecution, which left the victims without closure and finding it very difficult to move on with their lives. Since Eric's visit, it had been playing on my mind.

I was jolted from my thoughts by the girls' squeals of 'It's too cold, Adrian! You must be mad!' I looked over to where Adrian stood on the beach in his swimming shorts, surveying the water, ready for a swim. Although there were others walking along the beach, there was only one other person brave enough to swim, a little further along. 'One, two, three,' Adrian counted, psyching himself up. He ran down to the shoreline and into the water, splashing the girls as he went and causing more squeals of laughter. We all cheered as he dived in and a man walking by with his partner called out, 'Well done, that man!'

Adrian didn't stay in the water for long – it was very cold – but when he came out he was invigorated rather than shivering. We all turned our backs while he dried himself and dressed, and then we were ready for lunch. Brushing the sand from our feet, we slipped on our socks and trainers and crossed the road to a café overlooking the beach, where we ate a hearty all-day breakfast and drank hot chocolate. Once we'd finished, we decided to walk along the coastal path to the historic site of an old fort we'd been to years before. It was about half an hour away and there were others walking the path too. When we arrived we perched on the boulders, the last vestiges of the fort, and with seagulls circling overhead we gazed around. We could see a long way, including round the headland and partly into the next bay. The sea breeze and unadulterated view were refreshing and cathartic. We could have been in another country it was so different from where we lived.

Once we'd had our fill of the view, we continued along the coastal path a little further, and then turned and took a different path back, ending up at a tea house where we ate toasted sandwiches and a cream tea before setting off home. As often happens with a full day out, we felt we'd been away for much longer than a day. Clearly Toscha thought so too, as she wanted lots of strokes and attention before settling into her basket for the night.

It was only when I climbed into bed that night that I realized not only had Joss's behaviour improved dramatically since she'd disclosed the abuse from Eric, but she'd also stopped having nightmares. She hadn't had a single one since, whereas before it had been nearly every night. I'd seen this before in children I'd fostered who'd suffered from night terrors before they could tell what was worrying them. The mind is very clever and a little like a pressure-cooker, so that if the pressure builds up to an unsafe level it will release it in any way it can, including challenging behaviour and night-mares, in order for the child to function. Joss had been doing this, but whereas I'd thought it was solely due to her father's suicide and her mother remarrying, it was more because of the abuse she'd suffered, and then not being believed when she'd told her mother. Now her disclosures were out in the open and being acted on, she could sleep easier.

The following morning, when I mentioned to Joss that she no longer had nightmares, she said, 'I have nice dreams now. Last night I dreamt we were on the beach.'

'That wasn't a dream,' I said, smiling. 'We went there.'

'I know, but in my dream we were *all* there. You, Adrian, Lucy, Paula and my mum, dad and Kevin. It was a lovely dream, Cathy. We were having so much fun, I didn't want it to end.'

'That was a nice dream,' I said. 'I'm sure you'll have plenty more like that.' I knew from my amateur psychology that this was a good sign, a sign of recovery, and that the parts of Joss's previously fractured life were gradually coming together to be reconciled.

'Where do you think Mum and Kevin are now?' she asked.

'I don't know, love. I haven't heard anything since I spoke to Jill on Friday evening. I'm sure we'll know more when everyone is back at work tomorrow.'

'Can I phone Nana and Grandpa again? They might know where they are, and even if they don't, I'd like to talk to them.'

This was a decision I could make – I didn't have to phone my agency for advice – but I had some concerns.

'You can,' I said after a moment, 'but I'd like to make the call to check it's convenient with your grandparents. If it is, I'll put the phone on speaker while you chat.' I was playing safe. There'd already been too many mistakes and oversights with Joss's case; I didn't want to be responsible for any more.

'All right,' Joss agreed. 'Thanks.'

The two of us went into the living room where we sat side by side on the sofa. Adrian, Lucy and Paula were upstairs having a leisurely morning after our busy Saturday at the coast. I picked up the handset and pressed the number for Joss's grandparents, which I now had stored in the phone. Her grandfather, Andrew, answered with a rather formal, 'Good morning.'

'Good morning, Andrew. It's Cathy, Joss's foster carer.'

There was a short pause. 'I see. How can I help you?' he said reservedly.

'Joss would like to talk to you, but I wanted to make sure it was convenient with you first.'

'Yes, that's fine,' he said, relaxing. 'We're going to church later, but we've plenty of time.'

'I'll put her on, but I need to tell you that my phone will be on speaker.' (I was obliged to tell him I would be listening to the call.) 'I thought it sensible with everything that's been going on so there can't be any misunderstanding.'

'Most definitely,' he said reasonably. 'Quite understand. We've got nothing to hide.'

'Thank you. I haven't heard anything from the social services since Friday, and Joss was wondering if you knew where her mother and Kevin were.' I thought it best to ask the question.

'They're still here,' he said buoyantly. 'The social worker phoned and said Kevin could stay until Monday as long as we supervised Linda with him and didn't let Eric have contact with him. Let me say hello to Joss, and then if you put your phone on speaker I can tell you both what happened, save repeating it all.'

'They are there,' I said to Joss as I pressed the speakerphone button. 'He can hear you now.'

'Hi, Grandpa,' Joss said.

'Hi, sweetheart. How are you?'

'Good. We went to the seaside yesterday. Mum and Kevin are still with you?'

'Yes, they are, for the time being. After we spoke on Friday and Cathy told the social services they were here, a social worker telephoned us and asked lots of questions – about Nana and me, and your mum and Kevin, and whether we saw Eric. The social worker said that Kevin was going to be taken into care and I told her I wanted him and your mum to stay with us while everything was sorted out. The social worker phoned back later. It was nearly midnight and Kevin was in bed, and she said Eric had been found. She asked us more questions and then said that as it was very late it would be less disruptive for Kevin if he stayed the night with us. Then on Saturday another social worker telephoned and asked if we could keep Kevin for the weekend, as there weren't any foster carers available. She didn't seem to know that I'd already told the first social worker your nana and I wanted him and your mother to stay, but never mind, we got there in the end. So Kevin is with us for the rest of the weekend, and then tomorrow your nana and I are taking him to school in the car. After that, we're going to the social services so I can speak to a social worker in person and try to get this sorted out. I don't want you to worry, love. I'll take care of everything.' Again, I hoped he was right and wasn't giving the children false hopes.

'How's Mum?' Joss asked. 'Is she feeling a bit better now?'

'She's very low, pet, but we're helping her all we can. I'm sure she'd like to speak to you. Have a chat with Nana and Kevin first, while I go and see if she's awake. She's having a lie down.'

'Thanks, Grandpa. I love you,' Joss said.

'I love you too, lass. Here's Kevin.'

Kevin came on the line. 'Joss.'

'Hi, Kev, how are you doing?'

'Good. I miss you.'

'I miss you too, but you're having a good time at Nana and Grandpa's,' Joss said, upbeat.

'Yes. Grandpa plays games with me and shows me card tricks, and Nana makes chocolate cake and ice cream.' I smiled.

'That sounds great,' Joss said, keeping the conversation light. 'Lucky you. You'll never guess where we went yesterday – to the seaside.'

'Wow. I wish I could go.'

'We will when we're all together again – you, me, Mum, Nana and Grandpa.'

'Like we used to with Dad,' Kevin said.

'Yes,' Joss said with a sad smile. 'But you don't remember that, you were too young. You were only three or four the last time we went.'

'I do remember it!' Kevin said indignantly. 'I buried Dad's legs in the sand, and then yours and Mum's. You all looked so funny.'

'Yes, you did,' Joss said, surprised. 'There's a photo at home of us all. It was the last time we all went on a family outing before –' She stopped, and then said, 'We will go again, Kev, I know we will.'

They chatted for a while longer, mainly about what it was like living at Nana and Grandpa's, but Kevin also said they were taking him to church later while Mum had a rest. Then his voice fell. 'I may have to go into foster care, like you,' Kevin said. 'Grandpa told me he's going to try to make it so I can stay here, but if he can't I will have to live with a foster carer.' It was sensible of Andrew to prepare Kevin for this eventuality, painful though it must have been for him to do so. 'I hope I don't have to,' Kevin said. 'I told Grandpa to tell the social worker that if I can't live with Mum, I want to stay here with him and Nana.'

I think Joss knew it wouldn't be that straight-forward. 'Don't worry, Kev, Grandpa will do all he can. And if you do have to go into care, it'll be fine – we will still see each other.'

Joss changed the subject and asked Kevin what card tricks Grandpa had taught him, and they talked about those for a while. Then Kevin said he had to go and get ready for church, and that Nana wanted to speak to her now.

Joan's voice came on the line and she asked Joss how she was. She then said they were doing all they could to try to persuade the social services to allow Kevin to stay with them, and Joss too, if she wanted. 'Grandpa thinks it's best if we go and see the social worker in person tomorrow,' Joan said, as

Andrew had done. 'So once we've taken Kevin to school, we're going straight to their offices.' I hoped they wouldn't be disappointed, for I knew social workers' diaries filled quickly with meetings, home visits and court cases.

Joan reassured Joss that Kevin was fine and then said, 'Your mum has come down and would like to talk to you, so I'll say goodbye for now. Phone us whenever you want. We're always pleased to hear from you.'

'Thanks, Nana. I will. Love you.'

'Love you too, pet. Stay strong. I'll say a prayer in church that we can all be together soon.'

There was a short pause as Joan passed the phone to Linda, and then Linda's quiet, fragile voice came on the line. 'Hello, Joss,' she said tentatively, as if she hadn't the right to speak to her daughter. 'How are you?'

'I'm all right, Mum. How are you?'

'Trying to hold it all together.'

'Nana and Grandpa are looking after you?'

'Yes. They are.' Linda sounded depressed, as though each word was an effort. I assumed her parents would arrange for her to see a doctor if they thought it was necessary.

'We went out for the day yesterday,' Joss said, trying to make conversation.

'That's nice,' Linda said, her voice flat.

'And I've had a good week at school,' Joss continued. 'I've been doing my homework and paying attention in class. Miss Pryce saw me on Friday and said I was doing really well and that all my teachers were pleased with me. I'm going to work hard. I want to do well.'

'That's good,' Linda said.

'I feel better as a person,' Joss continued. 'I'm making new friends and I don't go out every evening any more. I stay at home with Cathy and don't get into trouble.'

'Good,' Linda said lifelessly.

'I know there's a lot of stuff to come,' Joss said, 'but if I take it a bit at a time, I think I can deal with it. The social worker is going to get me some counselling.'

The emotion Linda had been keeping a lid on now broke out. 'I'm so sorry, Joss,' she cried. 'It's all my fault. You were right to blame me. If I'd believed you from the start, none of this would have happened. I'll never forgive myself.'

'Mum, don't cry,' Joss said. 'I don't blame you any more. We can get through this together, and Nana and Grandpa will help us.'

Linda cried even more. 'I've been so stupid,' she said, her breath catching. 'I let you and Kevin down in the worst possible way. I'm not fit to be a mother. I keep thinking of what your father would say if he could see us now. If he knew how I'd let you down. I'm so ashamed. I brought a man into my home and let him abuse you. Then I didn't believe you when you told me. It makes me as bad as him.' And she wept uncontrollably.

CHAPTER TWENTY-SIX

BITTERSWEET

Joss's bottom lip trembled; she was close to tears, as indeed I was. Linda's grief was agonizing and I thought she must be near breaking point.

'Mum, it's not your fault,' Joss said, her voice shaking. 'I don't blame you. He was a good liar. I can see why you believed him. We'll come through this, I know we will. Nothing can be as bad as Dad dying, and we got through that, didn't we? Kevin and I need you, Mum, just as we've always done. I know if Dad is looking down on us, which I feel he is, he won't blame you. He'll be helping us get through this like he used to help us. He loved us, Mum, and we love you.'

I blinked back my tears and touched Joss's arm comfortingly. The poor, dear child, how brave she was being, trying to reassure and support her mother. Her touching, heartfelt words didn't ease Linda's distress, though, and her uncontrollable weeping was harrowing to listen to. I was thinking we should end the call and say we would phone back another time, but then Andrew's voice came on the line and Linda's crying receded into the background.

'Nana is taking your mum to have a quiet sit down,' he said to Joss. 'Try not to worry, love. We're looking after her. I'll phone you this evening.'

'Thank you,' I said.

Andrew and Joss said goodbye and the line went dead. We continued to sit side by side on the sofa and I tried to reassure Joss, as Andrew had, that her grandparents would take good care of her mother and she shouldn't worry. To be honest, I felt the phone call had done more harm than good, for although Joss now knew that Kevin and her mother were safe, Kevin could only definitely stay with the grandparents for the weekend and might then have to go into foster care. And to hear her mother so distraught was disturbing and an added anxiety for Joss, who was already having to cope with so much. Unsurprisingly, she was quiet and withdrawn for the rest of the day, and the good effects of our outing the previous day disappeared. Of course, it wasn't long before everyone else in the house knew what had happened, so the whole family was down. We ate lunch with little conversation and then later in the afternoon Joss came to me and voiced a concern that had been playing on my mind too.

'Cathy, I'm really worried Mum might try to do what Dad did,' she said, her face knitted with anxiety.

'No, she won't,' I said firmly. 'Your grandparents are looking after your mother and keeping a close eye on her. They won't let any harm come to her.'

'But they can't watch Mum all the time,' Joss said, no less concerned. 'And it doesn't take long to kill yourself. Mum was only out of the house for half an hour when Dad did what he did. Can we phone Nana and Grandpa to make sure Mum's OK?'

I glanced at the clock on the wall. It was 3.30 p.m. 'Your grandpa said he'd phone this evening,' I said. 'I think we should wait a while. He and your nana have a lot to do. If they haven't phoned by seven o'clock, we'll phone them.' I didn't want to keep bothering them, and Joss accepted this.

True to his word, just after six o'clock Andrew telephoned. Joss and I sat side by side on the sofa again with the phone on speaker. Joss began by asking about her mother.

'She's a bit brighter now, lass,' Andrew said positively. 'She came with us to church and she's had something to eat. She's having a rest now and she's going to see the doctor next week.' He didn't offer to put Linda on to speak to Joss, and I thought this was probably for the best. When Joss and her grandpa had had a chat he put Joan on, and she too was positive. They chatted about general things – what they'd been doing during the day – and then she reassured Joss that everything would be all right.

When Kevin came on the line he sounded cheerful and told Joss that Grandpa had taken him to the park in the afternoon, while Nana had stayed at home with Mum. He said that Grandpa had been on the children's swings and the roundabout with him, and then he laughed as he described their attempts at playing on the see-saw. 'Grandpa couldn't get off the ground because he's so much heavier than me,' Kevin said, chuckling. 'I was up in the air with my feet dangling and then I came down with a bump when he got off.' Joss laughed too.

It seemed that Andrew had also taken the opportunity to have a chat with Kevin about what he could expect to happen, for he told Joss, 'Grandpa says I will have to talk to a police officer about what Eric did, and he'll write it all down for the judge.'

'That's right,' Joss said. 'It's called a statement. I'll have to make one too. It's nothing to worry about. I've done it before. You have to tell the truth.'

'Yes. Grandpa says it's important I tell the police officer everything that happened. I don't think Eric was a nice man, was he? Not like a proper daddy. He pretended he was, but he wasn't really.'

'No,' Joss agreed. 'He wasn't nice. Not like a daddy at all.'

My heart went out to them; two children having their hopes of a family life shattered in the cruellest possible way, and after everything they'd already been through with their father's suicide. It was so unfair.

Then Kevin said, 'Will the police officer give me a sticker for being brave, like they do at the dentist?'

Joss and I both smiled. 'They might,' Joss said. 'But if not, I'll buy you lots and lots of stickers.'

'Promise?'

'Yes.'

'The shiny Batman ones?'

'Yes, whatever you like.'

Joss and Kevin chatted for a while longer and then the conversation ended with Joss saying she'd phone every day, which I assumed would be all right with the grandparents and social services.

That night Joss took a while to settle, so I sat with her, talking quietly about all sorts of things, until she dozen off. Once asleep, she slept through until I woke her for school the following morning. I felt relieved to have the school routine to fall back on, with its comforting familiarity, after all the trauma and uncertainty of the weekend. After breakfast and before we left the house, I presented Joss with a front-door key of her own.

'Oh,' she said, pleasantly surprised. 'Thanks. I guess I'm behaving myself and being responsible now.'

'You certainly are, love, and I'm very proud of you.'

She gave me a big hug and then told Adrian, Paula and Lucy that she had a front-door key like them. Even though Joss wouldn't have much opportunity to use the key, as I was collecting her from school and she didn't go out in the evenings any more, it was a sign that I trusted her and considered her mature enough not to abuse the privilege. When she'd first arrived I'd promised she could have a key when her behaviour had improved, and I always try to keep a promise.

I took Joss to school that morning and returned home. I knew there would be a lot going on and I needed to be contactable. I wondered how Andrew and Joan were faring at the social services, and if Linda was with them. I shared Joss's concern that her mother was so distraught she could harm herself, although I certainly wouldn't be telling Joss that.

Jill telephoned mid-morning but didn't really have any new information. She said she'd left a message on Amelia's voicemail to call her when she was free. Then she asked me how we all were, and if there'd been any new developments at my end. I told her we'd had a day at the coast on Saturday, and then gave her a brief summary of the two phone calls we'd made to Joss's grandparents the day before. Jill knew the rest from having been on duty over the weekend. She said she'd phone again when she had any news.

There were no more phone calls that afternoon, so when I collected Joss from school and she wanted to know if her grandparents had seen Amelia, I had to say I was still waiting for news. She accepted this with a sigh and then told me a bit about her day at school. When we arrived home she took her front-door key from her purse and went ahead of me to unlock the door. I could see how much having the key meant to her and I was touched. I also felt vindicated for the stand I'd taken. Had I bowed to pressure and given her a key when she'd first arrived, it would have been taken for granted and also created additional problems. Now Joss felt she'd achieved something worth having.

Jill telephoned at 5.30 p.m., just before she left the office, and she had plenty to tell me. Andrew and Joan had managed to see Amelia at the social services offices, having first taken Linda to the police station as the police wanted to interview her. Jill said Amelia was going to visit Joss's grandparents at their home the following morning to make a preliminary assessment on whether Kevin could live there for the time being.

'The alternative is a foster family right out of the area,' Jill said. 'So it will be better for him all round if he can stay with them. Amelia will need to be satisfied that the grandparents can cooperate with the conditions she's imposing, though.'

'Conditions?'

'That Linda isn't allowed out with Kevin by herself – in case she runs away again with him – and that Eric has no contact with the boy.'

'Where is Eric now?' I asked. 'Do you know?'

'At the matrimonial home,' Jill said. 'He says he hasn't got anywhere else to go. Make sure Joss doesn't go there. I know she has a key.'

'I'll tell her,' I said.

'The police need to interview Joss,' Jill said. 'Amelia is trying to arrange it for Wednesday afternoon. She's taking

Kevin for a memorandum interview in the morning, so he can give his evidence on video tape, and once she's finished she'll collect Joss from school – the time is still to be arranged. She'll bring Joss back to you when they've finished. Can you tell Joss, please?'

'Yes. Jill, do we know why the police didn't visit the grand-parents' home when Linda and Kevin went missing?' I asked out of curiosity.

'It seems there was a misunderstanding. Apparently two families with the same surname live on that street – Clark is a common name – and the police went to the wrong house. Mistakes happen,' she added philosophically.

'And did Amelia say why Linda has suddenly started believing Joss and Kevin? I have been wondering what changed her mind.'

'It was something Kevin told her about his stepfather,' Joss said. 'I don't know what he said, but it was enough to convince her that Kevin and Joss were telling the truth.'

'I see. Well, at least she believed them in the end.'

'Hopefully it's not too late. Whether the children will ever be allowed to live with their mother again remains to be seen. Not that Linda is in any state to look after them at present. She failed to protect them once, and the social services will want to make absolutely certain it can never happen again – and, of course, running away didn't help.'

'No,' I agreed thoughtfully.

'There is one more thing I need to mention, so it doesn't come as a shock.'

'Yes?' I asked, immediately concerned.

'Andrew and Joan have told Amelia they want Joss to live with them too, which is an option being considered by the social services. I thought it best to mention it, but don't tell Joss yet. Amelia will speak to her when and if it's appropriate.'

'All right. Thank you for telling me.'

We said goodbye and I went to Joss and told her what she needed to know: that her grandparents had seen Amelia and she was visiting them at their house the following morning, and also the arrangements for Amelia taking Joss to the police station on Wednesday afternoon – all of which Joss appeared to take in her stride.

That evening Joss telephoned her grandparents, but her mother was not up to coming to the phone. She spoke to her nana, grandpa and Kevin, but not for too long as it was a school night and Kevin was about to have a bath before going to bed at a reasonable time. It sounded as though Joan and Andrew had already established a routine for Kevin, which was good.

On Tuesday afternoon Amelia telephoned to confirm that she would be collecting Joss from school at one o'clock the following day to take her to the police station, and she asked me to tell Joss to be ready after the lunch break. I took the opportunity to ask Amelia if it was all right for Joss to telephone her grandparents every evening, and she said it was, as they were very happy to hear from her. That was all she said about her visit to them that morning, and when I collected Joss from school I told her the arrangements for the following day. She sighed but didn't comment. The evening continued as normal with dinner, homework, television and then a slow migration to bed. Lucy said she'd like to celebrate her birthday (ten days away) by going to the cinema with her friends and having something to eat afterwards. I said I'd arrange it, and of course we'd have a family celebration too.

On Wednesday morning Joss was naturally anxious about the police interview that afternoon, and I reassured her as best I could. I thought about her constantly during the day and anxiously awaited her return. It was 4.30 p.m. before Amelia finally brought her home; the interview had taken three hours. They both looked shattered, and Amelia said she couldn't come in, as she had to return to the office, having spent all day at the police station – with Kevin in the morning and Joss in the afternoon. She said the interview had gone well, but that was all she said. Joss didn't want to talk about it either. I didn't press her – she would tell me what she wanted me to know in time, and I appreciated that having to go over the abuse for the statement must have been very painful indeed. She took a while to settle that night, so again I sat with her, talking about general things, until she was ready to sleep.

On Thursday afternoon Jill telephoned to say that Amelia would be coming to see us after school on Friday, and one of the things she wanted to talk to Joss about was the issue of her going to live with her grandparents. Although the initial assessment had been reasonably positive, Amelia had some concerns. Andrew and Joan lived in a three-bedroom bungalow, and Joss would therefore have to share a bedroom with her mother (or Linda would have to sleep on the sofa, which she had offered to do). Amelia felt this wasn't satisfactory in the long term. Also, she had concerns that Andrew and Joan would struggle to cope with their grandchildren's and Linda's needs, as they were all going to require a lot of support for a long time to come.

'As well as everything going on surrounding Eric's abuse,' Jill said, 'the investigation into Zach is also continuing, so Joss has that to cope with too. Andrew and Joan are pushing to have Joss live with them, but they may not fully appreciate what is involved. It's a year since they've seen Joss and a lot has happened in that time. Amelia thinks it might be best if Joss continues to live with you and visits her family at weekends. She's going to discuss this with Joss when she sees her tomorrow, but could you mention it to her so she has time to think about it? She could stay over there on Saturday nights, beginning this weekend, if she wants to.'

'Yes. I'll tell her,' I said.

The time Joss and I spent alone in the car together going to and from school provided a good opportunity for us to talk uninterrupted, if she wished to. When I collected her from school that afternoon, I first asked her if she'd had a good day, and then I told her what Jill had said.

'So Amelia's saying I can stay with Nana and Grandpa every weekend?' Joss asked brightly.

'If you'd like to, yes.'

'Of course I would. Fantastic! I can be with my family. I mean, I like living with you, Cathy, but they are my family.' Which was the response I would have expected.

Following Amelia's visit on Friday afternoon, she left it to Andrew, Joan and I to arrange the exact time of the first weekend visit, so I telephoned Joss's grandparents, who lived fifteen miles away. We agreed I would take Joss on Saturday morning to arrive at around ten o'clock, and they would return her at around six o'clock on Sunday. That evening I helped a very excited Joss pack an overnight bag, and then the following morning we were up and dressed before everyone else, and called goodbyes as we left.

It was the first time I'd met Andrew and Joan, and it was a year since they'd seen Joss. It was a very emotional reunion – Joan was close to tears, while Andrew kept clearing his throat to hide his emotion. They were a delightful couple in their late sixties who reminded me of my own dear parents in their kind and loving ways. Linda was sitting in the living room, but she was very quiet and Joan told me she had been prescribed antidepressants by the doctor. She seemed a broken woman, a shadow of her former self, and I felt very sorry for her. The few times she did speak, she kept thanking me for all I was doing for Joss, and then kept apologizing to Joss for being such a dreadful mother, which made us all tear up.

That weekend went well. The following weekend, Joss stayed with us on Saturday for Lucy's family birthday celebration, and then I took her to her grandparents' for the day on Sunday and Andrew brought her home. We then fell into a pattern where Joss stayed with her grandparents from Saturday morning until Sunday evening every weekend for the whole of October and November. When I took Joss I sometimes saw Linda and she seemed to improve a little, but not much. Without her parents' support, I don't think she would have coped at all. Andrew and Joan had quickly established a good routine in their house, so that Joan stayed with Linda while Andrew took Joss and Kevin to school, which meant two round trips of thirty miles each for him, but he said he enjoyed doing the school run again.

During this time the police investigations were continuing in the background, but we didn't hear anything and I knew it would take time before they were complete and it could be decided if there was enough evidence to prosecute in court. At the end of November I was asked to make a statement in respect of Zach and Carl – not just about the night they had attacked Joss, but also the other times I'd seen them: in the car and at Chelsea's flat. I was pleased I'd kept good log notes, for I doubted I would have remembered all the details the police wanted without them.

At the beginning of December, as everyone was gearing up for Christmas, Andrew began putting more pressure on the social services to have Joss live with them full-time. It had rather slipped into the background as the weekend visits were working out so well, but he now threatened the social services with court action if they didn't make a decision. I knew he and Joan had already discussed it with Joss. I reassured them that I was happy with whatever was decided and fully appreciated why Joss would want to live with them – her family – although of course we'd all miss her. Two weeks before Christmas a meeting was held at the social services behind closed doors, without the grandparents, Linda or me being invited, which annoyed Andrew all the more, but the outcome was good. Joss was allowed to go and live with them.

'Can't she stay with us for Christmas?' Paula asked when I told her, clearly disappointed.

'Her family want her with them for Christmas,' I said. 'It's a family time and it's natural for Joss to want to be with them too.'

'But I've already bought her a Christmas present,' Paula said. 'So have Adrian and Lucy.'

'So have I. We'll give them to her nana and grandpa to put under their Christmas tree for her.'

So in secret we wrapped and labelled our presents for Joss and put them in a Santa sack, which I hid in my wardrobe. The moving date was set for the following Saturday – the schools were breaking up on the Friday, and it was one week before Christmas. We all helped Joss pack and stack her bags and cases in the hall, ready for when Andrew and Kevin arrived to collect her at 11 a.m. I put the Santa sack in a black bin liner and told Joss not to peer in or feel it. I noticed some presents for us had appeared under the tree. Parting from Joss was bittersweet, for while it was right that she should live with her family, she'd become so much a part of ours that we were going to miss her very much. And her leaving just before Christmas made it all the more poignant, with the house gaily decorated and our hearts full of festive joy. I told my children to put on brave faces, as we didn't want Joss to leave in tears. We all helped Andrew load the car, and then Adrian told Kevin he could choose two chocolate novelties from the Christmas tree – one for him and one for Joss. He'd been eyeing them since he'd first come in.

'Thank you,' he said, his little face a picture of delight. 'We're not allowed to have any chocolates off our tree until Christmas Day.'

'Neither are we,' Adrian said. 'So don't tell Father Christmas.'

And I could see from Kevin's expression that he wasn't sure if Adrian was joking or really did still believe in Father Christmas at his age.

Parting was difficult for Joss too. She was close to tears as she finally climbed into the passenger seat of her grandpa's car and we waved them off. Once their car had turned the corner and was out of sight, we returned indoors, our downcast faces at odds with the cheery decorations hanging all around us. I suggested we went to the ice rink later, which was now decked out like a winter wonderland for Christmas, and everyone agreed. So while they got ready, I took the opportunity to strip Joss's bed and dust and vacuum her room. I wasn't expecting another child, but family crises can happen at any time, resulting in a child or children coming into care. For while many families are involved in the merry build-up to Christmas, some are not, and I wouldn't be the first foster carer to receive a battered child on Christmas Eve – and believe me, it doesn't get more heartbreaking than that.

EPILOGUE

Joss, Kevin and Linda lived with Andrew and Joan for most of the following year, and during that time Joss often popped in to see us with Andrew and Kevin on their way home from school. While the young people talked, and played with Kevin, I made Andrew a cup of tea and we chatted, catching up on their news. Eric left the matrimonial home after four months and went into lodgings, as the house was owned by Linda. Once he'd gone, Andrew changed the locks, removed the rubbish Eric had left behind and gave the place a good clean and a coat of paint, ready for when Linda felt well enough to return.

Towards the end of that year both Eric's and Zach's cases went to court, Eric's first. He denied abusing Joss and Kevin but was found guilty on both counts. He received a prison sentence, and when he's released he'll be placed on the sex offenders register, so the police will know where he is living and be able to monitor him. Andrew said that in addition to Joss's and Kevin's statements, DNA evidence had been found at their home, which helped secure a conviction. He couldn't bring himself to tell me what that evidence was, but I later found out from Jill. She said that dried stains on Joss's underwear, taken by the police from a drawer in her bedroom when they'd searched the house, had contained traces of Eric's semen from when he'd masturbated over her pants. Little wonder Andrew couldn't tell me! I also learnt from Jill what had finally made Linda believe that Eric was abusing her children; it was also part of the evidence against him. In his interview with the police Kevin had said that when his mother was out at the charity meetings Eric got into the bath with him and played with his willy in front of him. Kevin was able to describe an old appendectomy scar Eric had just above his groin, which helped convince the judge that Kevin was telling the truth.

The case against Zach (and Carl) was always going to be difficult to prove, as it was their word against Joss's. Zach continued to deny he'd attacked Joss, claiming it was consensual sex – that she'd wanted to – and he hadn't known Joss was only thirteen. The police had done a thorough job of investigating, though, and were able to show that Zach (and Carl) were part of a group at Dave's flat who had groomed vulnerable young girls, plying them with drink and drugs and then abusing them. The court heard that there had been other complaints against persons at the flat, and a mother had reported that her teenage daughter had been given drink and drugs by Dave and was then assaulted by someone in the flat. A neighbour had also complained on a number of occasions about the comings and goings at the flat. There wasn't enough evidence to convict Carl, but Zach was found guilty of attempted rape and given a custodial sentence. When released, he too will be placed on the sex offenders register. Dave faced various charges, including supplying class A drugs. Chelsea was placed in a care home for teenagers but kept running away and returning to the flat.

I'm pleased to say that the police didn't interview Joss over the incident of the burning car – Andrew and I both felt this was the right decision. That behaviour had been part of a life Joss had led on the streets, when she'd been angry and confused from being abused but not believed. After the court cases, Joss, Kevin and Linda entered counselling, sometimes one to one with the counsellor and at other times together for family therapy. Andrew said the counselling wasn't only to help them come to terms with the abuse Joss and Kevin had suffered, but also to address the unresolved issues from their father's suicide – especially for Joss, who'd been with her mother when they found him.

Despite all that was going on that year, Joss continued to do well at school and made some new friends. She also took up ice skating again, going in the evening after school. I had to smile as I thought back to when I'd first suggested ice skating as an activity to keep her off the streets and out of trouble, and she'd begrudgingly agreed to go and then truanted. Now here she was, absolutely loving it and entering ice-skating competitions. Fantastic!

Linda, Joss and Kevin didn't return to live at their house, even though after a year Linda was considered well enough to parent her children on her own. I could understand why they didn't return. What had once been a happy family home had been scarred by the tragic and horrendous events that had taken place there; first with the father's suicide, and then Eric's abuse. Every room would have been haunted by ghostly reminders of what happened there. So once the social services felt Linda was able to look after her children, she sold the house and bought a bungalow on the same street as her parents. A fresh start, a new beginning, but wonderfully close to the loving grandparents who had done so much for their daughter and grandchildren, and without whom I'm sure the family would not have survived and been reunited.

Tragedy can strike any family, and Joss's family had more than their fair share of sorrow, but thanks to Andrew and Joan's unfailing support, they were able to come through it and look forward to a brighter future. I know from the many emails I receive that grandparents of children taken into care often have a very hard time trying to persuade the social services that they can look after the children when their parents cannot. The social services can be dismissive of grandparents, or get bogged down when assessing them with issues such as their age, the size of their home and other practicalities, which are factors, but not as important as what good grandparents have to offer: unconditional love, a wealth of experience, stability, endless patience and a life-long commitment to the family. At present, grandparents don't even have the automatic right to see their grandchildren if they are taken into care. This needs to change.

For the latest updates on Joss and the children in my other fostering memoirs, please visit www.cathyglass.co.uk.

Suggested topics for reading-group discussion

_____

Cathy blames herself for not spotting the signs that Joss was being abused by her stepfather earlier. Were there indicators, and if so should she have reasonably seen them?

Joss is very angry, as many abused children are. Why do you think this is?

How culpable is Linda? Should she have spotted the signs that Eric was abusing her children?

Why do you think Joss took comfort in the company of Zach, Dave and Chelsea?

Cathy is critical of the contract of behaviour. What do you think would be a reasonable contract of behaviour for Joss?

Cathy is concerned about how Joss's challenging behaviour might affect her other children. Is she right to be so? What is the likely impact on them, and what could Cathy do to minimize it?

Was Cathy right to go to Dave's flat and bring Joss home when she wanted to stay the night? What were Cathy's reasons for doing so?

Grandparents are often overlooked as full-time carers if the children can't live with their own parents. What are the positives and negatives of grandparents bringing up their grandchildren?

Did you feel that justice had been served to the perpetrators of Joss's abuse at the end of the book? Do you think our current justice system adequately supports victims of abuse?

Do you think Joss's family will be able to successfully rebuild their lives after everything they have been through? What could they do to move forward after experiencing so much trauma and distrust?

Cathy Glass

———

One remarkable woman, more
than **150** foster children cared for.

Cathy Glass has been a foster carer for
twenty-five years, during which time she has
looked after more than 150 children, as well
as raising three children of her own. She was
awarded a degree in education and psychology
as a mature student, and writes under a
pseudonym. To find out more about Cathy
and her story visit www.cathyglass.co.uk.

Saving Danny

Trapped in his own dark world, Danny doesn't understand why his parents are sending him away

Cathy must call on all her expertise to deal with his challenging behaviour, and discovers a frightened little boy who just wants to be loved.

The Child
Bride

**A girl blamed and
abused for dishonouring
her community**

Cathy discovers the
devastating truth.

Daddy's Little
Princess

**A sweet-natured girl with
a complicated past**

Cathy picks up the
pieces after events take
a dramatic turn.

Will you
love me?

**A broken child desperate
for a loving home**

The true story of Cathy's
adopted daughter Lucy.

Please Don't Take My Baby

Seventeen-year-old Jade is pregnant, homeless and alone

Cathy has room in her heart for two.

Another Forgotten Child

Eight-year-old Aimee was on the child-protection register at birth

Cathy is determined to give her the happy home she deserves.

A Baby's Cry

A newborn, only hours old, taken into care

Cathy protects tiny Harrison from the potentially fatal secrets that surround his existence.

The Night the Angels Came

A little boy on the brink of bereavement

Cathy and her family make sure Michael is never alone.

Mummy told me not to tell

A troubled boy sworn to secrecy

After his dark past has been revealed, Cathy helps Reece to rebuild his life.

I Miss Mummy

Four-year-old Alice doesn't understand why she's in care

Cathy fights for her to have the happy home she deserves.

The Saddest Girl in the World

A haunted child who refuses to speak

Do Donna's scars run too deep for Cathy to help?

Cut

Dawn is desperate to be loved

Abused and abandoned, this vulnerable child pushes Cathy and her family to their limits.

Hidden

The boy with no past

Can Cathy help Tayo to feel like he belongs again?

Damaged

A forgotten child

Cathy is Jodie's last hope. For the first time, this abused young girl has found someone she can trust.

Inspired by Cathy's own experiences...

Run, Mummy, Run

The gripping story of a woman caught in a horrific cycle of abuse, and the desperate measures she must take to escape.

My Dad's a Policeman

The dramatic short story about a young boy's desperate bid to keep his family together.

The Girl in the Mirror

Trying to piece together her past, Mandy uncovers a dreadful family secret that has been blanked from her memory for years.

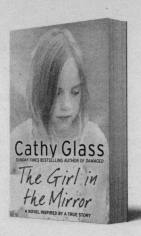

Sharing her expertise...

About Writing and How to Publish

A clear and concise, practical guide on writing and the best ways to get published.

Happy Mealtimes for Kids

A guide to healthy eating with simple recipes that children love.

Happy Adults

A practical guide to achieving lasting happiness, contentment and success. The essential manual for getting the best out of life.

Happy Kids

A clear and concise guide to raising confident, well-behaved and happy children.

Be amazed
Be moved
Be inspired

———